# Cross Purposes

*Reflections for Good Friday*

— KEVIN CAREY —

Sacristy
Press

**Sacristy Press**
PO Box 612, Durham, DH1 9HT

www.sacristy.co.uk

First published in 2018 by Sacristy Press, Durham

Sacristy Limited, registered in England & Wales, number 7565667

**British Library Cataloguing-in-Publication Data**
A catalogue record for the book is available from the British Library

ISBN 978-1-908381-11-8

# Preface

So perfect was my grandfather in his execution of the role of MC during the *Triduum* that I thought he had been performing the role during the whole of the fifty years he had by then served on the altar, for which he subsequently was awarded the *Benemerenti* medal by Pope John XXIII. He served daily from his seventh birthday in 1907 to his death in 1984 except when he was on holiday. The choreography of servers and celebrant was immaculate but the feat which I enjoyed most was the perfect timing of the fanfare for the *Gloria* of the First Mass of Easter which struck up precisely at Midnight to accompany the turning on of the lights, the tearing away of the purple shrouds and the invasion of flowers before the first words were sung, and this during a service which had already lasted for well over an hour, offering plenty of opportunity for an over-run or a hiatus. It was perhaps that detail, even more than the simplicity of the foot washing and the beauty of the Procession to the Altar of Repose on Maundy Thursday evening, the length and solemnity of the Good Friday observance which enfolded the "Creeping to the Cross" and the drama of the Easter Vigil with its fire, first light and résumé of the history of our salvation, which imprinted such a strong impression of the non-negotiability of Holy Week observance such that I could never understand why it was that otherwise apparently perfectly good and even devout Christians seemed indifferent to it, satisfying themselves with attendance at Mass on Easter Sunday morning. When I left the Roman Catholic Church for the Church of England I was even more scandalised by what appeared to me to be overwhelming liturgical indifference, the Saturday evening before Easter Sunday being at best observed by the lighting of congregational candles and the singing of a hymn at dusk and at worst by nothing at all.

The explanation, at least in part, which I discovered recently in Bradshaw & Johnson's superb *Eucharistic Liturgies*[1] is that the practice I began to observe in 1959, as a seven-year-old, was only begun when Pope Pius XII moved Holy Week ceremonies from the morning, where they had been marooned as collateral damage of the Eucharistic fasting regulations, to the evening, only completed in 1956, which cast a different light not only on the relative obscurity of the *Triduum* observance but also on the immense skill of my grandfather.

But for all my love of liturgical theatre which has never diminished, my personal focus has shifted from the "official" *Triduum* to the two hours on Good Friday before the *Liturgy of the Day* when I have been charged with delivering the extended reflections of which this book is mostly comprised and about which I have three comments. First, the theologically keen-eyed will readily observe that they are primarily concerned with our role in creating the kingdom of God on earth as it is in heaven (to borrow an apt phrase of N. T. Wright[2]) rather than on the personally focused mechanics of atonement which, if they operate at all, are a "downstream"consequence of Kingdom Theology as opposed to being the primary reason for standing at the foot of the Cross. Secondly, the typologically critical will no doubt have noticed that my characterisations of the protagonists are not entirely consistent because the characterisation is, necessarily, a work of the imagination which most resists the confinement of consistency. This might lead to the charge that I am using the participants as props to promote one particular standpoint or another to which I readily plead guilty, arguing that as long as my depiction is credible it is enough. And, finally, the dramatically attuned will note that I occasionally stray from the stricture which confines our thoughts to Good Friday itself which relies substantially for its drama on our ability to shut out the prospect of Easter. Sometimes the completist in me cannot be resisted, not least because I believe that the story which begins at the entry of Jesus into Jerusalem actually ends when he has left it and arrived in Emmaus. There is a sore need for a specially constructed Service of Evening Prayer for Easter Sunday when all the threads can be properly gathered together.

As the composer of a large number of Christmas poems it might seem paradoxical for me to protest at the shift in Christian sentiment (and sentimentality) from Easter to Christmas but the celebration of the necessary precondition should never abridge our reverence for the culmination. We are, after all, Easter children. The Incarnation is a matter of mysterious wonder but the Passion and death of our Lord are not only God's business but ours too. The real paradox is that we stand in horror at the foot of the Cross while something else in us is busy hammering in the nails. There is no better occasion than this for us to be absolutely bound up with the meaning of ourselves as necessarily flawed kingdom builders, necessarily because choice can only be operated in an ecology of personal and corporate imperfection and cosmic happenstance. The mistake of the Reformation was, I believe, to forsake its own rhetoric and rationalise the death of Jesus instead of simply being awestruck by the degree of God's solidarity with us in our created imperfection.

If this book prompts some thinking about the events it contemplates it will have done more than I could ever have hoped for.

**Kevin Carey**
*Hurstpierpoint*
*Feast of St Martin of Tours 2015*

# Notes

[1]   Paul F. Bradshaw and Maxwell E. Johnson, *Eucharistic Liturgies: Their Evolution and Interpretation* (SPCK, 2012).

[2]   N. T. Wright, *Jesus and The Victory of God* (SPCK, 1996).

# Contents

# 1. A Turbulent Day

*2005*

## i. Peter

Not again. Not again! Peter could not imagine how it could be worse; but that was his real problem; he could not imagine.

It had been such a turbulent day that he had been even less in control than usual. There had been the preparations for the Passover and friction with young John over where everyone would sit. He remembered the Master saying that he who put himself at the bottom of the table would be brought higher; but it hadn't happened, so John had kept the seat of honour. Then there was the foot washing; it was the most embarrassing thing that had ever happened to him, the Master behaving like a slave. He had got used to hearing him say all kinds of outrageous things but apart from the scene in the Temple with the traders he hadn't done anything really mad until this. Of course, like the rest, he had to go along with it, particularly as there was so much talk about the Master going away. He couldn't face that; whatever his faults, Peter had become so committed to Jesus that he could not bear the thought of leaving him. That's why he was so emphatic about never denying his Master. He could not imagine any situation in which he would deny him.

Then he had fallen asleep in the garden when he should have prayed; and then, flustered when that traitor Judas turned up with the Temple Police, he had lashed out and injured Malchus; and still the Master stayed calm, looking at him with that peculiar mixture of love and pity which he saved only for him.

The Master could see right inside him. When Peter had made a fool of himself, like that time when he broke the vision of Elias and Moses or the time when he jumped out of the boat, thinking he could walk on water, he would always go away quietly and perform some special task and try to pray even harder. He never told the others how many nights he had spent fixing things for people who could not afford to pay; and he never said how much effort he put into prayer and how hard it was; but the Master knew. And that's when he gave him that special look.

That was in the good days in Galilee before they had all come to Jerusalem, where people were so hostile and snobbish; they seemed to spend all their time trying to trap the Master so that it was really hard work teaching. Peter didn't like living in this hilly, arid place without a lake; and he didn't like the meat; and they didn't like the way his beard was cut or, rather, not cut, and the fisherman's coat and his Northern accent. They were always wrong footing him, trying to make him lose his temper; and they always succeeded.

He thought of the Galilee days as he walked down the hill towards the city, keeping the Police in sight. He was knotted up with hate and fear. He had never trusted Judas who was far too clever and full of stories about his great namesake; and he had been very clever to get hold of the money. But after the injury to Malchus he would have to be a bit careful.

As he came through the city gate his fear increased but he could not turn back because John came out of the shadows and signalled to him to follow. John knew everyone because of his Temple studies so Peter was not at all surprised when John pushed open a side gate in the wall of the High Priest's house and, after a minute, signalled him to come in. As Peter pushed past the woman who kept the gate she said: "Are you a disciple, like John?" and, without thinking, he said "No" and hurried on.

As usual, Peter had been so busy dealing with events as they happened that he had not thought clearly about what would happen to Jesus. The High Priest could make a big fuss and have him beaten but that was all; and perhaps Nicodemus could sort things out. He was a bit posh for Peter but he had got them out of a couple of tight corners before and this looked like the tightest yet.

Then he heard somebody mention Pilate and he felt himself getting out of control again. He had always been strong and physically fearless, but he could never remember a time when he had not been frightened of the Romans. Up in Galilee it was not too bad as long as they got their money but down in Jerusalem they were edgy and that meant trouble. The less certain they were, the more brutal they became.

A junior clerk said that the Romans were obsessed with what he called due process, but he was overwhelmed by critics who said the Romans would do anything to get their own way but, much worse, it was impossible to make a deal with Pilate because nothing ever stuck.

He had stayed against the courtyard wall until the cold got the better of him and he had to warm his feet. He did not want to be noticed but he had forgotten to get rid of his long knife and a Policeman roughly reminded him in a loud voice that it was strictly forbidden to carry unauthorised weapons on the High Priest's premises. Everybody looked at him and then, to his horror, a servant said: "I recognise that knife; you attacked my cousin Malchus with it."

Now he was really frightened as everybody looked at him and began to crowd around him. They could not shout in the courtyard because they would get into trouble but they started a low, menacing chant: "Kill Jesus! Kill the Galileans!" Then he completely lost control and charged blindly through the crowd, his knife flailing, until he got through the gate.

He would have to hide until he could work out what to do next, so he crouched behind a wall to get his breath back. He heard a cock crow somewhere on the Mount of Olives and then he remembered what the Master had said; and slowly he realised the enormity of what he had done. The Master had been in danger and he had pretended not to know him and run away. Not again! He had failed the test, his biggest yet, and he would never see the Master again if the Romans got him.

He heard a small group of soldiers marching round the corner. He crouched lower. They were passing him on the way to the Governor's house. Even in his fear he could not help looking; and the only thing he saw in the flaring torchlight was the face of the Master. The Romans had got him; that would be the end of everything. How could he possibly live once Jesus was dead?

Then Peter saw that look; that mixture of love and pity he saved only for him; and in that moment Peter knew that he would promise and fail and struggle and be forgiven; and would promise and fail and struggle and be forgiven; that the Master would be with him forever.

**Prayer**

Jesus, Saviour of the World, may we not deny you in word and silence when called upon to bear witness to your holy name. May we, like Peter, be contrite and humble when we have failed, seeking your forgiveness, turning again to you in prayer and good works. Even now, as you are condemned through false witnesses, we pray for your help that we may always be true to your earthly life in everything that we say and do. And, as you loved Peter's flawed love for you, may we never forget that our love imperfectly returns what you have given to us in your Passion and Death. Made sorrowful and joyful by your full and final sacrifice, may we ever thank the Father for being his creatures and for the gifts of the Holy Spirit. Amen.

# ii. Judas

Just for an hour, as Jesus rode down the Mount of Olives into Jerusalem, Judas saw a crown; things were going to be all right.

All the disciples had turned out with their families newly arrived from Galilee and there was a fair crowd of onlookers. Some were obviously foreigners and some were simply enjoying the spectacle, but there were many serious and then joyful faces; it might not be ideal but it was certainly a step in the right direction. Of course there would be opposition from the Jewish hierarchy and the Romans but Judas had seen enough miracles to convince him that if Jesus (he never called him "the Master", as the others did), if Jesus wanted the crown of Israel, he could have it.

Out of force of habit he kept an eye out for trouble. The Roman soldiers at the check points were not very interested in this motley procession, but he recognised some of the Temple Police mingling with the crowd and he thought he saw that slippery Nicodemus gliding away from the scene; which reminded him, he would go and see Joseph of Aramathea later to get a hefty donation for the fighting fund because even if Jesus could work miracles there would still need to be some sort of fighting fund; after that story of Cana you could imagine Jesus turning anything into anything, except into money.

No, Jesus had been decidedly ambivalent about money, though he did not mind eating and drinking what it bought. The disciples, on the other hand, were anything but indifferent to money; it caused more trouble than anything else except the rivalry to be close to "the Master". There was even a nasty incident when somebody accused him of stealing from the kitty. A stupid accusation because they all knew how fanatical he was about the cause; but when he reminded them of what Jesus said about the Pharisees who pretended to be pious when they were corrupt, it made no difference. The problem was that people exaggerated what they had actually given; the only one you could really trust was Joseph who gave quietly and never said anything.

He had seen Joseph as he left the High Priest's office after giving back the money. Joseph had been waiting outside the door and when he saw Judas he looked hurt and confused but Judas had stared him down. It had not been so easy during the short interview with Caiaphas as that oily cove Nicodemus was there. As Judas put the money down he could have sworn that Nicodemus gave him a contemptuous shrug but before he could take it in, the diplomatic mask slipped over his face, looking as if it had never moved; perhaps it never had.

Why had he taken the money in the first place? It seemed stupid now but it was his kind of revenge, his way of getting back at Jesus. After all, his problem was that he had seen through Jesus; the others, even Peter, still thought they would be courtiers of Judah. Just before the procession from the Mount of Olives broke up, Judas had manoeuvred all the young disciples, except for that dreamer, John, to form a kind of phalanx around Jesus; he had got them all chanting "Hosanna to the Son of David!" as they moved towards the Temple courtyard. If they could just get Jesus to the steps he could make his victory speech on the spot where all the kings had been crowned. But Jesus had told them to keep quiet and, before

Judas could do anything to intervene, he had signalled to Peter, James and John and had slipped away, leaving the remnants of the crowd; and Judas holding the donkey. That had been the last straw.

He took the wretched animal back to its owner and settled the bill. He had heard Jesus say something about borrowing it for nothing; but there was no such thing as a free donkey. Then he had found John and asked him how he could get in touch with Caiaphas and John, all innocent, had said he would have a word with Nicodemus who had been his Scripture tutor.

Judas had not quite known what he would do but there was no point going on with this charade. He had thought that the parables and coded statements were part of an elaborate plan to build support for a coup. Now there were masses of supporters from Galilee, there were sympathisers in the Council and, of course, those miraculous powers. And what was it all for? He did not know any more; he just felt cheated. He had wasted three years of his life, raising the money, making ends meet, haggling, putting some by for the big day; and now there was not going to be a big day. The only chance of preserving Judah from Roman absorption was to throw in his lot with the Temple authorities. His namesake Judas Maccabeus had fought to preserve the Temple rites against Melanisation and he would do the same against the Romans.

So Judas had steeled himself to bait Nicodemus with a story about reaching an accommodation between Jesus and the authorities, more necessary than ever after a recent nasty little incident in the Temple. Caiaphas had been cold but interested. It would be most helpful for the Jewish cause to keep Jesus under lock and key for a while. Nicodemus had slid back in and Caiaphas had changed instantly. It had been good to see a representative of Jesus; he hoped this would lead to a much better working relationship. Judas thought he saw Nicodemus give him a very old-fashioned look as he headed for the Treasury.

From the moment with the donkey he never wavered; better, as he heard Caiaphas say, that one man should die for the sake of the people; but it had been difficult because he knew that Jesus knew. It was like being in a dream. He went on with his secret life that was not a secret. It had been a relief when he had grabbed the piece of bread from Jesus and almost fallen down the stairs into the street.

Judas never wavered until he saw Jesus crowned with thorns. He had betrayed Jesus but then Caiaphas had betrayed him. Once Jesus was sent to Pilate the game was up but, much worse, Caiaphas had told Pilate publicly that he would not be a Friend of Caesar unless he condemned Jesus.

There was no way back: no way back to Jesus; no way back to the Temple; no way back to Maccabeus. Caiaphas had caved in; Jesus was about to die. All his life he had dreamed of a priestly king. It was all over.

He felt the rope tightening around his plunging neck; and then he saw the crown of thorns transformed into a crown of unbearable light.

**Prayer**

Jesus, Saviour of the World, may we not be lured away from you by our earthly entanglements. May we, warned by Judas, recognise how close we become to him if we do not stay close to you. Even now, as you are condemned to die for us as your final act of service, we pray for your help that we may be your humble servants, accepting the mission you will for us in your Church; and, as you declared the kingdom of your Father upon earth, may we, stirred by the Grace of your Passion, proclaim it steadfastly in your name. Armed with the sacred gifts of the Holy Spirit, may we never betray your obedience to the Father's love. Amen.

## iii. Simon

It had only been a chance remark, a throwaway line, when Simon had said that if Israel wanted a Messiah so badly, Jesus was as good as any.

He had been delivering a consignment of incense to the Temple and got into conversation with some of the clerks while the packets were being weighed and authority obtained for the payment from Joseph of Aramathea who always took his time checking the bills. Then the hot topic of the day, Jesus of Galilee, came up. One of the older men said that you had to maintain discipline; all sorts of people were claiming to be prophets or the Messiah nowadays; it was bad for the Temple; and if things went wrong at the Temple there would be no defence against complete absorption by Rome. As long as there was a Temple there would be a buffer, in the form of Herod and the religious elite, between the Jews and the Romans.

Simon had said that after the free and easy atmosphere in Cyrene, Jerusalem was getting the whole Jesus situation out of perspective, it was on the verge of hysteria over nothing. And then he said Jesus could be the Messiah; and the room went silent.

Simon had seen the so-called "Procession" on the previous day. Some of the followers of Jesus were shouting about the "Son of David" but it seemed good humoured and, as usual, the Temple spies had exaggerated the crowd numbers so that they would be kept on for more work; it was always best to keep everybody nervous.

Simon had been immediately drawn to Jesus because he had such an interesting face; he looked as if he could see everything but, at the same time, he was looking straight at you. No doubt he was holy, maybe a prophet, but Simon did not see how he could threaten the Temple and the religious authorities, a serene-faced, quietly spoken Galilean riding on a donkey. In fact, one or two of his followers looked a bit sheepish. There was one fellow, holding the donkey at the end of the ride, who looked decidedly embarrassed, almost angry. This did not look like a coup.

The awkwardness was broken by Joseph's messenger coming back with the tally and the authorisation; but because of some clause in the contract and the long weekend, he would not be able to pick up the cash until the morning after the Sabbath. When it came to Temple funds Joseph was a stickler, though he was said to be charming in private, in his own quiet way.

Almost a week in Jerusalem and nothing to do. He had seen the sights before, when he had come with his father to learn his trade; things were so expensive during Passover; and they did not know how to cook. He longed for some fresh Mediterranean fish. The only place he really liked was a shady courtyard near the Temple where the manuscript dealers gathered. His father, as the purchaser of new scrolls for a group of synagogues in Cyrene, had introduced him there. This time he had been asked to buy the Lamentations of Jeremiah—a curious little piece, it turned out—so he would study that to pass the time.

Simon could not sleep properly on Thursday night so he got up early and went for a walk. He heard a crowd shouting over near the Governor's Palace so he followed the noise. He then saw him, Jesus, beaten up and bleeding. Roman officials looked fed up with the whole thing and a couple of soldiers almost threw Jesus at the Temple Police. He stumbled and fell in front of Simon. That is when the disciplinarian from the Temple office saw him, gave him a nasty look, and talked to a senior official who signalled to a pair of Policemen who beckoned Simon to follow them.

He did not have any choice. They pointed at a rough, heavy section of a log and told him to take it over to Jesus. His rash words had caught up with him.

The man he had casually called the Messiah was struggling to stand up; a beaten up peasant. But he still had that look Simon had seen during the procession; he looked as if he could see everything but, at the same time, he was looking straight at you.

Jesus tried to say something but the police were threatening and clearly in a hurry. The wood had an awkward girth but it was so short that it was easier for one to carry than two. Simon put Jesus in front but they had only walked a couple of steps when Jesus tripped up; there was so much blood coming from the wounds on his forehead that he could not see and move at the same time. Simon put him behind and took all the weight so that Jesus could pretend to carry the log but he fell over again as soon as Simon moved off. And, anyway, Simon wanted to look at Jesus. So Simon let Jesus hold onto the log, walking a pace behind him and to the right; that way Simon could take most of the weight in his right arm and glance at Jesus whenever he wanted to.

"It is good to bear the burden when young ... to eat dust ... to turn your cheek to the assailant and be crammed with curses." The Lamentations echoed in Simon's head, in the face of Jesus, in the crowd; the Lament of the Prophet, the wickedness of the city, the yoke and the log fused in his brain. He was lost in the noise and the words within; his concentration lapsed and Jesus fell again.

This time Simon abandoned all pretence. He took Jesus under the arms and hauled him to his feet; he was deadly light. Jesus looked straight at him through the blood, the sweat, the hair and the thorns; Simon could feel his eyes through everything; and then he raised his hand and put it on Simon's head; just for a moment before the Policemen kicked Simon so hard that he fell over. Without thinking, he picked Jesus up and carried him to an empty pole, collected the wood and rushed back with it.

He could not bear the sound of the hammer. He went away and was sick. When he came back Jesus was on the Cross, still seeing the whole world and looking straight at Simon. "Is it nothing to you all who pass by?" He had never seen anything so sad.

He had been touched by Jesus. He knew it would change his life forever. He had been more right about the Messiah than he knew.

**Prayer**

Jesus, Saviour of the World, may we carry our Cross whenever you will it to fall upon our shoulder. May we, like Simon, show compassion to others when we are most under stress, struggling to Calvary. Even now, as you look down with compassion upon your persecutors, we pray for your help that we may be your faithful companions to the end. And, as Simon was touched by your love, may we feel your touch most fully when we are preoccupied and confused. Softened by your touch, may we walk quietly in the Way of the Cross, praying to the Father for holy strength and guided by the Holy Spirit that we may not fall. Amen.

## iv. Mary and the Women

Silent women. When Jesus was arrested in the Garden of Gethsemane all the disciples had fled and, later, Peter had denied him. Only the young John had crept back to the foot of the Cross to be commended to Mary and she to him.

So apart from John his only close friends were women; women who had followed him from Galilee, who had uprooted themselves from their homes to live a ramshackle life on the road. This itinerant and mendicant life was easier for the men who camped where they stopped; but for women who were subject to much stricter social rules in every aspect of their lives, travelling presented real problems.

The women ministered to Jesus and his disciples and, with the exception of Martha and Mary, they said nothing. Now they are silent, stoical figures, standing quietly amid the abuse, the spitting, the wanton, routine cruelty; standing amidst the stench of the rubbish dump that is Golgotha; standing in silent witness.

The men had been the inner circle for Jesus; they had organised the crowds, fanned out across the country to preach, heard the explanation of the parables, and shared the Last Supper; and now, when Jesus really needed them, they were not here; and the women who had been patient and silent, who had asked for nothing, who had said nothing, had stayed to the end.

That brave and humble girl who agreed to become the mother of Jesus was their unity, their strength, their magnet and their catalyst. After the Presentation of Jesus in the Temple Mary tried to fulfil the impossible mission of being the mother of God. When Jesus stayed behind in the Temple at the age of twelve she had to curb her terrible fear; when he said at Cana that his time had not yet come (though his mother knew better), she had to bite her tongue; and when she asked to see him after he had finished preaching, she could hardly control herself, gripped by a mixture of fear and joy.

And always in the background was Simeon's ominous warning that a sword would pierce her heart as the result of her faithfulness to her Son Jesus and that strange look she got from Hannah; and here is this sword now, piercing her heart, even before the soldier pierces the side of the dead Jesus, emptying the last drops of blood and water.

Mary has followed her Son every step of the way and many mothers must know how she feels with sons who are so mysterious: sons who talk in incomprehensible jargon; sons who are obsessed with the esoteric; sons who leave home to travel with hardly a spare shirt. Mary has such a Son who was old before his time; who spoke in parables and sometimes in riddles; who cured the sick and even raised the dead to life. How do you talk to a son like that?

Sons can be so gruff. Mary remembers Jesus in the Temple, aged twelve, telling her off for being worried; did she not know he had to be on his Father's business? She remembers trying to escape unseen from the wedding party at Cana to have a quiet word with the servants; and she remembers how often when she called him out of the Synagogue to give him a message that he was rather short with her. Although she knows he loves her more than anyone else in the world, she just wishes it was occasionally a little more lyrical, not quite so forthright; he is so full of love but a little short on sentiment. But, then, there were all those unbelievable moments when the sick were cured and the poor were fed; and he even brought the dead back to life; for all its trials, she could not imagine a better life and a better son.

She knew it would end in trouble; it was bound to, with all that preaching against the Scribes and the Pharisees. In an occupied land where people had to make unpleasant compromises, no leader was ever safe; the Jewish religious leaders had to be careful to balance their authority over the people and their unwritten deal with the Romans; and Jesus had steadily undermined their authority. Nicodemus had said a quiet word to her now and again but it had made no difference.

So here he is now, hanging from the Cross and here is Mary, patiently waiting for the end she knows will come soon; but she cannot quite see this end. She still believes the Angel who said her Son was the Son of God, brought into being through her by the Holy Spirit; she still remembers Simeon's promise that her Son would be a light to the Gentiles and she, with a mother's faith, always stored away what he said without wanting immediate answers. He has said he will establish his heavenly Father's kingdom on earth; and he has said he will rise again after three days.

Here, in this desolate landscape, amidst the rubbish rotting in the Mediterranean sun, amidst the blood and guts of another batch of crucifixions, within her there is an incongruous note of joy amidst the sorrow. Something will happen. Something must happen; she has to believe this or her whole life will have made no sense.

And as the men sat over the dregs of their cheap wine, stretching out towards the meaning of what Jesus told them, the women gathered quietly to comment on the day's events, strengthened by the conviction of Mary that they were on a special mission; and even now, when all seems lost, they are still there; something is holding them to the spot, keeping them next to Mary as Jesus cries out.

Being women, there has to be a plan past the immediate present. You cannot give way to total suffering; you cannot go into yourself and hope that the rest of the world will manage; because the disciples will not sort out the embalming and, in their distress and fear, they will not buy food and prepare it. Their emotional disintegration will be made worse by poor food and too much wine if the women are not there to put things right.

So, even as her Son is dying, Mary cannot be totally self-absorbed; the woman who has given life to Jesus and the whole of her life to Jesus is still giving it now, still making a sacrifice of her own emotional preferences, still thinking of others when she wants to focus on her Son, still seeing a tomorrow when today is such a disaster.

In excruciating agony, her Son's cry tears through the sneering hubbub around her; and he dies. For a split second there is nothing; and then she feels the movement of the Holy Spirit within her.


**Prayer**

Jesus, Saviour of the World, may we not run away when called upon to bear witness to your saving mission. May we, like Mary and the women, be faithful and humble as we now stand with them at Calvary. Even now, as you hang helpless on the Cross, we pray for your help that we may be your faithful servants in adversity to the end. And, as you commended your mother, Mary, to your disciples, may we take her into our hearts as an icon of what you want and what you have made possible for all your creatures. Fortified by your love, may we watch and pray in obedience to the Father and at one with the Holy Spirit. Amen.

# v. John

Suddenly, in the middle of the day, it had become pitch black; unusually black because there were no stars. John thought he must have been having another of his visions.

Ever since he came to the Temple School in Jerusalem John had been having visions. It was from reading too much Daniel. As the youngest in the class he had been the last to choose his special book and there were not all that many left, so he had chosen Daniel and its multiple variants; but it was the visions that gripped him not the exegesis. Of course, he said nothing; imagine what the other boys would have said if he had told them he was having visions. It was bad enough being an outsider.

John had been born so late that people talked about it: some said a child so late was a special gift from God; others said that no child born so late could be normal. John always thought he was different. He did not like boats and water and when it became clear that he would not carry on in the family fishing business he was lucky enough to get help from the local Rabbi to go down to Jerusalem. It had all been fixed by his Guardian Nicodemus and his friend Joseph who chaired the Scholarship Committee at the Temple.

At the beginning, the visions were disembodied flashes, huge infusions of light that made outlandish shapes; but when he first saw Jesus as he sat with James in their boat, he was overcome by a vision of light and water so that he felt sick. James, being phlegmatic, would say it was the angle of the sun and the movement of the boat but John knew it was a sacred vision and it had something to do with Jesus who, according to the locals, was turning into a fine interpreter of Scripture. John had known that he would follow Jesus and from then on he was rewarded with regular visions. Even though those who followed Jesus were much kinder than the group of boys he had now left behind at the Temple, he was still too frightened to mention the visions, even to Peter; but the Master knew. Peter tried to look after him carefully as he was the most sensitive but they never quite worked out their relationship and Jesus had to keep rescuing John when he was teased by the others for his affected Jerusalem accent, his soft hands and his tendency to daydream. Still, Peter was confused when Jesus had taken him, James and John—the leader, the fixer and the dreamer—up Mount Tabor. Peter could not keep still; he needed to do something. James had looked blank but knew how to keep quiet and keep a straight face; but John knew what was going on and just concentrated on the Master. There had been no jokes about visions after that. John had talked to Judas about it because he was the most intelligent of the Master's followers but Judas was still thinking about a coronation in Jerusalem. John was too young to argue but he felt danger.

He saw the Spirit around the Master and he could hear the Father. He knew that the Master was the Son of God, not just the greatest of the prophets; but the brothers were very muddled and defensive and it was best to say nothing and follow quietly.

Then, as they had made their regular trip to Jerusalem for the Passover, the visions grew darker; they were full of blood and the sound of torture.

The last few hours had seemed like one unbroken vision. He knew that the foot washing was a farewell; he knew that the breaking of the bread was the breaking of the Master's body; he knew before Judas got up to leave who the betrayer was; and, knowing all this, he needed the comfort of the Master who was to die. Without that comfort he would have fainted.

But in the Garden of Gethsemane, with all that emotion in the air, he did faint. The blood had become almost tangible, the noises had grown louder and the visions began happening while he was awake, not asleep; so the fainting and the darkness that followed were a relief. Then Judas came with the soldiers and John knew that Jesus wanted to be arrested. He could not work out the detail but he knew that the Master was just that, completely in charge of what was going on. That is why he wasn't frightened.

John knew how badly Peter would take it after the little skirmish with Malchus, so he decided to look after him during the trial and see if he could explain what was going on. But Peter did not understand the true purpose of the one he most loved or the politics in Jerusalem and he was so scared that he started saying really foolish things to the servants in the High Priest's courtyard after John had taken so much trouble to get him in. Then Peter had made an unearthly howling noise and rushed out, waving his knife. It could have been much worse but just as Peter ran away the news spread that Caiaphas was sending Jesus to Pilate. John knew what that would lead to; so Jesus must have wanted to be condemned both by the Jewish authorities and the Romans, by the spiritual and temporal rulers.

He could not find Peter, who had not gone back to their Jerusalem headquarters, but he did find the Master's mother and the other women who had heard nothing. They were still clearing up after the evening meal, growing anxious about the men who had gone out to pray. It was hard for John to tell his story but Mary's calmness helped him. They did not like going out, particularly not when there were crowds about but they had no choice. They reached the Governor's Palace in time to see Pilate showing the Master to the crowd before he was bound over to be crucified. John thought he saw Nicodemus slipping out of the side door but a soldier blocked his line of sight.

John walked with Mary because they both seemed to know that the whole series of terrible events were somehow under the control of her Son. The women were very upset but they said nothing. They followed the Master, careful not to fall within his eye line but once he stopped suddenly and saw them and comforted them.

It was when they put the Master on the Cross that John knew he really was having a vision; but he knew he would not faint. He was the only man with Mary and the women; he must try to be more mature than his age.

In the dark the noises carried much further. John could hear the Master's slowing, shallowing breath; he could almost hear the beating of his heart. And then he said: "Mother, here is your son" and to John he said: "And this is your mother." She held his hand.

Then the Master gave a deep sigh and said: "At last, it is finished"; but John did not hear the rest. He felt Mary's hand suddenly tighten, as if seized by a spasm, and he felt the Holy Spirit's life passing from her to him. Then his vision of the dark was transformed into a vision of unending light.

## Prayer

Jesus, Saviour of the World, may our lives not be rooted in earthly things but remain faithful to your heavenly vision. May we, like John, be sustained by the promise of your kingdom, enshrined in your redeeming love. Even now, as you ascend into heavenly glory, we pray for your help that we may be seekers after eternal truth through prayer, Sacrament and Holy Scripture. And, as you Commended your Mother Mary and your beloved disciple John to one other, may we accept what you commend without doubt or hesitation. Filled by hope of salvation, may we hold before us the vision of the Blessed and undivided Trinity. Amen.

## vi. Jesus

Where did it all go wrong? How did so much love become transformed into so much hate? How did he become separated from the lovely lakeside of Galilee and end up, dying between a pair of thieves on this rubbish dump? But, more important, where was the Father to whom he had been so faithful and obedient for the whole of his life?

Relatives always will reminisce about the birth of a child but nobody had said much to Jesus; they were obviously ashamed of something. He remembered childhood trips to Jerusalem which broke the monotony of village life as an odd job man but it had all been calm until his wild Cousin John had burst out of the wilderness to preach the kingdom; and he knew at once that John meant the kingdom of his Father. He knew this when he was baptised by John; he heard his Father and he felt the Spirit within him. He knew it when he fasted and prayed in the wilderness before those magic days by the lake when he had felt totally free, recruiting his followers; and he knew it when he performed his first miracles. Of course there had been scepticism, and even some small minded opposition, but he had everything in front of him. He knew, of course, that it would not always be easy; but those first few months with all the raw faith of the people, the rows of sick and broken humanity made whole, encounters with Gentiles and strange people; it was like a blur now, with flashes of sun and water, boat trips and scenes of wild jubilation as thousands were fed.

It had all become more serious as opposition hardened and became organised at the top of the religious hierarchy. He knew he had to go on but it became more edgy; he had to say what he had to say but was tempted to speak less directly, sometimes choosing enigmatic sounding statements rather than the homely and hard hitting parables he most liked. Slowly, as the time went by, he saw that he would have to work out the choreography for his own death; it could not be allowed to be a messy chapter of accidents; it needed to happen in a certain way in order to show the world the love and power of his Father.

He had not been travelling the length and breadth of Palestine for more than a few months before he knew that he would die at the third Passover, to make a neat alignment with the Scriptures. It haunted him constantly but there was still the companionship of the disciples and the somewhat unsteady love of the crowd; but as the time drew nearer, the disciples were not such good companions and the crowd was ever more fickle. Even as he sat at table for the final Passover, he knew that his ordeal would be lonely; he knew that Peter would not have the nerve to stick with him, that the others would flee; and that, as usual, it would be his mother and the women who would stay. His mother; what a miracle she was!

The physical pain since his arrest had been alternately excruciating and numbing; the noise and mockery and mess had been unrelenting. He had known how it would be; every time he visited Jerusalem there were crucifixions. It would soon be over; and then, what?

Where had it all gone wrong? Where was his Father to whom he had been so humbly and unswervingly faithful? He had preached the kingdom of his Father, he had always deferred in everything to his Father; he had claimed nothing for himself which did not come from the Father; he was acting now in painful obedience to the Father; but he could not see why; he could not see what it was for.

Even in pain he liked the ironic plaque that the old rogue Pilate had caused to be put above his head; King of the Jews in three languages; he liked it because he had spent so much of his time telling people that he was not going to be the King of the Jews; and that had been the killer blow for poor old Judas who could not bear his airy fairy promises about a heavenly kingdom and wanted him to be the King of the Jews here and now. Poor Judas; and it had all ended like this with Judas dying before him.

He saw his mother trying not to cry; he saw young John pretending not to cry; he saw the women who had been so quietly faithful trying not to cry. He wished they would cry because he wanted to cry, too. He had known all his life that there was something special about him and his lifelong mission. He had somehow known from as soon as he could speak that he was a very special child of his Father in heaven. He had felt it with every visit to the Synagogue, as he was allowed to untie the scrolls and read from the Torah. He had read and understood very well for a boy of such humble origins. He knew, when his spirit was freed to travel and preach, that he was doing the right thing; He knew as he prayed alone whenever he could find respite from the crowds, that he was doing the right thing, that he was a special child of his Father in heaven. He had never felt embarrassed using the sacred language of Godhead; he had never felt that he was overstepping the mark, that he was being blasphemous, even though that was the charge most often levelled against him. He had said he would rise in three days; that was the Spirit in him; but where was the Spirit now?

He had known that his mission was special right up to the time when he was condemned to die; and then his certainty had forsaken him. It was all very well to say that his kingdom was not of this world and that his accusers would learn the reality sooner or later; but here he was, about to die, with his disciples fled and nothing lasting accomplished.

Where had it all gone wrong? How had so much love turned to so much hate? With his last breath he cried out to his Father: "Why have you forsaken me?"; and in the split second after he said it, in the split second before he died, he wished he had stayed quiet. In that split second he saw that it had not gone wrong; that he was not forsaken; that his unswerving obedience to his Father, even in death, had earned him a unique place in his Father's love that would spill over Golgotha, over Palestine and over the whole world; he did not know how; but he knew in that instant that he had not been abandoned but had simply been left to show love in the way that only the lonely can show love. And then he died.

**Prayer**

Jesus, Saviour of the World, may we learn true obedience, through your example, to our heavenly Father. May we, in imitation of you, be brave and steadfast in the face of mockery and, even more committed in the face of indifference to your word. Even now, as you are suspended between earthly life and heavenly glory, we pray for your help that we may stand daily within the shadow of your Cross. And, as you were unswervingly obedient to the Father, may we, strengthened by your example, temper our obedience with love so that we may be his true children. Secure in his love, may our obedience be deepened by your Passion and death and broadened by the calm of the Holy Spirit. Amen.

## vii. Nicodemus and Joseph

What did it mean? He cried out through the sneering hubbub: "My God, why have you forsaken me?"; and then he died.

Well, at least that is what Nicodemus and Joseph thought he had said. Sometime later somebody said that he had commended himself to the Father but that sounded a bit unlikely given the lasting impression of desperation they heard in his distant cry. Distant, of course, it was distant; they were frightened; they did not want to get too involved. The place was infested with fellow Pharisees, Sadducees, minor officials, soldiers and cranks; and you could not be too careful. Caiaphas was clearly in a filthy mood; he had probably overstepped the mark in calling for the death of Jesus. They heard strange laughter from a passer-by who said Pilate had proclaimed Jesus to be King of the Jews. Well, he was so unpredictable; you never knew where you were.

They always had kept their distance except for the night when Nicodemus secretly visited Jesus to ask him about the kingdom. Ever since then he had been in the background, quietly pulling strings; arguing for moderation when the authorities wanted to arrest Jesus; sending discreet warnings when things were getting too hot; urging the disciples to take Jesus out of Jerusalem for a few days until things quieted down. Yes, Nicodemus had always been there and thereabouts in the corridors of power, quietly doing his earthly bit for this unearthly prophet; but always careful not to be identified as a follower; just doing his cautious bit on the Council to keep the temperature down.

And Joseph, well, he had always been too shy to approach Jesus directly but he had quietly tipped Judas the odd donation, for the poor, for the disciples and for Jesus; he had never been one to put himself forward but business was good and he always had a little something to spare. He would have liked to do more but he never could quite work out how; Jesus was so odd when it came to money; so gentle and yet so forthright. Joseph did not know whether he would ever quite come to terms with the incident in the Temple courtyard when Jesus had expelled all the traders.

They knew each other, Nicodemus and Joseph; in the hothouse of Jerusalem religious politics that was hardly surprising; they had even sat on the same Temple fund-raising committee for a while. Each also knew that the other knew Jesus; but they had never brought themselves to mention it as they exchanged pleasantries at social and ceremonial occasions.

Now, as this horrible, almost unbearable scene drew them together, they still found it difficult to drop the pretence. They knew they had not done enough for Jesus; they had been content to be discreet, like fellow travellers, tacitly supporting a good cause. Each of them had suspected Judas but had sat on their hands.

It was too late to show their hand now to Jesus but things had to be done. Pilate would have to be approached for the body and you never knew what sort of a mood he would be in; it was a bit awkward but they would have to talk to the women about the burial of Jesus. There was not much time to waste as the Sabbath was rapidly approaching.

They forgot the horror in the flurry of activity; filing a writ for the body of Jesus, making all the burial arrangements; and Mary was so quiet and calm, making them feel that she was looking after them instead of the other way round, so gently that it was not embarrassing.

On the way home it really hit them. They felt that they had missed a once in a lifetime opportunity to find themselves spiritually. Jesus was like nobody else they had ever heard but they had never quite managed to commit themselves, there was always a tiny cord of caution holding them back; they could have broken it but that would have broken the cautious habits of a lifetime; so they had watched, and listened and waited; then He had cried out with a loud voice; and it was too late.

So before they parted for the Sabbath they agreed to meet regularly with the disciples, if they could find them, to go through the whole life story of Jesus to see what they could salvage from it. They would try to be brave; they would try to face up to their own caution, or perhaps it would be more honest to call it cowardice; they would commit themselves to the memory of Jesus and see that his wisdom would not be forgotten; and they would do their best to help those he had left behind.

It was a miserable Sabbath; the most miserable they had ever known. They kept hearing his distant, desperate cry; they wished they had been closer, to hear what he had really said. Nicodemus could hardly bear the moonlight; it reminded him so much of that night he had talked with Jesus; Joseph could not bear the darkness when the moon disappeared because it reminded him of the tomb. Nicodemus could not get the strange riddle out of his head that Jesus told him on that mysterious night: "God loved the world so much he sent his only son; all who believe in him will not die but will be saved; for God did not send his Son into the world to condemn it but that it might be saved through him."

What did it mean? Well, whatever it meant, it was meaningless now.

As Joseph tossed and turned during that desolate night, he, too, remembered Jesus saying something; something about coming back again after three days, something curious about destroying and rebuilding the Temple. What did it mean? They could make no sense of it when they met on Saturday evening. They were haunted by an opportunity missed. Only God, looking down on his broken world, knew their broken hearts; only God knew that they were not too late; that they would get another and another and another chance; only God knew that his Son had not died in vain, that his unswerving obedience would bring him to unimaginable, everlasting glory. Only God knew.

**Prayer**

Jesus, Saviour of the World, may we be bold and brave in your service, loving your Father without restraint, loving our neighbour with cheerful generosity. Even now, as you are taking your leave of this cruel world to be ever glorified with your Father, we pray for your help that we may lose our earthly inhibitions and grow in our desire for the heavenly life. And, as you loved all your Father's children in spite of their timid strivings, may we feel your sacred love, born of the Father and radiated within us through your Holy Spirit. Amen.

## viii. Mary Magdalene

Such small feet. The nails had not so much pierced them as smashed each of them into two, jagged halves; but Mary could still make out a tiny scar which she remembered from that time when she had tended his feet.

For so long she had literally sat at his feet that it had become her natural vantage point. She liked to watch him pray in the quiet of the early evening while supper was being prepared. She liked to pray with him because she felt his spiritual energy. Martha occasionally grumbled but she would not have liked sitting at his feet any more than Mary liked cooking. The Master said you could come into the kingdom as a mystic or a cook; and she, by temperament, was a mystic, as totally unaware of her beauty as Martha was unaware of her plainness. That is why Mary got on so well with John whereas Martha liked to be with Peter and James.

She could not help thinking, as she opened Joseph's big jar, of the time they had embalmed Lazarus. This time they would have to do everything in a hurry before the Sabbath was about to begin but that time they had waited as long as they dared in the hope that the Master would arrive and do something. They were not sure, in a focused kind of way, what he would do; but they felt he would do something.

The waiting was terrible but the entombment was even worse. They still went on waiting, even after mourners began to arrive. Martha covered her anxiety by looking after everyone but you could see she had not given up hope. Mary tried to get closer to the Holy Spirit, leaving herself as open as she could to receive strength.

And then he came. Martha had gone out immediately but Mary knew she must wait, that nothing they said could change things; that only the Master could make a difference. Martha came back trying to look calm and said he had asked for her. So Mary went and knelt at his feet, noticing how sore they were. People would think that she was crying for Lazarus but she was crying for him; nobody understood him. All that love that he sent out and so little ever came back. She could feel it then, as she knelt at his feet, worshipping, not pleading.

He went to the tomb and some of the men reluctantly opened it; and Lazarus came out, frightening everyone but Jesus and Mary; and John who was in a kind of trance in the middle distance. Somehow they got everybody away and gave Lazarus the peace and quiet he needed but just before Passover they arranged a small party. Lazarus, who was still in a state of shock, said nothing; Martha was busy making everything comfortable; but Mary felt that a gesture was called for; friendship, food and wine were not enough. She anointed his feet; that is when she had noticed the small scar; it was amazing that there were not more, the amount of walking he had done in the past three years. She wept in gratitude for what he had done and fear for what would happen to him. Then she sat nearby on the floor. She was so upset that nobody understood him that she could not eat. She just sat there, half praying, half grieving.

She went with some of the other women into Jerusalem to assist at the festivities; but nobody was very festive. She fetched hot water from the fire and a large towel but it caused dissension; Peter was upset though she could not immediately work out why. As she left, she caught sight of Jesus as she stood at the angle of the stairs; he was bending down in precisely the way she could see herself doing; then she knew exactly what was going on and why Peter was upset; he would be; but John would know what was going on. Later, when they left the dining room, they did not look refreshed; they looked shattered as they went out to pray. She wanted to go with him but knew that she could not; they had no time for women and, except for John, no time for mystics. She put the towel into some more hot water.

They worried when the men did not come back at their usual time; but most of them managed some sleep. Mary felt the tension in the air; she could feel his love being twisted and returned to him in hate, but she was still shocked when John rushed in and said what was going on. She asked no questions and only stayed long enough to see that Mary had everything she needed; of course she did, even under such pressure.

Mary stood uncertainly near the Cross. It was not the cruelty, she had seen enough of that, and it was not the hostility which she could blank out; but she felt as if she was waiting for something, as if what was going on in the real world was a dream, a feeling greatly enhanced by the unearthly darkness.

And then he died.

Such small feet. She worked more quickly than she had ever done before. The whole process was unearthly: the strange environment; the febrile activity; the important men looking at her. But Mary made everything real; you would have expected a mother, even one as serene as she, to give way a little; but she was intent on looking after everyone; she would save her grief until later when the job was done. This was not nature working of its own accord before the impact of shock, she was using her reserves; you could see how the ethic of service was something that she and her Son had shared.

Seeing Nicodemus, such a staunch Pharisee, standing nearby reminded Mary of her brother Lazarus and his return to life. Jesus had told Mary afterwards that he had deliberately waited some way off after he heard about the death so that he could bear witness to the greater glory of his Father by raising Lazarus. She had understood what he meant. As the raising of Lazarus passed through her mind, Lazarus who was nearby, helping Joseph to find a rock that would fit the entrance of the tomb, she wondered how the Master would be raised from the dead. She knew that he, like all true believers, would be raised; but she thought he would be raised in a special way. He might deliberately stay away for a few days but he would be back, for the Greater Glory of God. She felt the Holy Spirit coming back to her as if he had been bearing company to the Soul of Jesus, and, in that moment, Mary knew he would return.

**Prayer**

Jesus, Saviour of the World, may we stay with you to the end, no matter how hopeless our lives appear to be. May we, like Martha and Mary, find our way to your kingdom by uniting your redeeming Grace with our human wills. Even now, as your earthly body is entombed, we pray for your help that we may once again faithfully re-enact our own earthly entombment in Baptism. And, as you gave strength to Martha and Mary's faith in you, may we recall their faith that you would raise Lazarus from the dead, their hope of the life to come and their love of your earthly sisters and brothers. Grieved by the pain you suffered for us, yet may we be joyful in your Resurrection, through our faith in the Father and our obedience to the Holy Spirit. Amen.

# 2. Who Was to Blame?

*2006*

## i. Palm Sunday—Self-Interest and Generosity

*Blessed is the Coming One, the King in the Lord's Name,*
*in heaven peace and glory in the highest places.*

**Luke 19:38**

In an age of unquestioned elitism tragedy was epitomised in the hero who suffered from a fatal flaw. Such was the stuff of ancient Greek and Shakespeare plays such as *Hamlet* and *Othello* and yet there are other Shakespeare plays, notably *Julius Caesar* and *Coriolanus*, which anticipate a different, more volatile and demotic age when the mob would have a decisive role in politics. That age was feared throughout the eighteenth century by the emerging bourgeoisie and seemed justified by the mad lurch in the course of the French Revolution from Utopianism to mob-induced state mass murder. Tragedy passed from cathartic inevitability to cynically murderous manipulation. Fate gave way to the state.

Today we are accustomed to the "virtual mob" of the mass media which routinely makes and breaks celebrities for our entertainment. In an age of vicious competition for sales in dwindling and fragmenting markets, those who want to devote themselves to public service or any kind of creativity risk monstrously presumptive glorification and degradation.

It is therefore against the historical background of mob-induced and mob-inflicted violence and the mass media acting as a surrogate mob that we tend to view the entry of Jesus into Jerusalem, but before we consider the interaction between Jesus and those who greeted him it is important to note that the Gospels are not entirely clear about what actually took place. The safest assumption is that the crowds which greeted Jesus were made up both of his followers and sight-seers not only from Jerusalem but from the diaspora newly arrived for Passover, a mixture of devoted admirers and sceptics carried away by the moment. Looked at dispassionately, what they shouted was, in the Jewish historical context, quite extraordinary; Luke's rendition of the shouting suggestively echoes the angelic address to the shepherds.

The standard charge that is laid against the crowd which greeted Jesus is that it was fickle, that it cheered him during his entry into the city and within a few days called for his Crucifixion. This rather glib two-part proposition makes all kinds of assumptions: first, it is not clear that there really were crowds on either occasion; secondly, even if there were, we do not know that the same leaders or agitators were in both crowds. Alternatively, the same people who praised him might have turned against Jesus but with very good reason. Between his entry into Jerusalem and the call for his Crucifixion he had, depending on the different chronologies: rampaged through the Temple, attacking the merchants; insulted religious leaders and accused them of being impostors; publicly supported the payment of taxes to the Roman Empire; roughed up the Sadducees over the Pharisaic doctrine of life after death; and forecast the destruction of the Temple. By any stretch of the imagination that was a charge sheet of enormous weight in a politically charged and instinctively conservative religious culture. For some people at least, a naive Northerner, a healer and teacher from Galilee, said to have performed some mighty acts and said some memorable things, achieving the status of a folk hero, had transformed himself into a religious and political radical. From the standpoint of the Synoptics this was a plausible if sudden development; from the point of view of John it was absolutely inevitable from the beginning; the locating of the rampage through the Temple is significant. All four Evangelists agree that the fate of Jesus was bound up with prophesy but they did not maintain that this was a separate and somehow different development from the confrontation between Jesus and the authorities, a narrowing of options which ultimately left them with no room for manoeuvre.

By performing an act of historical and social imagination, we can see many reasons why the resolve of the religious leaders to curb Jesus might have been strengthened and the resolve of the people to support him weakened. That the precise opposite should have taken place, that the hierarchy would have felt more drawn to Jesus and that the people would have found it possible to set aside the radical things he said, is almost unimaginable. That is why the attempt to drive a wedge between the people and their religious leaders is futile, no matter how admirable it might be as a device for defusing anti-Semitism.

The first lesson to be drawn is not that the mob is fickle and dangerous but that our perception of our own self-interest, paying little regard to intellectual consistency, can shift radically and summarily. It did not take long for the somewhat enigmatic prospect of a Messianic revival to be replaced by the leadership closing ranks to ensure a stable polity. Nobody knew better than the Jews who suffered when there was a rebellion. If they temporarily, and against their better judgment, believed that Jesus could restore the Kingdom of David without violence and social upheaval, they soon thought better of it. From the perspective of the impartial outsider, Jesus steadily increased the political stakes while the leadership he confronted stuck to a consistent line, a line which had been summed up by Caiaphas in a phrase which resonated with his people; better that one man should die for the whole people.

At a very basic level, disregarding any underlying theological purposes in the Gospels, there is, in spite of some post hoc wedge driving already noted, an attempt to place the blame for the death of Jesus jointly—though in different proportions—on the religious leadership and the mob. So, having considered the position of the people, what of the religious leadership? The first thing to say is that in spite of a massive shift in the Jewish theological focus from an earth-bound, here and now, religious practice to one which looked forward to a Messiah and even an after-life, there was no mechanism for recognising the Messiah and very little theology of the after-life. There were assumptions about the Messiah which depicted him as an actual descendant of David who would overthrow the Romans but it was a piece of shallow assertion which resembled the Medieval dichotomy of heaven and hell or the contemporary dichotomy between liberals and evangelicals. It was not theology as a process or as a personal journey, it was theology as theatre. What had started out as apocalyptic vision had become a cliché, a piece of convention, a common, conventional cultural object, a logo, an icon, a simple way of summing up a complex of ambition and resentment, propaganda and scholarship, history and promise. If you had asked the first-century man in the Jerusalem street about the coming of the Messiah he would have given you much the same kind of answer as you would receive today if you asked a Worcester woman about heaven.

For this reason, when Jesus presented himself in public as a different kind of Messiah there was no procedural way of dealing with the claim. This lack of process was severely complicated by Jesus' possible claim that he was the second person of the Jewish Godhead. We conflate these two ideas in Christology but to the Jewish mind they would have been quite separate. We might imagine a parallel situation of a woman proclaiming that she is the saviour of the contemporary church from all its terrible weaknesses and that she is also the fourth person of the Christian Godhead. Even most liberal Christians would find it difficult to arrive at any kind of procedure for assessing the second and more radical of these claims. From the standpoint of the Jewish religious authorities, Jesus was outlandish; but as long as he was only that then there was a degree of latitude which could be allowed. The Jewish people, led by their priestly class and political leaders, had not infrequently killed prophets who became too radical for the security or self-regard of their targets but on the whole Judaism allowed a great deal of latitude in religious controversy and speculation.

The more serious charge against the religious leadership—much more serious than its lack of a process for a largely hypothetical situation—is that it had elevated religious practice into a largely clerical monopoly. This charge can easily be exaggerated because of the necessarily partial accounts of the Evangelists but the religious observance within which Jesus grew up was losing contact with its earthliness. Apocalyptic, Messianism and interest in the after-life are only three examples of this shift in emphasis which was given added impetus by the improvement of transport and the economy under the Romans which made Temple-based, priestly officiated religion much more viable and the need for local improvisation much less acceptable. Like all maturing religions, Judaism was tending towards a Platonic desire for uniformity, the accomplishment of which is always made easier by means of communication and transport (the building of roads, for example, is the largest contributory factor to the destruction of languages previously protected by isolation). Uniformity and sterility are rarely far apart; the vigour which diversity brings to arguments about fundamental principles is usually replaced by febrile disputes over detail. Given the Jewish definition of work, it is highly unlikely that Jesus would have been condemned for healing on the Sabbath, but this is simply a metaphor for rampant legalism and hair-splitting.

The most serious charge against the religious authorities, however, is the simplest; they had lost any way of being self-referential; they had no way of understanding themselves. Their religious practices and theology seemed to lack any element of self-criticism, of doubt, any sense of things having gone wrong, of things being open to uncertainty.

If we accept Luke's implication that Jesus was only greeted by his own circle of followers when he entered Jerusalem, the charge against them of being fickle must be taken far more seriously than the charge against the common people or the religious leaders. Jesus' followers had, depending on which Gospel you read, been working alongside him in his mission for at least one (the Synoptics) and maybe three (John) years. They may not have understood everything he said. They may have been puzzled in a similar way to that in which we are puzzled by a poem that makes sense in our being but does not make sense syntactically. They may have felt that their sacrifice had not been rewarded adequately. But it is difficult to see, in spite of the pressures they underwent in that fateful week, how there could have been such a complete breakdown of empathy and trust. Surely the practical, political arguments, already mentioned, which might have swayed the people to change their minds should have had little sway with the close followers of this charismatic man. It is impossible to know but there are a number of possibilities which might have influenced them, individually or in combination.

First, did they stop praying under the pressure of events as they came up to Jerusalem, took part in the ceremony of entering and then embarked on a hectic round of teaching and controversy before the Passover? Secondly, did they simply suffer from spiritual fatigue? Had it all been too much? Thirdly, and in my view by far the most powerful question, did they simply run out of patience because there was no clear relationship between what they put into the mission and what they got back? There are hints of this in the second half of all four Gospels. Had they been weakened by one or all of these factors to such an extent that they were simply too vulnerable when the time of trial finally came?

Having looked at the situation from the point of view of the people, the clergy and the Apostles, let us now look at ourselves in those three roles, as citizens, ministers of Christ and disciples, granting that they are not really separate, that citizenship and discipleship are one and that discipleship and ministry are one.

The charge against us as citizens is that we collude with caricature out of self-interest. The most obvious symptom of our double dealing is that we consume the media we condemn. No newspaper or television channel which oversimplifies our lives, reducing public figures in cynical caricature and concentrating on creators rather than on what they create, can survive without our patronage. There is a breakdown of trust between us and our media and politicians because we would have it that way. We know when we are being lied to but prefer to pretend that what we are being told is true; and when public figures dare to tell the truth at our hectoring insistence, we turn against them. Could any political party that tells the truth win an election? Would any newspaper that provides a balanced picture of our society remain economically viable? Would we take any notice of the work of a writer or painter if the only criterion was what was created?

The cynicism and trivialisation with which we collude provides us with the cover to please ourselves. Having denied that anybody has anything to tell us that we do not know, having renounced any notion of authority or wisdom, it is but a short step to crowning ourselves with authority and robing ourselves with wisdom. Such self-aggrandisement quickly leads to wild swings of opinion based on extremely short-term perceptions of self-interest. One day we want to be there when the big event takes place, when the hero rides into town; this satisfies our craving for celebrity, for the immediate, for the kind of quasi religiosity which accompanied the death of Princess Diana and which still pervaded us almost a year after the abduction of Madeleine McCann. Days later, having been there, having drunk from the heady sugar-fix of celebrity, the effect wears off and we turn on those who fail to satisfy us. Like any other addictive drug the only course of action open to us is to increase the dose to avoid even further depression. The peaks become ever higher, the troughs ever deeper, until we lose any sense of self-reality. In the end, our relationship with the media turns into a dangerous syndrome; we are what we consume. Instead of being cool observers of a diversity of opinions, more or less manipulative, we allow ourselves to be swept along. Too late, we find out that we have been duped, that we have been left with nothing, that the roller-coaster has taken us on its giddy course and landed us back where we started, shaken, depressed and poorer.

That same charge, in a slightly different form, can be held against us as Christ's ministers. Abandoning service for leadership and then abandoning leadership for control, our quest for uniformity evades the big questions which at root show us that the creation of diversity cannot be subdued in favour of ephemeral issues that generate more heat than light, which promise solutions to our insecurity. But the fix is no more beneficial in church matters than it is in secular society. The apparent depth of our divisions, arising, we say, from a fundamental difference about the nature and meaning of Scripture, avoids the most basic issue of all, the difficulty that we necessarily have in building a personal relationship with God. Controversy is a snare which easily cheapens doctrine, but doctrine is itself a snare which frequently reduces the nature of our relationship with God to philosophical dispute. In other words, instead of engaging theologically, we confine ourselves to the philosophy of religion.

This leads to the charge against us as disciples. Does the flux of controversy and the inevitable disillusion with the provisionality and imperfection of doctrine lead us into a situation of mistrust? Do we begin to think that the very imperfection of our human understanding of God is God's fault? And does this in turn lead us to think that the whole enterprise is shallow? Was the struggle to understand so overwhelming for the Apostles that they forgot how to trust Jesus?

Returning to the moment of departure, Jesus rides into Jerusalem to a cry of collective liberation. Whether this was the cry of the people or the Apostles, it was a moment of pure, intuitive perception, of something tellingly right even if, to paraphrase Eliot, it was right for the wrong reason. It might later have been clouded by doubt and self-interest, its reality might have been distorted by real events and self-delusion; but just for one moment there was a conceptual and a perceptual breakthrough that justified the struggles of the journey from the Lake to the hilltop fastness, from the peasant North to the cosmopolitan South, from the hum-drum Synagogue to the very gates of heaven.

The Apostles were carried along on a wave of enthusiasm which ultimately broke before it could sweep its way over the hill of Calvary; and for us such waves break too soon, failing to carry us as far as their promise. Yet trust is not a matter of abandoning ourselves to the wave in the passive hope that it will take us all the way to where we would go; trust lies in knowing, at the very heart of our being, that wherever we are deposited, broken and disconsolate, we will be given the resources to prepare ourselves for the next wave, whenever it comes; and that we will have the strength to survive for long periods when there is no wave at all. That kind of trust is the opposite of millenarian optimism, it is the trust of eschatological uncertainty. It takes us back to the religious frame of mind of that very David of whom Jesus was the son. David had no Messiah, no thought of everlasting life; to be a Jew meant leading the holy life now and for as long as life lasted. The trust was not in the promise but in the present.

Life in the theological street, where the trumpets sound and the hero rides triumphantly to the cries of his followers, is nothing if the events are not re-lived in our homes. When I stood for Parliament, even though I lost we were carried along on a surge of collective adrenalin as the loudspeaker van went through the streets, as the votes were counted and the speeches were made. Even as a defeated candidate I felt the pulse of presence in a tiny piece of historic drama. Next day I went to the campaign headquarters to pick up my belongings and found my agent clearing up, a worthier act than any he had performed in the heat of the campaign. It is those who serve in silence, in the twilight of affairs, who have most taken the message of the street into their hearts and homes who are closest to the reality of mission. The steady response to the call of the moment, the answer to the call to serve, the honouring of personal integrity, are the best answer to hysteria and self-interest.

I like to think that, although Jesus asked his followers to fetch the donkey, he stayed with it for a while when the ride was over, seeing that it was rested, fed and watered before it was returned to its owner. I also like to think that if there had been media coverage of the day he would have smiled benignly at the pictures and the pundits; and thought them of little account.

The root of our troubles, of the inadequacy of our collective response, caught up in the crowd, to the arrival of Jesus, is the triumph of calculation over generosity. We generally use the latter to mean supererogatory donation, doing something that we need not do, giving something we cannot afford to give; it is much more rarely applied to our frame of mind, to our frame of reference with respect to otherness, to difference.

No doubt Jesus was different; it is one of his characteristics which most often gives rise to comment. He is an erudite carpenter's son, a miracle worker, a constant friend, a fearless critic and, whatever the theological niceties, a favoured child of God. Yet all the time there is pressure to force him to conform, to be an earthly king, an orthodox believer, a magician, a judge, a pragmatic operator. He is rarely given the benefit of the doubt, rarely the beneficiary of the exercise of social imagination. When the polarities of created diversity and doctrinal uniformity meet head on it is the uniformity that is urged upon him; as it is urged upon us. Our society gives itself away by its erroneous use of the term "different to" instead of "different from"; for all the rhetoric of individualism we are pushed towards uniformity, denying the generosity of creation.

Yet we are in no position to require the generosity of the Jerusalem crowd or the religious tribunal if we, as children of the Resurrection,

with our salvation under-written, cannot be generous to each other as
citizens, ministers and disciples.

Our lack of generosity as citizens is now so ingrained that we hardly
think about it: we collude in the pillorying of politicians who can only
speak for themselves through the very media that condemn them and
which we condemn; we have forgotten the legal principle of innocent until
proved guilty; we have made racism respectable under the guise of self-
protection; we think our nugatory contributions to reduce inequality are
the best we can do. We have deformed the grand civic virtue of scepticism
into the mean and selfish vice of cynicism. Our lack of generosity has,
inevitably, rebounded on us, individually and collectively, so that we live
in an ecology of weak and declining trust. This, in turn, leads to more and
more regulation, codes of conduct, monitoring, auditing and suspicion.
We have reached the stage where generosity itself is suspect.

Our lack of generosity as Ministers is so obvious that we believe we
have to live with it, that it is an inevitable consequence of deep feeling.
Reflecting the world of secular politics, we have elevated doctrinal
ideology over personal generosity. We have almost lost the ability to
be cautious in speech and patient in listening; we think of dialogue as
competitive not collaborative. The charge against the religious leaders
who threatened Jesus is that they elevated doctrine over behaviour,
that their view of perfection was radically separated from, rather than
a synthesis of, personal experience. If we were to start by conducting
ourselves with generosity, with respect for difference, prepared to leave
judgment where it belongs, with God, we could not get ourselves into
the position where we use exclusion or self-exclusion from the Eucharist
as a political weapon. Like secular society, we have tried to mitigate the
worst excesses of mistrust with a structural fix; but by ignoring the root
cause, the failure of generosity, we will only make the situation worse.

As disciples, our lack of generosity manifests itself in a two-way
failure of communication with Jesus: we fail to give him enough room
to be himself and to be in us. There is an inevitable problem that arises
because of our necessary imperfection as creatures—the imperfection
which makes us free to choose to love or not to love—and which
manifests itself most crucially in the imperfection of the tools we have
for making sense of the divine. We only have language and our quest, in

recognising and making patterns, is precisely to "make sense" when we need to do something much more generous and open-ended. We have become suspicious of what Karen Armstrong would call Mythos and have imprisoned ourselves, in her sense of the word, in Logos; instead of being disciples of theological praxis we have become scholars of philosophical theory. We have trapped ourselves in narrowing language instead of freeing ourselves in broadening language. Just as the word "criticism" has come to mean negative commentary, so theology has become an arsenal when it should be a form of mine clearing, expanding the space within which we can contemplate mystery and allow it to operate in us.

As Jesus entered Jerusalem to the sound of the cheering crowd it is difficult to see how matters could have ended differently; the whole history of salvation from Eden to Olivet is a history of calculation from which Jesus came to liberate us. The free gift of God's self-communication, promised to everyone forever, is the guarantee which allows the risk of generosity without fear of reprisal or exploitation. As Christians we can, even in our human imperfection, live generous lives in the certain knowledge that we are free of calculation. The difference for us, as we stand in the Jerusalem crowd, is that we know how the story will end, an end brought about not by the fatal flaw in a man nor even by the mob but by the inevitable incompatibility of perfection and imperfection.

## ii. "Spy" Wednesday—Guilt and Assurance

*Surely, it's not me, is it?*

**Mark 14.19**

Franz Kafka's *The Trial* is one of the emblematic books of the twentieth century. It plots in almost addictively intricate detail the way in which manipulative power can make a nonsense of self-reference until the victim begins to think—and in some cases actually does think—he has committed a crime he did not commit. This became the pattern of the totalitarian show trial in which innocent victims and even activist supporters of a regime condemned themselves to death. Because most places in which the practice persists are either politically unimportant or very important, we take much less notice than we should. Even so, the sad fact is that the sham of the show trial has given way to open torture and genocide.

Our contemporary show trials are less catastrophically terminal than those with a view to judicial murder but the corollary is that we are more implicated. We are the consumers, through our mass media, of a different kind of self-condemnation in which would-be celebrities, chosen for reality television shows, chat shows, "show and tell" exposés and even trivial competitions, compete in self-abasement. If virtue commands no attention then vicarious vice must suffice.

In spite of a deep feeling of moral paralysis brought about by the layering of post-modernist complexity and ambiguity (irony, games, self-parody and undiluted hype) on top of modernist, inexorable mechanical industrialism, we still retain some notion of volunteer collectivism. The Marxist paradox of imposed altruism never quite overcame the Christian solidarity of earlier generations. In spite of the aggressive assertion of liberalism as a reaction to government centralism by such political figures as Ronald Reagan and Margaret Thatcher, we can still not bring ourselves to believe her dictum: "There is no such thing as society." We still think there is and we carry with us all kinds of distributed—re-insured, one might say—guilt about oppression, poverty, colonialism, child rearing and even our own affluence. In spite of more than three decades of reaction to collectivism, we still cannot quite be persuaded that we are not to blame.

Was it any of these kinds of guilt which elicited that most remarkable question from the Apostles of Jesus: "Is it me?" There they were, sitting down to a solemn meal with Jesus (either the Passover or the eve of Passover, depending on whose Gospel you read) when he drops a bombshell. He has already said that he has come up to Jerusalem to die; he might even have hinted (we do not know) that a follower might be implicated; but suddenly he confronts them point blank with the accusation that one of them will betray him. Our normal reaction to such a situation would surely be: "Is it him?" So why was the reaction so self-referentially guilt ridden?

Each of the Synoptic Gospels has its turning point from optimism and wonder to a narrative inevitability that will involve suffering and death. At some point the rippling blue waters of the Galilee Lake are replaced by the unforgiving, golden stone of Jerusalem. The earthy Northerners will ultimately be sucked into the dangerous world of Southern metropolitan power politics. For Jesus' lieutenants, Peter, James and John, not even the hazy consolation of the Transfiguration is enough. Something is going to go badly wrong. It is almost as if the adulation on the entry into Jerusalem was a delusion, an attempt to escape momentarily from the impending horror. In John the dynamic is the same but the fuse is much longer and brighter; we have known almost since the beginning that it will end this way.

The Apostles, then, preparing for the meal, know what is to come in general terms though not in specifics. The Evangelists, looking back on events, add detail which was surely not available to those who nervously prepared to eat. Then Jesus dropped the bombshell and all they seem able to do is to condemn themselves.

Jesus was the opposite of manipulative; he was open to the point of scandal. There is no evidence that he ever held a sin against anybody or that he tried to exploit weakness. There is plenty of evidence that he condemned a lack of penitence and that he expected more from the strong than the weak, that he took authority, leadership and service seriously; but there is no sense of a game, a manoeuvring for personal advantage. The totalitarian impulse and the self-condemning response are both distorted forms of altruism exercised on behalf of a collective utopia at the expense of individual happiness. For Jesus there was no conflict between these two; the ultimate eschatological Utopia was integrated with personal and collective self-respect and freedom of action. In spite of what some of his successors might have said (and in the case of Paul and Augustine what they actually said has been caricatured in controversy), Jesus followed in the strict Jewish tradition of rooting virtue in earthly praxis, exercised for its own sake rather than as a down payment for a utopian settlement. The kingdom of heaven is now; it might take an eschatological form at

some time in the future; but it is now. We can see this most clearly in
the behaviour of the Pharisees who, in Evangelical hindsight, seem to be
far too concerned with the present; but even if you were a Pharisee who
believed in the after-life, its theology was not a serious counterweight to
the deep Jewish sense of the present obligation. Jesus, then, is not using
people as pawns in an eschatological game, demanding that they wreck
their lives on the altar of distant hope. The Apostles could hardly have
thought that they were being asked in some imprecise way to absorb the
guilt for the fate of Jesus which they feared above all things. This is not to
say that later Christians did not fall victim to the kind of over-stimulated
self-abasement which they thought would bring them eternal glory; but
the Apostles were operating on a much less rarefied plane; they did not
have to induce religious experience, they were living alongside Jesus.

Nor is there any evidence that Jesus responded to attention seeking
through self-abasement. There are some rather troubling incidents, such
as the behaviour of the woman with the haemorrhages and the Syro-
Phoenician woman which seem to go against the whole tenor of Jesus'
teaching and actions but perhaps these odd fragments of Evangelical
inconsistency only go to highlight the serene even-handedness of
Jesus with regard to those who sought his service. He called for faith
and penitence but nothing more. Occasionally those whom he served
worshipped him but that was a gift not a bribe. There was no league
table of woe, no competing to be the most degraded, in order better to
secure a reversal. The Apostles did not compete for attention by showing
themselves to be the worst of men. They frequently showed that they had
the same kind of moral compasses that we have—a little pride, a little
self-pity, a little misdirected energy—with an overwhelming wish to do
good in a practical way, to struggle to pray, to please their Master. It is
therefore not competitive attention seeking that caused the Apostles to
ask their extraordinary question.

Even more unlikely is the idea that the Apostles were suffering from
a form of unfocused, collective guilt, the feeling that if they had acted
differently somehow everything would be much better. They were
brought up to emphasise individual responsibility within the family
and community collective, but there was no sense in which they held
themselves responsible for the way things were. Extremely conservative

societies have very little sense of the connection between individual action and social change and are much more concerned with preventing decline. The mind-set which the Apostles brought to the radical mission of Jesus was therefore incompatible with his frame of reference. This certainly caused tensions. Time and again Jesus asks whether they understand what he is doing. In a sense the question is rhetorical because it is not really understanding that he needs; what he wants, and what they try to give him, is a loyalty which goes far beyond calculation. There is a sense, then, in which the guilty question relates to incomprehension, to a simple incompatibility of ways of seeing and talking. It may be that the Apostles somehow think that they have done something wrong but do not know what. They have so often made "silly" mistakes before, failing to understand what they are told.

It is, however, a much deeper incomprehension that lies behind the guilty question. When Jesus says that one of them will betray him, they think that they are guilty of a failure of love. In some way they cannot specify, they have let him down. Somehow their wrong choices or their failure to act or speak have led to a situation in which Jesus feels betrayed. I doubt that they were thinking that one of them was about to arrange for Jesus to be handed over to the authorities who would kill him. No doubt Jesus was in trouble with the authorities for his public challenges—the repeated taunting and its climax in the murderously direct story of the vineyard murders, the attacks on the Temple cult culminating in the fracas with the traders, the threat of political instability—but fear was not yet focused and the notion of an individual traitor would have seemed far-fetched.

So ingrained is it in our expectations—and perhaps even in our psyche—that we no longer notice that we live in a world deliberately delivered into our lives as dysfunctional. We shrug when we are reminded that good news does not sell newspapers, but we need to take our addiction to disaster seriously because it distorts our view of creation. If society breaks down, as it has in such places as Bosnia and Iraq, the pulse of life is easy to monitor negatively—in the same way that when we look at a piece of old film we soon lose consciousness of flicker and hiss—as long as we hear nothing on the news the place at the back of our consciousness is doing well; we are sure we will hear if it is not. The public positions adopted by brave people in favour of humanity, ethics, god, integrity, are only rarely reported; the wonder of creation is deliberately distorted for profit; and yet it is our addiction that lies at the root of the economic gain that results.

In addition to the darkness which we find comfortingly familiar, we live in a world of broken narratives, of incomplete stories. At the very basic level, our ancestors, whether nomadic or sedentary, lived in dispersed but tight knit groups, aware not only of the change of the seasons but also of the life processes of friends and family from birth to death. At a personal level we live disrupted geographical and emotional lives, overcoming the difficulties of dislocation by choosing to spend time with people we like; we choose our friends the way we choose everything else. In a wider perspective, and related to the previous observations about news, our view of the world leans forward: we are fed endless predictions by people impatient with the present. We live in a culture of stories, of dramas, and particularly disasters, that have spectacular beginnings but no endings.

At many levels, then, our view of ourselves and our world is broken, incomplete, and almost incoherent. If we were asked to give an account of the world in which we live, of the town in which we live, of the family into which we were born, we would find it very difficult. We are perpetually watching kings marching their troops up to the top of the hill without ever seeing them marching them down again. We come to know the notorious parts of our community where youths threaten but we have no idea about quiet places within half a mile of where we live. We lose track of relatives and cannot picture children as they grow far away from us.

What this amounts to is a lack of texture both to hold us and to absorb shock; we live in such an exposed, vulnerable way, that a retreat into self-indulgence is understandable. This forces a retreat from a frame of critical reference, an understanding of how our behaviour relates to the behaviour of the rest of our world. In spite of warnings, under-written by centuries of piety, that our besetting sin is pride, the suspicion must be of our contemporary frame of reference that our besetting sin is guilt. Unable to assess ourselves objectively, we chronically take responsibility for failures that are not our own.

As if our sense of incompleteness were not enough, we are chronically goaded into self-reproach by images of impossible "perfection". Whenever our fire sinks low it is fuelled with faggots of envy. Nothing sums up our pursuit of false comfort as an escape from gnawing guilt as the twin images of obesity and anorexia.

Again, it is important not to take responsibility for the danger; businesses would not spend money on advertising if it did not produce an economic return. The extent to which we are "helpless" victims of advertising is a controversial area, but it would be hard to argue for either extreme, that we cannot help ourselves or that we are immune. It is difficult to argue, for example, that we are not aware of the lurid vacuity of many messages. If we care to be reflective we know that buying a certain car will not improve our sexual "performance"; a hinterland of upbringing will persuade us that we will never be radically different in shape; a sense of our comfort zone will warn us against an apparently desirable object that will be out of place. We have a whole social commentary about the limitations of advertising, about our self-awareness and our determination to be caught out; and yet the advertising budgets do not falter. Perhaps it is the image of a monkey or a pelican that nudges us from one brand of beer to another; and perhaps that is harmless enough. The danger, however, is that the purpose of advertising is not simply to persuade us to switch brands in the context of fixed consumption but to reinforce addiction as an escape from perceived inadequacy. Thus, the danger may not so much be in any consumption arising from self-indulgence but in the damage to our self-image as we compare ourselves, in the true tradition of Plato, with archetypal figures which display a perfection we can never achieve. Again, this has been portrayed traditionally by moralists as competitive consumption, as an attempt to "keep up with the Joneses" but that is to be deceived by the competitive exterior. The danger is in the internal corrosion; the desire to "keep up" is not to impress the Joneses or others watching the competition, it is a futile attempt to make good what we see as the failure in ourselves.

This perceived failure, this futile attempt to achieve a perceived perfection, is bolstered by two other factors. First, because the culture in which we live is still deeply influenced by rationalism, we think that phenomena are "caused" by other, traceable phenomena. Everything is

the result of something and so when there is a disaster of any kind we
look for the human failure of perception, judgment or ethics; where there
is no guilt we need to find it. Secondly, there is something profoundly
egotistical about guilt; it latches onto the notion of causality and assigns
it to the self. These are very powerful cultural forces; I remember being
sceptical of the subtitle of the first part of Christine Edzard's monumental
*Little Dorritt, Nobody's Fault*. Where there is fault, we argue, there must be
guilt. Where there is incompetence or catastrophe there must be a culprit.
Just as the show trials in the Soviet Union were linked in a sinister way
to agricultural failure, our need for guilt is linked to perceived failure on
a major scale as if we cannot tolerate an unexplained disaster.

It is, I think, this unfocused guilt, this need to find a cause, that most
gripped the disciples. It was not that any one of them had betrayed
Jesus, but that any one of them might somehow have betrayed him, that
something each could not see in himself might have been the trigger for
impending disaster. They were, after all, living in dangerous spiritual
territory; how can living alongside God on a daily basis be risk free? These
devout Jews, brought up in a conservative tradition, were confronted
with such a plethora of new ideas about God and themselves that they
were bound to suffer doubt and self-doubt. In Holy Week we are forced
to concentrate on failures of discipleship but we rarely compensate for
this by concentrating at other times on its difficulty as tensions break
through the narrative. Only in John do some of the followers of Jesus
actually walk away, stunned by his claims, unable to square them
with what they know. Although we might take advantage too often, it
is vital that we are able to walk away from our direct involvement in
discipleship and watch ourselves as if we were a third person. Sometimes
the demands are so great—proportionate to how scrupulous we are in our
self-criticism—that it is better to turn away; yet this was not an option
open to the followers of Jesus, particularly as the tensions mounted and
the commitments became more congested as they approached Jerusalem.
There are echoes, particularly in John, of the timeless worry which
confronts country people visiting a metropolis for the first time, places
with corners and shadows, daunting space and frightening constriction,
the body language imposed by congestion, the compression of variety
into small spaces, the unnatural juxtaposition of wealth and poverty,

splendour and squalor; and, above all, there is the detachment from the reliable bonds of community, of friendship and family and even from familiar animosities and frictions. In the city, who can you trust? It is not far from this insecurity and the affectation of superiority with which the new arrival is confronted to a sense of inadequacy. Is it my fault?

It was all too much for the disciples. They were far from home in a large and threatening city, they had seen Jesus triumph and then they had seen him under attack from the authorities, they were out of control, they did not know what would happen next; and then Jesus told them that one of them was about to betray him.

It is the sense of exaggerated, vague culpability which the disciples felt which is the core of what we call guilt. We should not be confused by the legal terminology which suggests an opposite of innocence; in the sense in which the word is used here the opposite of guilt is refuge or assurance. Guilt is our damaged view of our damaged selves.

Christ is our refuge, particularly during this week when we concentrate on his brokenness. We are faced with the incommensurable paradox that we who have broken him will be comforted in our brokenness. There is enough genuine cause for sorrow without manufacturing false guilt; humanity collectively killed Jesus, is that not enough? The charge could not be more serious; in an act of apparent ontological impossibility we have accused ourselves of killing God in the person of Christ and yet we affirm that he is our refuge.

The impossible magnitude of the charge should not free us from careful self-examination. In what way have we crucified Christ? Is it through excess consumption or self-assertion? Is it even through cruelty and indifference to humanity? Which one of the many offences which we can list is central to the accusation? There are enough charges against us from outside and within to make life seem like a permanent failure. One of the severe penalties of living in a religious environment is that it brings with it the dual pain of self-criticism, just or otherwise, and the gratuitous censoriousness of clerics. We are forever being asked, or asking ourselves: "What would Jesus do?" to which the usual answer is: "not what you are doing" but to which the proper answer is: "Don't presume; you can't possibly know in a particular way" although in a general way we know that Jesus refused to judge people, particularly on the basis of a dry legalism or external appearances. Because of this moralistic claustrophobia we tend to focus on the wrong things, on what are—without devaluing the importance of the way in which we behave towards each other—trivial symptoms of a profound underlying condition. Instead of focusing on the broken figure of Jesus on the Cross and wondering how he got there, we think of how we got where we are; and then stop. The crucial link is not made between how we have ended up where we are and how Jesus ended up where he did.

Whatever our ethical failures, these are symptoms of the deeper failure of love. Yet behind that failure there lies perhaps the deepest mystery of all. We were created to fail in love; there is no other way in which we could be free to choose to love; imperfection makes freedom to love possible but that brings with it inevitable failure.

That is why Christ is our refuge; because we were made to fail we stand in permanent, chronic need of consolation; and the broken Christ tells us that it does not matter how badly we have failed, how often we have chosen not to love, that even though we killed him, he is still our refuge. There is just a tiny part of my consciousness that speculates that we might have been made to kill him.

A refuge is not a process or a purpose, a theory or a belief, a competition or a contract; it is an unconditional state of openness. In a tragic breach of understanding we bind those in search of refuge—refugees—with crippling conditionality. We have ceased to provide refuge but instead grudgingly construct makeshift prisons for new arrivals. In failing to understand unconditionality we are failing to understand Jesus. For it is that very unconditionality of refuge which is the space in which we are able to love freely, to choose to love.

The disciples who walked with Jesus, brought up with the law, could never bring themselves to grasp the unconditionality of Jesus and, even though we are children of the Resurrection, neither can we. St Paul, St Augustine and Martin Luther all tried to articulate the idea of unconditionality but in doing so they accidentally, in a form of theological collateral damage, overturned our sense of our moral selves; in trying to describe unconditionality they took away our freedom; they thought that the Cross was the ultimate guarantee of our salvation but it is not; it is the concrete expression of the worst possible human failing resulting from the exercise of choice which defines what we are; it says that no matter how hard we try to destroy God's love for us it is indestructible. The refuge of Christ will always be there; it is as inevitable as our flawed exercise of the freedom to love.

So when Jesus hands us the piece of bread which says that we have betrayed him, we need not flinch. This is not the accusation of a lawyer nor the condemnation of a judge, it is the sad acknowledgment of our autonomous, flawed condition. Without the refuge of Christ we are alone and bewildered, beset by wordless guilt, by a feeling of incompleteness which gives us an inkling of how Adam might have felt when his innocence collided with worldliness. In a way that Paul intimates without being explicit Jesus, through his death and Resurrection, lifted Adam's bewilderment from us and put us back into direct contact with innocence; but as the Incarnation is part of history it cannot undo history. We were put back into contact with the divine but could not reclaim innocence. To know that there is good and evil is not to be trapped in a state of incomprehension, on trial for an unknown offence which implies, without anything ever being said, that we cannot escape being evil, it is to know that we must choose.

### iii. Maundy Thursday—Flesh and Blood

*This is my body . . . This is my blood.*
**Mark 14.22–25**

"It was the best of times; it was the worst of times!" So begins Charles Dickens' novel of the French Revolution, *A Tale of Two Cities*, in which the authorities are gripped by murderous fanaticism which leads to the voluntary death of Sydney Carton, a lawyer who thinks he is beyond redemption. The actions of the authorities were unpredictable: the hero, Charles Darnay, is put on trial but then triumphally released; he is almost immediately apprehended and the same tribunal sentences him to death. Although he is a lawyer, Carton's legal skill is useless; his effective response is subterfuge and sacrifice.

That portentous opening could have been written for Maundy Thursday, the day in the Church's year which presents us with the sharpest contrast of feeling, when we celebrate the Institution of the Eucharist and then carry the newly consecrated bread to the Altar of Repose, signifying Gethsemane, the place of the second sacrifice, before the arrest and trial of Jesus and his final sacrifice. His body and blood, sacramentally sacrificed forever, are sacrificed again in historical reality, in blood at Gethsemane and in blood and water on Calvary. The sequence is, of course, illusory; it always is in narratives where you know what is going to happen. As a culture we are much more attuned to narratives of surprise where we are "on the edge of our seat" or rapidly scanning the "page turner" because of our need to know; but this is a relatively recent form of culture. From the beginnings of Greek drama until the end of the seventeenth century, cultured people knew just about every story there was to know; and what fascinated them was the working out; the "how?" rather than the "what?". Whereas the narrative of surprise encourages a forward projection which tends to skim over the present and over the complexities of motive and accident, the narrative of working out, in such plays as *The Tempest* where all the action takes place before the curtain rises, encourages reflection. When we read a complex novel, such as *A Tale of Two Cities*, for the first time, we are naturally curious about how it will end and we rarely look back. We know that it will end happily, or at least not disastrously, because that is the way of nineteenth-century fiction but there are points where we cannot see how different events link and other points where we cannot see the end in detail. If we read the novel for a second time we will pay far more attention to the subtleties of the dialogue, the shades of feeling, the interplay of characters, the possibilities which present themselves to protagonists and, of course, the role of accident and coincidence, the novelist's licence to twist the terms of trade.

In a well-known narrative such as that describing the events for today which we have read so regularly from childhood that it is an integral part of our sense of ourselves, the complexities are even greater because we do not experience the events in sequence, they are all there together; that is why we cannot help thinking of Gethsemane while we are watching the wine being blessed and cannot escape the lash of the whip, breaking the flesh of Jesus, as we watch the bread being broken. Conversely, while we are watching Jesus bend his back as he trudges up the hill of Calvary, we see him bending his back to wash the feet of his disciples. It is important that we should accord the text this kind of attention, tracing the threads of symbolism, hearing echoes of past events and marking premonitions of the future, because that is how the Evangelists wrote. It is all too easy to see the gospels—of Matthew, Mark and Luke at least—as events strung together in a haphazard way with the minimum of narrative catch phrases such as "and then". We also have the added complication that our story comes from four sources which only overlap in part so that, if we are not careful, over time we meld the narratives into a single sequence, a contemporary *Tessarion* (in the same way that we put shepherds in the crib and leave the kings upon the road until the Epiphany). There are four accounts of the Institution of the Eucharist, three in the Synoptics and the fourth, the first to be written down, in 1 Corinthians. All four narratives are different, as Paul Bradshaw demonstrates in his *Eucharistic Origins*, and we need to ask whether the differences call into question any of the theology we have built on top of this fractured foundation; and we need, incidentally, given the chronology, to consider whether Paul heard about the Institution from colleagues or whether what he said had a serious influence on the Evangelists. Given his unique theologies of Baptism and of the atonement, the latter sequence is intriguing. John does not mention the Eucharist at all, possibly because his transcendent Christology could do without such complexities. All four Evangelists describe the arrest and trial of Jesus, subtly analysed in Rowan Williams' *Christ On Trial* and, again, there are differences of incident as well as emphasis. In the interlude between the Institution of the Eucharist and the Crucifixion, the Gethsemane narratives of sacrifice are remarkably similar although Luke is more dramatic than the others (and more generous to the leading Apostles).

We are therefore considering a human and theological story written from different standpoints where all the incidents and symbolism are being played out simultaneously. Looked at in this way, we can see that a lazy narrative sequence is not good enough. As we are so familiar with all the elements, we need to take our time, to understand what we are being told. The vivid presentness of the narrative is not for dramatic effect but to bring us closer to the events we need to understand. If we are to have a personal relationship with God, which is why we are here, that is best achieved through a personal relationship with Jesus; and coming to terms with the incident and drama of the Gospels is one of the most important ways of helping us to stand alongside Jesus as his three sacrifices, once separate, fuse in our consciousness. In every incident we witness, on every step of the way, we need to be conscious as the images and emotions pile up, that gaining some kind of general impression of benevolence and suffering is not enough; for what is at stake in the drama of Maundy Thursday is the nature of salvation, the out-playing of the event, if we may call it such, of the creation of humanity.

There are four charges against us as we consider the events of Maundy Thursday. The first is that we oscillate between rejecting Jesus the servant and then wanting him to do everything for us; first we do not want him to wash our feet and then we want him to wash us all over. This is a serious charge because we so easily drift into a mind-set which operates as if there had been no Incarnation, concentrating on the idea of the all-powerful God, the God who drowned Pharaoh, not the God who walks weeping across the battlefield. The second is that we feel unfocused guilt, a vague sense that we did something wrong which brought Jesus to his death. Of course the disciples were not sure in what way they had betrayed Jesus but we know. Our responsibility should not be unfocused nor egotistical, it should be sharp and to the point; the perfect Jesus was bound to come into conflict with imperfect humanity and his death at our hands was therefore inevitable. The third and related charge of the failure of our duty of care is simple enough; even though we were created for the specific purpose of being able freely to choose to love God through each other and directly, we too often forget that purpose and wander off, physically and mentally, into self-indulgence and carelessness. But what of the final charge, of direct rejection of Jesus? We would find it hard to accept this;

and we would be right. None of us would betray Jesus with a kiss; we are
not in the realm of the Brothers Karamazov. We will accept the first three
charges but not this one. I think that is right. I think that we spend too
much time, again in a kind of self-aggrandisement, personalising and
magnifying guilt.

There can, after all, be no more serious charge than the collective blame
we carry for killing God in the person of Jesus to which the act of Judas is
simply a lurid precursor. It was the best of times; it was the worst of times.
That the language of killing God is difficult, even extreme, is impossible to
evade but so, too, is the counterbalancing language of Eucharist. We say
that humanity was collectively responsible for the death of the Incarnate
Christ; and we say that the Incarnate Christ was responsible for giving
himself to us until the end of time in the Eucharist. Each is not possible
without the other. We could not imagine the worst sin of all, killing Jesus,
without a profound reverence for the mystery of Incarnation; and we
could not survive our part in the events of today and tomorrow were it
not for the Eucharist which forms the centre of the Maundy Thursday
drama and which forms the centre of our Christian lives. It is through the
Eucharist that we can come to grips with the massive two-part drama of
our responsibility for Christ on earth and Christ's responsibility for us on
earth. For just as Jesus was God Incarnate we are God's creation incarnate;
the Creator became incarnate for us and creatures became incarnate for
the Creator. That contract, which gave us freedom and the imperfection
that necessarily goes with it, is made tolerable by the perpetuation of the
Incarnate Jesus in Eucharist.

It was the best of times; it was the worst of times. We will accept our
part in Christ's suffering and death; but we are only able to do this because
of the part he has in us. For just as the mystery of the Incarnation ended
in the scandal of the Cross it also, simultaneously, perpetuated itself in the
Institution of the Eucharist. It is therefore overwhelmingly significant for
us that as we leave the room where our feet have been washed to climb
the Mount of Olives to the Garden of Gethsemane at the beginning of our
most harrowing journey, that we carry the Blessed Sacrament with us to
the Altar of Repose; for, in the profoundest mystery of all, Jesus ensured
that he would never die before we killed him.

The kind of "rational" difficulty which we face in coming to terms with the mystery of the Eucharist and our part in the death of Jesus which, in turn, makes us participants in the Institution of the Eucharist, presents itself when we consider the plea of Jesus to the Father that his prospective suffering should be withdrawn. The prayer of Jesus in Gethsemane is frequently down-graded to an interlude between the more dramatic sacrifices of the Eucharist and Calvary but it is a sacrifice in its own right because it is the ultimate kenosis. Jesus, having emptied himself of all his divine attributes, then empties himself of all of his human strength. He places himself in prayer in obedience to God whose instruments are human hands. This form of submission echoes the use by God of foreign civil powers in the punishment of the Chosen People for their unfaithfulness. The very correspondence of the language of Jesus with that of the prophets serves to underline the unique position of Jesus whose faithfulness was beyond question and beyond limit. Notwithstanding our limited capacity to imitate Jesus and to live as he lived, Gethsemane is the exemplar of our kind of sacrifice; it is the sacrifice self-made in prayer. The mysteries of the Eucharistic and Golgotha sacrifices inhere in Christ alone but the offering back of the human will to God is a creaturely mission to which we must continually aspire. We were made freely to offer our own kenosis, to make space in ourselves because space is a precondition of love. Today most people think that to love is to act but it is the opposite; to love is to allow others to act in a state of total freedom. Jesus gave himself by emptying himself of divinity; we give ourselves by emptying ourselves of what is earthly.

One obstacle to understanding our kenotic mission is the tendency of the Gospels to establish an absolute dichotomy between Jesus and his followers. Jesus is unique in being both divine and human and then, in his post-Resurrection state, divine and human but not human. If we are to aspire to imitate Jesus in our lives we have to be convinced, in some simplistic way, that this imitation is possible and is not just a metaphor; to rule it out of possibility is to relegate the significance of the Incarnation and to put us back into the Old Testament relationship with God.

The three sacrifices, of Eucharist, Gethsemane and Golgotha, present us with different ways of coming to terms with the Incarnation and its sacrificial apotheosis; we are to be inspired by the Incarnation, sustained by the Eucharist, challenged by Gethsemane and chastened by the Crucifixion. Throughout our consideration of these different aspects we must never forget the decisively binding power of the Incarnation which unites the sacrifice of Jesus as God and man with our sacrifice as creatures formed to love and, therefore, to suffer.

While the Eucharist bears within it the comfort of nurture and the sharpness of sacrifice, it also inherently bears within it the solidity of bread and the volatility of wine. For those of us whose life is centred on the Eucharist—the benign addiction—it is too easy to associate it almost exclusively with the deep satisfaction of worshipping with those who broadly share our views and our background. Indeed, our attention to this tendency has recently been sharpened by the use of withdrawal from Eucharistic solidarity as a weapon in Church politics. Such actions miss the central point of Eucharistic solidarity which is that we are all children of God and sisters and brothers of Christ whatever our attitudes and actions and we are all invited to the Lord's table. It is not for us to write the guest list and put people through a moral or doctrinal test as they come to celebrate. Jesus asked no questions of those who were present at the miracles of the loaves and fishes; and he did not exclude Judas during the Institution of the Eucharist. Conformity and uniformity are not preconditions for Eucharistic solidarity; in Christ difference is celebrated and judgment suspended, pride is subdued and prejudice overcome.

Yet the mystery of the Eucharist demands more of us than a celebration of solidity and solidarity; it demands that we take risks for Christ. Just as bread represents solidity, wine represents risk: it is the element which becomes blood, the substance sacred to the God of the Old Testament, it is the symbol of passion and temperament; it is the substance that gives life and can so easily slip away and lead to death. It is therefore appropriate that blood which could, theologically, be realised from many substances, notably animals, should be realised from wine. For wine is the substance of joy and risk, of companionship and excess, of exaltation and depression, of palace celebration and slum addiction. Wine reminds us of the vicissitudes of being human, of how a substance can be both uplifting and degrading. To think of the Eucharist as bread alone is to take false comfort from it.

There is a scene in *A Tale of Two Cities* where a cask of wine falls from a cart and breaks open in the filthy street. The starving and apathetic people suddenly spring to life in the pursuit of wine; this is the wine which they hope will give them some escape from the lack of bread. This is where the wine of risk and the wine of oblivion can be dangerous, just as an excess of bread's stolidity and solidity tends towards complacency. The Eucharist should neither be an escape nor taken to be a confirmation of the lives we have chosen for ourselves; there is as much danger in the hysteria of wine as there is in the self-satisfaction of the bread. Perhaps the Roman Catholic tradition of the consecration of both elements but the distribution of bread alone has led to an almost domestic comfort in the Sacrament. We need a better balance, a better way.

To be incarnational is to affirm Christ in everything. The structures of established religion have tended to obscure this because their ostensible purpose is to refine and abstract our spiritual experience into dogmas that begin as questions but end up as answers. At every stage of the process, whether we are thinking about dogma, ethics, worship or ministry, the process inexorably closes down questions, eliminates risk and builds up uniformity and exclusion; there is a conflation of useful coherence and crushing uniformity. We are not asked to take risks for Christ, to obey him, but to obey for him. Instead of using poetry and music, imagination and speculation to ask questions about the mystery of God, we are forced into technical and legal language, Credal and dogmatic, which remains under the control of a self-perpetuating oligarchy operated under the guise of a "holy spirit" who is apparently a guardian of procedure and orthodoxy. We have mistakenly anthropomorphised the Creator as an imperial figure; we have anthropomorphised Jesus as a liberal or a fundamentalist, depending on our personal temperament and outlook; but that is nothing to the way in which we have anthropomorphised the Holy Spirit to reflect the positions of power which we hold. The Holy Spirit does not operate in the Church but through the clergy, not the voice of Christ in us but the voice of Bishops above us. The Spirit is not so much the fire which might rage through the secular rubbish which almost suffocates us but the right word in the right place. Yet the Epiclesis at the Eucharist ought to inject into it the actual unity of the diverse priesthood of God which the President is there to represent; and that priesthood bears within it elements of risk as well as elements of stability, elements of hysteria as well as elements of stolidity. Surely we, as incarnational people, come to celebrate the apotheosis of Incarnation in Eucharist as pilgrims on a dangerous journey rather than as bureaucrats who will receive their due if they follow the correct procedure.

Having called to mind the tension between solidity and risk, we should acknowledge that this represents not only the differences within ourselves and between us, we should acknowledge the way in which the Eucharist reminds us of the contrast between the perfect Christ and imperfect humanity. We need the perfect flesh and blood of Christ to sustain us on our journey towards our own ultimate perfectedness, with bread for food and wine for joy, for comfort and courage. It is that very perfection which allows us to take risks for Christ, to go to the edge of speculation to come closer to the core of the mystery, to risk losing a part of our worldly selves by spending more time with those who have not yet come to know Jesus, to risk rejection from the very people we are trying to help. Jesus told us that we would never be asked to do anything for which we would not be given the resources and the resource which is most tangible is the flesh and blood of Jesus himself; being human, we need Sacramentality to complement Scripture. It is hard to imagine the mystery of the incarnate Word of God living with us, dying and rising again and then simply leaving us with a library of Scripture. The Bible is the written record of our dialogue with God but Christianity is not a society for keeping records; from the Bible we have derived ways of asking questions about God but Christianity is not a society of philosophers; from the Bible and from the questions we ask, we have come to understand the legacy of the Incarnation in Sacrament and, above all, in the Sacramentality of initiation and Eucharist. The Bible speaks but the Eucharist lives.

When I was a child it was the custom at my school to process behind the Blessed Sacrament on the Feast of Corpus Christi in an act of public affirmation; it was literally taking Jesus into the world. The practice was condemned by many good Christians who were confused about the nature of Eucharist, who confused their received version of Transubstantiation with the doctrine of the Real Presence of Jesus Christ in the host, a confusion (in an ironic isomorphism of Thomist distinctions) of the essence, of what happens, with the mechanics of how it happens. In rejecting a narrowly philosophical view of the Eucharist they simultaneously confined the "real presence", if they accepted its validity at all, to the chancel.

The criticism, however, misses the missiological point, that incarnational fulfilment is not a privilege to be shared in private. There is a special feeling as we walk from our places to the altar to receive Christ, but surely there is a more special kind of movement where we take the Eucharist out of church and into the community. There is always a tension between the tranquillity and restlessness of existence and both need to be held in balance. There is a danger that this balance will be rejected by many Christians: on the one hand, those who claim most to venerate the Eucharist tend to be inward looking, to place the higher value on tranquillity, whereas those who are restless, who wish to advance mission apparently believe that they can do this best by abandoning the Eucharist, leaving it in church in the care of those who are theologically rooted to the spot.

I suspect that the root of the misunderstanding is a deep symbiosis between Protestantism and liberalism to fashion a form of religious observance that hardly troubles the spirit; perhaps it is no accident that the essence of the Church of England is encapsulated in The Prayer Book rather than a Confession. For all the benign consequences which flow from a lack of dogmatism, the danger of spiritual weakness—epitomised in German liberal Protestantism—is acute. Secular liberalism, with all its state resources, has failed to mend the nation; and although there is an unfocused yearning in many for something other than the physical, with the exception of vulgar programmes on the paranormal, our mass media are fiercely materialistic. Empiricism has descended into consumerism. Religion must be privatised lest it makes selfishness marginally uncomfortable. We must not give way, subconsciously acquiring the traits of those who oppose us; the missiological task before us is so daunting that we could not possibly attempt it without the strength which the Eucharist supplies.

The attempt to separate the tranquillity of the liturgy from the turbulence of life is a denial of the reality of the incarnational being and life of Jesus. The chronology of Maundy Thursday, of all days, is restless except for the meal where the Eucharist was Instituted and during which Jesus gave his final discourse. There was preparation, foot washing, the meal, then the walk to the Mount of Olives; even there, even as Jesus prayed in Gethsemane, the atmosphere was not tranquil; and then came the arrest and the sinister comings and goings in the night. Perhaps in this context our mistake is to refer to the destination of the Maundy Sacrament as the Altar of Repose; we might better call it the Altar of Commitment which encapsulates both the sacrifice of prayer in the garden and the sacrifice of self, of life, which followed. The rite requires that only the consecrated bread be moved because, uniquely, on Good Friday the Eucharist is delivered in one kind only; on the day when the blood of Jesus flowed as the consequence of his flesh being broken, only the flesh is broken, the blood is somehow hidden away. On this day of all days, we need not comfort but risk, not tranquillity but outrage, not the sedentary comfort of the table but the restlessness of climbing feet. The initial reaction of the disciples to the arrest of Jesus was to run away; but some of them scrambled back, dragged themselves to the fringes of the drama. That is what we do when we walk from the chancel to the Altar of Repose, with the strength of the Eucharist to sustain our vigil, to keep us on the fringes of the drama of the night and the morrow; until it is over.

"It was the best of times; it was the worst of times." Without casually falling under the twin charms of easy dichotomy and elegant paradox, we can see that in the Eucharist, the best and worst of us is fused for all time.

## iv. Emptiness and Silence

I first noticed the phenomenon of what I might call narrative slack when reading D. H. Lawrence's *Sons and Lovers*. At that time I thought it was a peculiar flaw characteristic of a novelist whose achievement could never hope to match his ambition for what the novel should be, but since then I have identified it as a common structural failing in novels and films. The narrative—let us say it consists of 400 pages—starts promisingly and then builds steadily to its crux, usually about halfway through. The second half of the work is then supposed to resolve what the author has deliberately entangled but many such exercises are not symmetrical. All the painful construction of complexities can be resolved with two or three easy, dramatic strokes in a maximum of 50 pages. In most cases of stories written before the midpoint of the twentieth century, you know how they will end: happily ever after, or getting just deserts. However many the twists and turns there will be a resolution and the concern is not with what will happen but with how it will happen. Today, in our self-styled postmodern era, it may be that nothing is really going to happen at all. A story, or strands of stories, begin at some indeterminate point and end at another indeterminate point, having followed an apparently random course; here it is the process, not the outcome, that matters in narratives of emptiness. In many traditionally constructed narratives we reach halfway and then the author appears not to know what to do between page 200 and page 350 when she can begin to pull all the threads together or simply slice through the knots. In the meantime, while we are waiting, he can bring in a fresh sub-plot, some new characters or, worst of all, get the main characters to perform some kind of diversion.

That is how I feel about Holy Saturday except that the intermediate pages between the entombment of Jesus and the discovery of the empty tomb are completely blank. Nothing happens.

If we look at the narrative of the last few hours it is strangely thin. After the turbulent scenes of crowds calling for crucifixion and then streaming up the hill to Calvary, the scene at the summit is almost eerily quiet: a few people pass by and mock, Pilate has his joke at the expense of the priests over the Crucifixion plaque, there is a knot of soldiers and some bit part characters who offer unpleasant beverages. John, Mary and some women arrive just in time for the last few moments of a life; and then it is over; and then there are only the women; and then nothing.

And then, precisely 38 hours later, the same women re-appear, to complete what they started when we last saw them. Last time it was a temporary embalming and the hurried rolling of a stone. This time it is the very final embalming and the definitive entombment.

After the tumultuous emotional and spiritual journey which starts with the entry into Jerusalem and ends in silence, only made tolerable by the Institution of the Eucharist, we are left with nothing. To close the church door at five minutes after three on Good Friday is the strangest experience of my spiritual self-narrative. It does not matter that this Friday will be almost the 50th occasion, it is always the same. This is not the silence contained by physical or musical architecture, not the silence of wide open space, of big skies, it is the emptiness I feel after the funeral, before life, as they say, goes on; but in this case it is an externally imposed hiatus and there is the difference. It is not, like the return from a funeral, a space which will slowly be filled by the wonderful weeds of life which will grow no matter how heavy the marble slab, this is a span which we know will be completed very soon. Yet, in the hours before it happens, there is some spiritual reticence which keeps me from imagining the lighting of the fire and, most triumphant of all triumphs, the lighting of the candle. Of course, for the Apostles it was like the return from the worst funeral they had ever attended; the women would have to finish off. For them physically, mentally, psychologically, spiritually, it was finished. Only they knew how badly they had played the hands they were dealt and they would have to live with that knowledge for the rest of their lives.

But for us, there is this day to get through. I know that there is an element of self-delusion in this: after all, on the Saturday we buy lamb, arrange flowers, check the Easter egg supply, make phone calls about tomorrow; but there is still a compartment in my brain which is stubbornly concerned with the emptiness of the present.

The question in the construction of a narrative must be whether it would be better to shorten the whole thing by resolving the first 200 pages in a final 50 without the 150 in between. I used to think that this was the appropriate solution. Today I am less sure. Perhaps there is the need for sub plots, strange new characters, or a diversion so that we can come to the final pages with an added sense of relish; perhaps novels, reflecting the way we really live, should contain periods of ennui in contrast with the high drama. Perhaps, too, there is a time for reflection between the novel's crux and final unfolding; and perhaps we are not self-disciplined enough to put the book down and undertake the reflection; it has to be narratively forced on us. In the case of this narrative of death and new life, I want the hiatus because, if the closing of the door on Good Friday is the most alienating, the saddest experience, the lighting of the candle at the Easter Vigil is the most resolving, the happiest experience. When the primeval fire of Genesis 1 is to be refined in the purposeful fire of the Paschal Candle, the only preparation is emptiness, not the architectural silence made by human hands, nor the dwindling natural silence of the tundra, but the emptiness of nothing, the most difficult emptiness of all.

This is the day without Jesus.

Silence is enclosed in life, emptiness has no edges; silence is defined by what it is, emptiness by what it is not; silence can be chosen or broken, emptiness is non-negotiable.

Perhaps the most tangible silence is that which we experience in architecture, a silence that relates to stone and space, a silence that inhabits as an intention of the architect; a silence that communicates, as intended by the composer. Musical silence is as integral to the experience as the notes and the relationship between the two is frequently an architectural phenomenon. That is why John Cage's 4'-33" is such a powerful musical statement; its sustained silence is a calculated antithesis. Self-styled purists often overlook the way in which composers such as Mahler altered the performance characteristics of symphonies depending on the acoustics of the hall. Durham Cathedral, built to broadcast Gregorian Chant, produces a single, split-second response which is evenly sustained at a declining volume whereas the circular environment of St Paul's Cathedral, built to broadcast preaching, produces a series of reverberative, gradually receding waves. Sound and silence can be shaped to increase mutual impact.

To shape silence requires great skill. The person leading public prayer has to work out how much silence to employ but quite often the result depends on self-confidence; in general, the length of silences is in direct proportion to the confidence and authority of the leader. A comedian uses silence to produce timing and, again, this requires technical skill and self-confidence; and the actor, playing a sustained role, has to work out the rhythm of the character and alter it according to the situation. In our personal dealings, particularly with people we know well, we can read a massive degree of significance into the length of a silence in the same way that we read significance into the intonation of a single word. If we ring up somebody to whom we are very close and ask how they are, a silence followed by the single word "fine" will immediately put us on an intelligent footing.

There are silences which can last days but we always know when we live in silence that there will be an end to it just as there was a beginning. We experience the tangible accompaniment of silence as a different experience from sound but we know how closely the two are symbiotic.

One of the reasons why we seek a surrounding silence is that we want to find the silence within ourselves.

Silence should be most intense in prayer. The usual mnemonic for prayer is ACTS: adoration, contrition, thanksgiving and supplication but an equally important part of prayer is attuning, listening, reflecting and resolving: tuning to God, listening to what we are being told, reflecting on its meaning and deciding what we should do. We often say of our relationships that we like people who are on the same wavelength; and the reality of this is more satisfying than the metaphor. God self-communicates to us not as a broadcaster with a uniform output but as individuals and as such we do not know what to expect which is why listening is so important. That listening may comprise periods of silence and bursts of sound or sustained sound and fragments of silence; frequently it will sound aleatoric and even confusing; but there will always be moments of supreme communication within the silence if we are prepared to open ourselves to the possibility of God's self-communication. Like the refining of gold, the precious outcome does not come from a casual event, it results from mining or dredging, crushing and sorting, firing and moulding; and much of this will be enhanced by silence. As for resolution, this is often forgotten; it means that no prayer is complete unless we work out what we are to do: there is no supplication, for example, unless we work out how to help the person whose plight we "lay before God"', for in laying it before God we are actually allowing God to lay it before us.

In prayer it is not always easy to create the silence we want and might need. Some people are skilled at blocking out the world, others, such as monks, have trained themselves to pare down their consciousness into silence and there are some who can lower themselves gradually into a state of deep silence. I have never—in a sphere which is profoundly personal even though we may help each other with techniques and frameworks—been able to manage my external environment so that it recedes from my consciousness; I let it play over to me because it is almost always a benevolent list. I am not, for example, listing the worldly goods I covet or the people I am going to hurt; I am listing the good things of life I wish to enjoy and share and the positive ways in which I can help people. Most of us are like this and one option, therefore, is to let the world in which we live holy lives run its course until it leads us, if it will, to silence.

When people say they are frightened of silence it is important to help them work out whether what they are really frightened of is emptiness or whether they lack enough solidity to make silence a viable element; after all, the depth of silence depends on the solidity of the structures it inhabits. A solid building will exclude noise and enfold silence whereas a tent will absorb the external environment uncritically. As people, the degree to which we can accommodate silence depends on our spiritual architecture, whether we need the distraction of noise and movement or whether we can nurture the core of silence at our centre. The idea of the soul is a dangerous dualist misconception but if I have what other people think of as a soul it is the silence at my centre.

During the hours from the commitment to the ignition, from the closing of the door until the lighting of the flame, I know that silence is impossible, that my sprawling, seemingly limitless emptiness has to be filled with the activities of preparation to stop it taking over. There are times when the only possible course of action is to tread water, to stay afloat, to force a smile, to be satisfied with the apparently trivial, to take undue care with detail. Not unsurprisingly, too, this is not a day for music, or at least not serious music. There is some purchase in an almost nostalgic hearing of a Bach Passion in the late afternoon of Good Friday but then I find that the emptiness corrodes the substance and the sandbagging has to begin.

Emptiness has no edges. Far from being contained, identifiable, like a wound, a trajectory or a pattern, it is the mental equivalent of liquid, it seeps into every crevice but it resembles weak acid rather than water so that it has a slow but irresistible power of corrosion.

This is the emptiness of Holy (such a strange term) Saturday. It is impossible to do anything when emptiness is at work: colours lose bloom, sound loses definition and words lose charm. Whatever we are in contact with presents us simply with a form, like a tapestry that has faded so that the colour has leeched and there is only the conceptual ghost; we know the theoretical, abstract meaning of what we perceive but not its reality. That is why the moment or arrival at church continues to be a surprise. As we wait for the time to come we can describe what is going to happen in every detail; we have, after all, been participants in the great feast many times before; but although the future has a shape that we can predict, it lacks content, it bears a relationship similar to that between a map and a drive along a road, the difference between a love letter and a kiss.

When we say we are bored we are suffering a lack of feeling close to emptiness. Boredom is a failure of perception which empties everything with which we come into contact of its content (an unintended but apt double meaning). There is a sense of a sequence in this which begins with an injection of emptiness, the beginning of corrosion, which might arise because of a failed love or a thwarted ambition. Lacking self-confidence and self-esteem, we aim lower but still fail, and before too long we suffer from the leeching process which we see in Anita Brookner's novels. We see the fading as it happens, wondering why the pretence of the compensation of small pleasures is so stolidly and meticulously maintained, sceptical of the reality of hope which, like everything else, is a shell of an idea. Our automatic reaction to emptiness, our means of survival, in the first instance, is to fill the space. Many lives are lived almost entirely in this way, in a feverish effort to generate words, objects, patterns, incidents, crises, in order to mask the emptiness. Holy Saturday is a good time to watch ourselves to see whether what we are doing on this day makes us feel warm or cool. If, as is likely (as voluntary attendants) we feel warmth, is this nostalgia, the satisfaction of a familiar ritual, or do we feel the surge of new hope?

There is a point at which, in an echo of the Bach Passion nostalgic valediction of Good Friday evening, that we can begin to arrange time as a part of what we are to enjoy. Whether it is the point at which we bathe or have finished dressing, or have taken up the Liturgy to survey the words or the music, the hope of what is to come, the irresistible pressure of content to fill the shape becomes blessedly irresistible. The sun goes down, as it must, before the Vigil can begin, and we know, as the Apostles did not, that there will be such an outburst when it rises again that nothing will ever be the same. Hope is the great bulwark against the encroachment of emptiness, it seals the space and then pumps new resolve into the vacuum. Sometimes we call this the Holy Spirit because she is the comforter. She pours content back into empty places which emptiness has eroded; she puts lustre into colours and intonation into sound; she informs (or perhaps enforms) the abstract with life. For me, not uniquely in realising the narrative force of the New Testament, there is a trick of time. The idea that the Resurrection, whatever that might mean, anticipates the coming of the Holy Spirit is incomprehensible, for the occasion on which she is most powerful is on this night, and I can feel her restlessness within me as I turn the pages of the words to come.

Thus, in the space of just over 24 hours, we experience the profound tragedy, the closing silence of the drama of the life of Jesus, followed by a descent into emptiness and then, through a process of rising hope, an ascent out of that emptiness towards the silence that precedes the night; for by the time we reach church it is no longer empty, it is filled with anticipation, in the opening of the flowers, in the lustre of the organ keys, in the new candle waiting to be lit. Jesus who had left us is returned and in living through the absence we learn how much he is woven into the fabric of our daily lives. As with so many phenomena, we only notice him by his absence but this is surely not enough. The one day without him should prepare us for our Easter recognition, an emotional as well as a theological, liturgical or creaturely response, to his renewed presence with us. Each of these responses is necessary but the emotion is a necessary part of rejoicing for the restoration of wholeness, for the defeat of emptiness. To be truly creaturely is to be both emotional and rational, to be and to give of ourselves in fullness.

For me, the silence before the priest begins the Liturgy of the Easter Vigil is the profoundest silence of all, more weighty even than the silence at the end of Mahler's 9th Symphony; for that silence contains all our hope, the joy of the Easter Proclamation, the story of our Redemption, the Gloria and, above all, the Eucharist celebrated for the first time since its Institution in its proper post-Resurrection context.

Was the tomb empty or silent? Both words are used, apparently interchangeably, to describe the state in which the women found it (although it is obvious that a full tomb can be silent). To understand the question we have to think back to the first visit of the women to this new tomb when they hurriedly prepared Jesus for his temporary entombment. Then everything was lost; they were not caught in the silence between words or actions, they were faithfully, dutifully carrying the dead weight of the body and all their fears. For them, at least for now (and we must not assume forever as we do not really know what their understanding was of Messianism or Resurrection) their hope had gone; it might return with memory or replacement but for now it was gone. It must have been the most miserable Saturday (Sabbath or Passover) they ever spent; and then, the new week and the need to make all things complete.

There was nothing in the tomb except the grave clothes. Did this suggest a renewal of hope, the anticipatory silence of things to come, or was it an extension of their emptiness, just another piece of bad news, an assault upon their religious and cultural need to make all things complete? Describing that moment the Evangelists, except Mark, find it impossible to eliminate a note of anticipatory triumph; but Mark is surely nearest to the actual situation when he describes a scene of initial shock and fear which the later addendum to his Gospel and the accounts in the other gospels never entirely mitigate. The Lord has been judicially murdered; they wish to do him final reverence but are denied. The tomb is empty; they will have a great deal of explaining to do, to themselves and then to their menfolk. The sheer horror of their plight is individualised in John in the person of Mary Magdalene who is distraught at the loss of the body. They are all caught in the fear not of what Resurrection might mean—they have no means of imagining what that might be—but in the open-ended misery of incompleteness. When we read Resurrection accounts we too easily get ahead of ourselves. At the point when the women discovered the empty tomb they suffered yet another dreadful disappointment.

Viewed in this light, the story of our Redemption told in the readings from Scripture after the Exultet and Easter Proclamation feel rather odd. For as we listen to the story from Genesis 1 onwards we are part of a process whose end we have already celebrated in the lighting of the candle; restored from our emptiness to the fullness of life in the risen Christ, like the readers of fiction before the nineteenth century, we know where we are in the story and we know the completeness of it. The women knew nothing of the sort.

Then something happened. There is no denying that the idea of a risen Jesus, bodily and yet not bodily in the way we are or he was before his Crucifixion, is very difficult to grasp; and we have to acknowledge that the account that is most detailed and concrete in John 20 is the last to have been written but this needs to be balanced against our first record of the Resurrection from Paul who seems to have known and/or cared little about the details of the life of Jesus except that he died and rose again. Whether the later additions to Mark and John are "fixes" or affirmations; there is no denying that the mood of Jesus' followers shifted radically between the discovery of the empty tomb and Peter's Pentecost sermon.

In an increasingly fascinating paradox, non-Christians are much more worried about the debate encompassing the actual form of Jesus' Resurrection than we are. The sterile debates about the mechanics of the Eucharist (Transubstantiation, consubstantiation &c) and our Redemption (penal substitution) should warn us against trying to describe the mechanics of the Resurrection; for us the central point is what happened not how it happened. What happened was that the followers of Jesus were, without warning, without a preparatory sign or a pregnant silence, electrified into a new sense of hope. Their loss of emptiness was not gradual, it was instant and total. They were not restored to the plane of their mission with Jesus but projected in a unique spiritual trajectory to a higher state of being and knowing, of human and salvific assurance. Whether they apprehended a physical presence or visions, whether they could read Jesus' lips or simply knew what he was saying to them, whether they all experienced a personal atunedness or lived the same events with different levels of response, built up through mutual support, there is no denying the reality of the massive injection of Christological acuteness. They knew, more definitely than any human being has known anything before or since, knew in a way that transformed every facet of their lives, knew in a way that brooked no subordinate clauses, that the life (they had not reached back to the logical starting point of incarnation), death and return of Jesus to them was the means of their fulfilment. It was not long before that under-writing was extended to Jews and then to the whole world. God's self-communication to his people had, through the means of historical intervention, taken a new, sharper and, above all, more definite form; the purpose of existence, the self-understanding of our creatureliness, was given, in Karl Rahner's classic formulation, an irreversible forward projection. As they struggled with the immense consequences of their hope, giving it shape which ultimately became the theology of Paul and the Evangelists, they stayed together, integrating and re-integrating what they had learned in their lives with Jesus before his death and their lives with Jesus after his return. Whatever the mechanics, the process seemed to them then and seems to us now, to be gracefully and simply complete.

It is vital in considering where we are now that we do not forget the narrative sequence. There was no rejoicing in front of the tomb; there was no obvious solution to the mystery of its emptiness. Subsequently there were a number of appearances but what happened to the followers of Jesus between that first Easter day and Pentecost was as radical as the Incarnation itself and was itself the Incarnation's completeness. The fusion of God in man in the Incarnation was confirmed for all mankind in the Resurrection.

## v. Easter Day—Form and Substance

*Our heart burned within us*

**Luke 24.32**

Empiricism and a certain kind of metaphysical fastidiousness have, between them, radically undermined a coherent sense of being. The empiricists, on the one hand, have relegated being to chemistry so that being is a matter of physical presence whereas some metaphysicians, on the other, have sought to question the very concept of being by asking whether what we think of as being is a form of sleep from which we will wake into real being. In their different ways both these kinds of understanding of being are dualist: the scientist thinks that being is solely physical and the dream theorist thinks that being is entirely non-physical. That distinction, which goes back to the Gnostics and, before them, to Plato, is responsible for the Christian notion of the soul as a separate entity from the body, leading to such questions as: when does the soul enter the body? It is not a very great leap from this dualist position to one in which the body is made inferior to the soul and becomes an obstacle to the soul's purity. The problem with this idea is that a disembodied soul, a purely spiritual entity, would not be able to exercise and execute choice; the soul is simply a metaphysical device for describing that aspect of humanity which is not physical; but in trying to work out the relationship between the physical and non-physical, the ranking of the two is to misunderstand their relationship which is symbiotic. We receive information through our senses and we transmit information from our senses; the same is true of moral and spiritual impulses. God does not communicate with our "soul" but with our body.

We might start a more fruitful discussion by thinking back to the earlier consideration of silence which is quite a different entity from emptiness. Silence has a presence, a known-ness but it is not physical; it is created by humanity deliberately so that it can be transmitted and received by humanity to fulfil an authorial intention. Equally, when the music which surrounds the silence is played, there are certain combinations of notes which induce extraordinary reactions in some listeners, inspiring a sense of awe or deep sorrow. The same impact is made by the use of certain combinations of words or images. Now it might be objected that a theory of non-physical being cannot be based on these phenomena because they are all physical—the musician writes and the listener hears; the author writes and the reader hears or sees; and the painter paints and the viewer sees—but the point is that even if that is true, the reactions are not predictable as they would be in the empiricist's laboratory. Something happens to make us behave differently towards music, literature and art than we behave towards, say, gravity, heat and food. To reverse the argument, if we come across people who behave in a purely predictable, selfish or even utilitarian way, without variation or nuance, we think them uncivilised at least if not downright inhuman. In spite of the supposed sharp distinction, then, which we owe to Descartes' sharpening of Plato, we know in some way that to be human is to be both physical and non-physical. Rather, however, than separating the non-physical—the aesthetic, the spiritual, the altruistic—from the physical, we might consider them to be so symbiotic that they are impossible to separate: the artist's imagination is expressed in paint, the viewer's imagination is fired by paint, and so on. There is no awe without the pain but the pain is nothing without the awe. That is a good working model for the way we operate socially but does it tell us enough about ourselves? I doubt that we would find it easy to understand ourselves to consist of two symbiotic parts, a physical and a non-physical.

At a deeper, level, however, we begin to find more difficulties with dualism which can be summarised in the question: why would God create anything in which some part was inferior to the other? Put differently, was the human body of Jesus inferior to the divine nature of Jesus? If we grant that God's creation is all of a piece, that it is all in the same class of existence, that it is, in other words, all createdness, we have to agree with the Councils of Nicea and Chalcedon that Jesus consisted of what they called "two natures" in one person. They were entitled to draw a distinction between the human and the divine in thinking about Jesus but we have mistakenly mistranslated that to try to separate the physical (which we think of as human) and the spiritual (which we think of as divine). This doctrinal haggle gives us a clue to a different way of understanding being, by separating form (how we describe something by reference to our ability for pattern recognition) from substance (what something is of itself): Jesus came to earth in the form of a man but was still God. God can exist in the form of a man or, as Christians believe, in the form bread and wine. It is the relationship between form and substance which ultimately defeats empiricists because they only accept the form which is physical. In order to sustain this narrow view they reduce their own passions and aesthetics to physical phenomena: I love Mary because something physical in me recognises something physical in her; I support Manchester United because a variety of anthropological and socio-economic factors have aggregated to turn a potentiality into something actual; I cry when I hear the outer movements of Mahler's 9th Symphony because certain combinations of notes induce a physiological experience; but, of course, this is not true. You only need to look at studies of identical twins to disprove that crude causality. The next line of defence is to argue that the causality is much more complex, even infinite, but still to retain the single assertion that the causality is purely physical. It is much more intuitive to turn the proposition on its head and say, parodying Aquinas in the words of St Theresa of Avila, that the spiritual can only be given expression through the physical. To that extent the "soul" cannot be superior because, by definition, a phenomenon cannot be superior to something it depends upon but, if anything, vice versa.

We, therefore, being created by God out of Love for the purpose of choosing to love and worship, understand our relationship with God and the way we make choices through spiritual power operating within us as creatures. Why would we as the creatures of God require a separate "soul" to legitimate us spiritually in some way? It is, perhaps more than any other single factor, the tendency towards dualism which makes our understanding of God so difficult. We want to make ourselves inferior to God rather than simply different, and we want to constitute that inferiority in a hierarchy which puts the spiritual above the physical. God is better than that; God cannot be ranked with us nor we with God in any meaningful way; and we are better than that because anything created out of love must be as good as it possibly can be; that is what love is like.

My fascination with T. S. Eliot's *The Waste Land* long preceded my fascination with the story of the followers of Jesus on the road to Emmaus; but as I have gradually come to see Eliot's poem as a series of puzzles valuable in themselves rather than valuable in their solution, Luke's account has taken an ever tighter grip on my imagination.

Here is the story. Two people, Cleopas and companion, probably his wife (who was probably, therefore, present at the Institution of the Eucharist), are walking home to Emmaus when they are joined by a stranger whom they naturally suppose is a human fellow traveller. He asks them why they are sad and they tell him of the death of Jesus and the appearance of Angels. The man then explains all that has happened and, being invited into a house, breaks bread, at the very least implying that the bread is his body, and he then disappears. Here is a veritable feast of form and substance problems. The key questions are: what form did the traveller take; why were the eyes of his beholders unequal to their task; what happened at the breaking of the bread; and how did the traveller "disappear"? The first and last questions are identical to those we pose about the form taken by the risen Christ. To an empiricist this question makes no sense; but neither does it make any sense to the impartial critic to state flatly that nothing of significance happened between the discovery of the empty tomb and Pentecost. Jesus was real to Cleopas and his companion and he was real at the instant when he broke bread; and, in a paradoxical way, he was most real at the moment after he had disappeared. As with silence and music, his very absence, the space he left, was more real than the substance that had filled it a moment before. The second question is the easiest to answer; the viewers simply did not know what they were looking for. Most often "seeing" is a matter of discerning patterns from apparently random phenomena. Jesus was such an outlandish figure that it was not possible for them to see a pattern; they could not match up the traveller with their experience of Jesus and their knowledge of his death. Even when Jesus had completed (if he had) his narration as they approach Emmaus, they still did not see. What, remarkably, created the discernment was the repetition of a single act which had only been undertaken once before in this special form, although, no doubt, as the head of his travelling companions, Jesus must often have broken bread.

The third question is the most important because it is that which marks the story of Emmaus as crucial to our understanding of Jesus and our self-understanding as Christians.

Perhaps the best way to understand the significance of Emmaus is to ask what the four post-Resurrection accounts would add up to without it. The key feature which the Emmaus story adds is the inclusion of a Eucharist ceremony which points backward to Maundy Thursday which, in turn, points forward to the end of time. Emmaus is a confirmation of the promise made on Maundy Thursday. Resurrection without Eucharist is tenable and some Christians even find it tolerable but the placing of this Emmaus story is so strategic and so closely tied to the Resurrection event that it is not possible to see the two apart.

If we tell the narrative in a slightly different way: the substance Jesus, buried in physical, human form, was replaced by Jesus in a different, undefined form who appeared to the women who told the men, one of whom, with a companion, left Jerusalem and met Jesus in an undefined form who, in the course of receiving hospitality, gave himself in the form of bread and then withdrew his undefined form. The whole sentence is a series of statements about form but there is no doubt about the substance: the body of Jesus was buried but a recognisable Jesus appeared to the women who told the men, one of whom and a companion recognised Jesus when he gave himself in the form of bread and then disappeared.

If we can be clear about substance and form this, in turn, clarifies other areas of theology. Most often Christians seem to be worried about mechanics, about how things happened. Thus, when many people struggle with the question: "What happened at the Resurrection?" they are more likely asking "How did the Resurrection happen?" They therefore think that they have to have faith in the form the event took rather than having faith in what the event was. As Christians we are not expected to affirm our faith in the mechanics of Resurrection any more than we are expected to hold a particular view on the mechanics of "Redemption" but we are expected to affirm the reality of the event; Jesus rose from the dead, was with the Apostles in a way they could grasp, promised to send and then sent the Holy Spirit.

We must be careful neither to be empiricists struggling with the empirical evidence for the Resurrection nor to believe that we live in a dream over which we have no control until we wake up in another place, better or worse. Perhaps the key obstacle is the sequence specified by John that Jesus would only send the Spirit once he ascended into heaven I take this sequence, this chronology to accompany the geometry of the Trinity, to be metaphorical. I do not see how the followers of Jesus can have so quickly grasped the post-Resurrection reality without the presence of the Spirit; indeed, without the infusion of the Holy Spirit I doubt that the Emmaus event could have been recognised by Cleopas and his companion for what it was. There is no doctrine that says the Eucharist is only of effect with an Epiclesis at a certain date defined by theologians; either the sanctification of the Spirit is necessary for the consecration of the elements, rendering the real presence of Jesus, sacrificed for us all, or it is not.

If we can try to distance our theological metaphors from a strict dualism and to see form as the presenting pattern which helps us to recognise substance, and if we can understand that recognition of the divine as the work of the Holy Spirit, then we will be less troubled by the empirical claim of scientists and the illusion claims of some thinkers. Unfortunately, Plato is still alive and well and still wreaking havoc within the Christian core of self-consciousness.

It sometimes appears that the only real purpose of the Holy Spirit, the Sanctifier, is to satisfy the Greek numerological requirement for three, rather than two "persons" or major attributes of the deity. This phenomenon, being entitled "spirit", has always been characterised as having no form or substance but that is where the major error lies; anything that is, that exists, has substance even if we cannot use our powers of pattern recognition to discern its form. In other words, the inability to discern form does not mean that something does not have substance. If we think of the history of the way in which we understand the universe, for instance, we started with a totally formless view which evolved into an understanding of the earth as a flat planet beneath the sun, the moon and a canopy of stars which came to have astrological significance; then we became aware of planetary motion around earth as the centre of the system. Gradually, however, the earth, and then the solar system, were seen in the context of the Milky Way and then in the context of an even wider universe which began to take on a temporal as well as a spatial aspect and these two aspects were finally linked. Thus, the universe may have had a constant substantive existence (although this is problematic in itself) but the form of the universe and its components developed according to our powers of pattern recognition. Equally, although in a different way, our understanding of the "form" of the Holy Spirit, our ability to recognise the Spirit at work, changes over time, not so much as a corporate but as a personal phenomenon.

If we try to unimagine the Greek Tripartite view of the Christian Godhead, the outstanding question is why there needs to be a Holy Spirit. We can intuitively understand the idea of a Creator and we have no problem in recognising the Incarnate Redeemer; but why could the Creator not be the Sanctifier? The classic answer is that the Sanctifier is the product of the love of the Creator and Redeemer for each other, a divine reflection of the erotic, but that is surely to conflate love with procreation. At the very least it is a view of love in which the participants are proactive, again reflecting the way human beings think about love, based both on the biological imperative to impose and, biological or otherwise (this is a matter of debate), on the demonstration of supererogatory benevolence. My answer to the question is more distanced from the biological patterns of behaviour which we have characterised, in one way or another, as love but it is not altogether separate because it suggests a female antithesis to the idea of a creator that is male. It is that the Spirit is the repository of human love brought about by divine Grace which is not, as so often appears, a product delivered to humanity, like wheat or gold dust, but is the space which allows us to choose. When we say that people have the "good grace" we generally mean that they are allowing, not that they are imposing.

It is, of course, easy to read a pattern across from the biological to the moral and then to the divine: there is a "male" aspect that proposes, projects and creates complemented by a "female" aspect that accepts, receives and, and what? Here is where the neat antithesis breaks down because just as there is an egg in the biological and an acceptance in the moral, so there is a dimension of reception in the spiritual but it is not passive but creative in the way that the egg is creative, in the way that acceptance is creative. There is no generation without the egg, no giving without receiving, no creation without the capacity to receive the love freely given. If we think of God simply as creating and Redeeming and then think of the Spirit as some kind of dispenser we have to ask how that part of God is to be thought of which receives the love we freely give for which we were created in love.

Although, as I have pointed out, it is oversimplifying matters to think purely in biological terms rather than thinking of them, as we do with all formulations of God as metaphor, there is something fundamentally, intuitively, attractive in thinking of the Spirit as a female metaphor. Much of what has gone wrong with Western religion has been its hopeless imbalance of "male", spiritual testosterone, forever expressing, projecting, organising, problem solving and, of course, controlling and exercising power and not, conversely, enough emphasis on patience, acceptance, humility, healing and just being there, often silent, contemplating God in itself and in the world. Of course males will object that they are capable of all these "female" characteristics and vice versa but the point is simply to characterise two sets of complementary outlooks with which we were created. It is not that we have made God in our own image but that we were made in the image of God and can therefore proclaim that we are as we are made. There is no point protesting, as some moralists do, that we should behave differently, that our behaviour is somehow immoral or unfitting; rather, we should simply behave more in balance, as suspicious of too "male" an outlook as of too "female" an outlook, equally worried, for example, about power and fatalism.

It is pointless pretending that these ideas, even as metaphors, are simple or tidy but their virtue is that they might help us to understand that aspect of God (to use that idea explains why the term "person" is difficult in this context) which receives what we freely offer which is the justification for our creation. This, in turn, will lead us back to ask how redemption fits into the pattern, or the "economy" of God to which my answer is that which I pointed towards on Maundy Thursday and which is under-written in the return of Christ at Easter. The Crucifixion proclaims and the Resurrection confirms that there is no act which we can collectively commit as the result of our deliberately perverse exercise of freedom that takes us away from rather than towards God, including the murder of God, which will result in our rejection; having been created in imperfection in order to love freely, we will be enfolded back into the Creator after our sojourning here in the struggle to realise our purpose. There is no point saying that the Redeemer "conquered sin" unless we know what this means; it means literally what it says. Sin will not separate a single one of us from God; we will all be saved.

The Emmaus story is crucial in our understanding of the life, death and return of Jesus because what it describes, better than any other account of that return, is the process of recognition, an understanding of a form which allows the participants to perceive the substance. To say that Emmaus is the post-Resurrection enactment of the Last Supper or the First Eucharist of Easter, of the new era, is not to go far enough. Emmaus encapsulates the purpose of the whole divine enterprise from the Incarnation of Jesus up until this point in the narrative and that is to enable us to recognise the substance of God both in the life of Jesus the Redeemer and in his own perpetuation of himself in the Eucharist. We might understand this better by again asking ourselves how the accounts of the Resurrection would "stack up" without this account of scriptural and Sacramental illumination. If I try to imagine which incidents Jesus recounted to the downcast travellers, I would not settle on the tortuous correspondences of the life of Jesus with the Prophets but rather on the vivid moments of recognition in the Old Testament, the awakening of Abraham, the struggles of Jacob, the burning bush and the peculiar meteorology of Horeb, the "domestication" in Samuel, the aberration of kingship and the forward trajectory in Nehemiah. At a critical point of nadir, the Chosen People experienced a shift from the nostalgic to the anticipatory. At the very point when they were tidying up their law and their history, consolidating their collective identity, they found themselves in the untidiness of expectation which is, as we know, not so reliable a source of literary inspiration as history. I like to think that Jesus explained how God was there to be seen but was only recognised in a limited way; but that that recognition was infinitely broadened by his presence (what we call the Incarnation) and under-written forever by his death and return. "Yes, Lord," I hear them say, "but how do we know?" "Wait and see," he might have replied, "what happens when we eat together." Luke's account, perhaps because of its brevity, implies surprise but I prefer to think that what really took place was confirmed recognition of what had been promised.

If we ask ourselves what characterises human beings, one serious contender is pattern recognition, the ability to see form. This is often expressed in the specific ability to use language but it goes much deeper than that. Unlike the empiricists, on the one hand, who draw our scope too narrowly and those who question the very concept of reality, on the other, who make us helpless dreamers, Christians (and many others) know from our own personal and collective experience that we have the power to recognise forms which tell us of reality, of substance beyond the empirical that is more solid than the dream. It would be strange indeed if a god who created out of love would arrange matters in such a way that we could not recognise the substance of the creator in the forms which surround us. Without recognition there would be no way for us to fulfil our purpose of choosing to love, we would not know why we were here and would revert to the empirical or the dream. But the whole of human history shows us the intermittent recognition of form and the struggle to see the substance it represents, to see the patterns behind what is apparently random. The history of the human race is not primarily one of scientific endeavour (although that is important) nor of trance-like fatalism (although that provides a sometimes necessary "playful", scepticism) but it is, above all, a history of our outer and inner dialogue with existence which has resulted in an account of ourselves far beyond the empirical or the fatalistic. There is a school of thought which says that our purpose is to forge, to make form, but that is secondary to recognising it; even transformative creativity arises out of recognition. Action without recognition results at best in waste and at worst, and most often, in failure. Just as there is no effective writing without reading, no painting without seeing, no sound without hearing, so there is no constructiveness without a recognition of structure.

As we stand, therefore, outside the house at Emmaus, looking down the road in the gathering gloom, wondering where the traveller went, we should recognise that we have just seen a form of God which helps us to imagine the substance. God is with us forever, however we choose to acknowledge this, and that presence is not simply in the Word, in Scripture, in the account of the Jewish dialogue with God but also in Sacrament, a presence in simple bread and wine; and Word and Sacrament are bound together, made complete in the openness of God to our expressions of love for which we were created. The ultimate mystery of God is that we, who are created to love, cannot love without recognising the lover, but the lover is a space, a pregnant silence which we can fill with our creativity. We can only infer the substance of God through form and that form is given shape in what we do, but the space inside the form, the silence, is the essence of the "receiving" aspect of God, the corollary of creation. We might better say, rather than thinking of a Father and a Son whose mutual love generates a Spirit, that there is the God who gives and the God who takes whose purpose was Incarnate in the God who lived in Jesus and lives with us now in Word and Sacrament. In these forms I recognise substance and respond as I was created to respond. Recognising God and recognising myself are one.

# 3. The Seven Last Words

*2007*

## i. Doubt

*My God, My God, why have you forsaken me?*
**Matthew 27:46**

Every so often in the middle of a period of quiet prayer, my brain asks the question I least want it to ask: "Do you really believe this or is it just a massive superstructure of comfort to give your trivial life some kind of meaning?"

Doubt is possibly the most misunderstood Christian attribute because it loses all its dynamic force when it is separated from faith. If an atheist says that she doubts the existence of God it doesn't mean all that much; but if a Christian, struggling with faith, says that he doubts, then the statement has true vibrancy, true value.

The mystery of the Passion and death of our Saviour is only one of the sacred mysteries into which we have been initiated in our Christian life by virtue of our Baptism. Yesterday we witnessed the re-enactment of the mystery of the Eucharist; today we witness the working out of that mystery in the physical death of Jesus.

Ironically, looked at from a Christian perspective, the mistake we most often make is thinking that we understand God, that there really are no mysteries in connection with the creative, salvific and sanctifying purposes of the Trinity. In a very real sense the problem for many of us is that we do not doubt enough.

Yet there are some Christians who walk in our Saviour's Church of Doubt with a list in their hands of the great certainties, as if there is no mystery at all, as if it is all perfectly clear. They say what is true and that anybody who disagrees with them must be wrong. They say that Scripture is as plain as plain can be; that our sin is in not seeing what is obvious.

God created us with brains so that we might think, so that we might choose, so that our love might be consciously given, so that we might leave ourselves open to the Holy Spirit in a state of intense calm; and in creating us to choose, in creating us to reflect God, in creating us to explore the mystery of God's love and our creation, God created doubt. But doubt is suffocated by pride, pride that human knowledge can penetrate the sacred mystery of God. And doubt is corroded by cowardice.

I have doubted but instead of pressing on towards the core of doubt, towards the zone of acute discomfort, I have stood back. I have been prepared to forsake my Saviour and live in the comfortable world of Jesus the fairy story, the story which starts so beautifully, goes through a horrible episode, as all fairy stories will, but ends happily ever after. I have left my Saviour hanging on the Cross instead of getting closer; I have read my Bible and prayed my prayers and flinched when it has become too difficult to face. I have wanted to be in command of myself and of the Holy words and books; yes, I have wanted to be in command; and at the same time I have only wanted comfort from this enterprise. I often fail to flex my inner self to see where the sharp edges of commitment might be. Because I want to be in command, the prospect of being out of my depth is too daunting with which to live. So I have exchanged the challenge and pain of doubt for the relative comfort of dogma.

There may be some technical problems with dogma but the Creed sounds so comforting if we don't think too carefully about it; and we have become comfortable in our Sacraments; and we feel such warmth in the fellowship of the Lord's Supper; but unless we flex our commitment, unless we examine its cost, unless we stretch to the limit for its healing, we are taking refuge in a formula, something familiar and comforting, something that is a social ritual rather than a journey towards faith.

Given the centrality of doubt in the condition of human holiness it is inevitable that Jesus should have suffered from doubt. We must always remember that although he was fully God, Jesus was also fully human.

He knew what he was doing in obedience to his Father but he did not know how this would end and for what ultimate purpose. He knew that he was dying for the forgiveness of sin, to absorb in himself as a Sacred vessel, all the wrong choices, all the choices not to love, that had ever been made and would ever be made; but he did not know precisely how this transaction related to his Father. In taking human form he had denied himself knowledge, he had been cast into the human condition of doubt. We might go further and argue that Jesus had temporarily lost his faith altogether, that he thought that he had been abandoned.

This is the most searing consequence of doubt, the moment of blankness, the moment when we are most human, living as we were meant to live, living as we were meant to live because one of the consequences of being created to choose is that we must confront the extremes of certainty and doubt instead of living halfway along the spectrum, managing to rub along with the Divine as if it were a rather anomalous but comfortable "given" in the way we see the universe.

When we go to the extreme, we face the prospect that there is no God, that our lives are shapeless and meaningless, that within years of our death the memories will have faded, the photographs will have been thrown away, stories once funny will be left untold. Nothing.

Only then can we begin to leave ourselves open to the Holy Spirit, to begin to know God from a position of humble creatureliness. Only then can we see every doctrine as a question not as an answer; only then can we understand that all human enterprise is a question, not an answer; that the Church is a question not an answer but, hopefully, the right question.

There are those who tell us that we can be risk-free Christians, that as long as we believe in God all will be well. But not to take risks is not to know what it might mean to believe. All our lives we must take the risk of walking towards the Cross, of trying to work out what it means, of trying to understand why Jesus hangs there in front of us and why we still have the strength to walk towards him. All our lives we must face the inevitable discomfort of not knowing, of not being in control, of being made small, of having our intellectual powers overwhelmed by the mystery of God's love. But because the only way in which we can really relate to God's love is through the incarnate Son, the only way we can really know why we are is to keep on flexing ourselves out of complacency, to keep on walking forward towards the Cross, to risk the horror of that tortured face, to look into the face and see our own imperfection. For there is a paradox in the Cross which we have to confront; it is our comfort that has brought about the torture of our Saviour which we are looking at now.

Let us come closer. Closer.

## Prayer

Lord Jesus, as you hang upon the Cross in the loneliness of human doubt, forgive us our pride in the refuge of human doctrine: may we struggle towards the Cross, abandoning comfort for commitment, so that we are alive to the mystery of your Grace. Amen.

# ii. Faith

*Into your hands I commend my spirit*

**Luke 23:46**

Faith is not the opposite of doubt, it is the flower that can only bloom where doubt has been sewn; but whereas doubt will always be there, the flower of faith will bloom and fade before it blooms again. The Church sustains "the Faith" because it is a corporate enterprise, a huge garden of questions where, through the Grace of our Saviour, there are always some flowers blooming. Hopefully, it is never completely winter in the garden of Jesus; and, hopefully, in the way of divine institutions on earth, there will be times when the array of flowers is stunning, like one of those magical, searing summer days when Van Gogh was lucid.

Because it is a flower that blooms and fades, faith commands the greatest care: the thought and love of the gardener, the right nourishment, the balance between sun and shade. Yet, as different flowers of faith, we all need different kinds of fertiliser, different balances of sun and shade. Some of us grow in clay, others in sandy ground, others in chalk. Some of us are gaudy and long for the summer sun; others, more delicate, long for the misty days of fine rain and winter's pale sun.

Our gardener, our Saviour, will give us all the nourishment we need, the right balance of sun and rain to suit our needs, to help us best accord with God's purpose for us as flowers in the earthly garden. But we turn to other gardeners, to other nourishment; we crave more sun than is good for us or more rain; we see another flower in the distance and think we should be like that flower and not simply be ourselves.

This is not a parable about beauty or earthly pride, this is a parable about the way we have come to misunderstand faith. We have persuaded ourselves that faith is robust and uniform instead of seeing it as fragile and highly differentiated.

Yet there are some Christians who walk in our Saviour's Church of Faith with a list in their hands of all the essential ingredients, who think that God is one kind of gardener and that all of us are not delicate and different flowers but are cabbages to be forced into uniform ugliness and utility. We are not in a garden where the blooms vary and where our own flowers fade and revive, we are not individual believers in a corporate church; we are identical plants that react in a uniform way to the correct dosage of divinely approved but humanly manufactured fertiliser.

We have all grown familiar with the idea of faith as some kind of production line that begins at Baptism and ends at the crematorium or cemetery. In this we have misunderstood faith in two serious ways. First, as I have said, faith is not a production line where standard nutrition is poured in and a standard product is forced out. Faith is a risky business. One year a flower will not bloom at all. Sometimes the ground is too dry, at other times too wet. Sometimes there are blights and infestations. More often, however, we have abandoned our gentle gardener and opted for a supposedly more reliable, hermetically sealed greenhouse. Secondly, faith is individual to us but the garden in which we bloom is as old as mankind. We grow in the soil of saints and martyrs, of those who went before us in faith, who bloomed in a different time but in the same place, whose flowers look strange and exotic.

Those who went before us as saints and martyrs lived that they might be worthy of our Saviour, that their spirits, too, might be commended, through him, to the Father. When we listen to our Saviour as he hangs upon the Cross we do not hear him say: "Father, into your hands I deliver my spirit as part of a spiritual job lot." There is, in his word, the humility of commendation, the possibility in the word that what he has to offer might not be good enough.

Our ultimate act of faith is to doubt our worthiness, to flex our capacity for self-knowledge and look at our self-image. It is so easy over time to mould our self-image so that it adjusts to new circumstances. The young person that demands an answer and searches feverishly is replaced by the older person who has found an answer that is good enough; and in turn that older person becomes increasingly desperate as time wears on. Is the faith which we have now going to carry us into the presence of God or have we been too complacent?

Unfortunately for our sense of stability and comfort, faith is reflexive; we have to have faith in faith; and, at the same time, faith is indispensable. Just as true wisdom is to know what we do not know, true faith is to know the limits of our faith, to know that we have been unable to take the step of abandoning ourselves to God. By this act of abandonment we do not give up trying to lead virtuous lives, it simply means that we know the virtuous life is not enough, no matter how virtuous. We must count everything we have done as nothing compared with what God has done for us through our Saviour.

What is this Spirit which, reflecting the cry of Jesus, we commend in faith? It is, above all, the spirit of courage. We are not called upon to be right for our Saviour; we are not called upon to be prudent for our Saviour; we are not even called upon to be pious for our Saviour; we are called upon to be brave for our Saviour, to commit, to take the risk, to risk being unpopular, even to risk being wrong. While the fashion is for this or for that, that spirit of courage might involve staying still and waiting until the gardener reaches us.

I am restless, I am full of ideas, I strive but the striving usually amounts to an assertion of the human will. Instead of faith in stillness, in subjecting myself to the sun and rain, instead of being content to be in the ground where I was planted, I long for a programme of forced virtue, to make me fat with grace, to make me shiny with virtue, to make me ripe with advice, to make me rich with learning and, oh, the consequence, to make

me feel fitted in all my ripeness and richness, to judge all those plants that
never seem to flower, that are limp and bedraggled.

How easily we are moved by the rich and the colourful, the perfumed
and the pretty; how much we value the aesthetic and under-estimate the
healing powers of unglamorous plants. Yet only our Saviour who tends
us, nourishing us with that endless Grace which flows from the reservoir
of his blood, only he can commend us to the Father as he commended
his own spirit as he hung on the Cross, ready to die for us. We cannot,
no matter what we do, commend ourselves.

A flower blooms; a flower fades and dies; and a new flower blooms,
nourished by the blood of the Cross.

**Prayer**

Lord Jesus, as you hang upon the Cross in ultimate obedience to the
Father, forgive us our resort to a coarse and cold faith: may we struggle
towards the Cross in soul as well as mind, learning to grow in submission
to you so that our frail flowers of faith may bloom in your tender care.
Amen.

## iii. Forgiveness

*Father forgive them; for they know not what they do*
**Luke 23:34**

Recently I have been dipping into *The New Oxford Book of Christian Verse*,
paying particular attention to the words of hymns. The most striking
discovery I have made is the extent to which the compilers of the hymn
book we use, Hymns Ancient and Modern Revised (New Standard), have
omitted beautiful verses from initial compositions which refer to Satan
and to sin. I have some sympathy with the omission of Satan whose
depiction with horns and a tail can be a distraction from our deeper

understanding of sin as deliberately distancing ourselves from God; but if we are to eliminate sin from our vocabulary, what is today about?

We must be careful to understand the relationship we have with God. Sin, as a symptom of our capacity to choose, is inevitable in imperfect humanity, but no individual sin is inevitable. We have to take responsibility, today is the day of responsibility, our responsibility to God and the responsibility which God, through Jesus, has taken for us.

Let us begin at the beginning. We were created by God so that we might choose to love freely; and, naturally, as human beings possessing, as Genesis picturesquely portrays it, the knowledge of good and evil, we frequently choose not to love rather than to love.

That is the essence of sin. There is not a ledger with sin on one side and virtue on the other; it isn't the outcome that matters. There are virtuous people captivated by their own goodness and there are struggling people torn between almost impossibly difficult choices.

Yet there are some Christians who walk in our Saviour's Church of Forgiveness with a list in their hands, claiming to know from external appearances who is a sinner and who is saved. But they are forging disastrous caricatures of God's purpose. Nobody but God knows what we chose and how; they only know what it looks like; and what it looks like can be fatally misleading.

Today, then, is the day for facing up to our sin. But we must not face up to our sin in an intellectual way, admitting that the human race frequently chooses not to love; nor is it good enough to admit that we, collectively and individually, often choose not to love. This is the day to flex our notion of sinfulness so that it becomes alive in us as a self-reproach instead of simply being a dispassionate social commentary.

Because I have chosen not to love, Jesus is hanging on the Cross; because I have chosen to be proud, to give myself credit for an act well done, a thorn is pressed into my Saviour's head; because I have chosen to be cruel in what I say, my Saviour is being mocked; because I have used power instead of love, a nail is being driven into my Saviour's hand; because I have stood by instead of acting out of love, the crowd are standing by as my Saviour dies.

Yet, the searing mystery of this day is that the very sin I have committed can be forgiven because of what my Saviour suffered. Through his

Incarnation, Passion and death, Jesus created the possibility of forgiveness for sin. His blood is the reservoir from which Grace flows.

As he hangs there, on the Cross, he articulates the meaning of what he is doing through forgiving. He is ostensibly forgiving those who are throwing dice for his clothes but his forgiveness surely encompasses all of those who have been a part of this terrible human betrayal from Judas up until this moment of impending death; but that forgiveness spreads out in time and space from the Cross to the whole world from the beginning to the end of time.

The forgiveness which we hear granted through the waves of pain is not the cramped forgiveness we bring ourselves to utter through clenched teeth. This is not the cold forgiveness of duty, the fruit of severe moral schooling; this is the generous forgiveness of the one who has lived without sin. Jesus even goes as far as to excuse his persecutors and us: "They know not what they do," he says. True, those on the spot did not know what they were doing. They thought they were dealing with yet another zealot, another awkward customer in the tortured history of military occupation. Jesus had said he was the Messiah, the Christ, the Son of God but he was not the first and no doubt he would not be the last. These were difficult times for the Jewish authorities. So to that extent Jesus was correct when he said that these people did not really know what they were doing, but can we plead the same ignorance when we sin? Do we know what we are doing?

Often at the end of the day I begin to examine my behaviour, to see where I might have done better; but so often there is an excuse, an extenuating circumstance, some mitigation. So often the decisions about loving and not loving feel as if they are at one remove; the sense of loving and not loving is not flexed, not tried.

So often the admission of sin does not hurt, it becomes an item on a salvific balance sheet. And why? Because we have come to know, deep in our psyche, that the reservoir of the blood of our Saviour is the source of unending Grace. We forget the price that was paid; and we forget the part that we played; and that we play. We have absented ourselves from the drama; we are watching our Saviour hanging on the Cross as if it were a television programme; but it is not. We are there: we have pressed in the thorns, we have mocked our King, we have driven in the nails; and now we are watching, at a distance. And in those dreadful moments before death, we are forgiven.

Not for us the remission that we do not know what we are doing. I know. We know what we are doing but that does not mean we are allowed to assume that other people know what they are doing. If we are to be worthy of our Saviour we must forgive in the absolute conviction that we are not entitled to judge those who trespass against us. We must accept that they are innocent, that we must leave them in the hands of our Saviour as the intercessor between the created and the Creator. Forgiveness is not a statement of accounts where we magnanimously wipe the slate clean. In the truest sense it is not for us to forgive or withhold forgiveness except in the sense that we try to treat all of God's creatures as our Saviour said we should treat them. We forgive in the sense that we have nothing to forgive.

Forgiveness belongs to God alone, made lively in the death of our Saviour, and because forgiveness lies solely with God we will never be able to measure it. We tamper with God's prerogative at our peril. We may well have attained the knowledge of good and evil in an external, human sense; but we cannot measure forgiveness, we cannot match it with a deed.

We are not worthy to forgive. We are not worthy.

**Prayer**

Lord Jesus, as you hang upon the Cross full of forgiveness for the thief and for all who have persecuted you, forgive us our part in your suffering and death; may we struggle towards the Cross passing from cold judgment to warm forgiveness of all those who have injured us so much less than we have injured you so that we may be worthy of the fruits of your sacrifice. Amen.

# iv. Hope

*Truly, I say to you, today you will be with me in paradise*
**Luke 23:43**

How could we dare to hope without forgiveness? What would it mean to think of shaping our whole existence as a journey towards God or, at least, a struggle not to be pulled any further away, if we thought that this was simply our personal struggle? Surely it would mean nothing very spiritual. It would mean an endless calculation of how we were doing: up yesterday, down today. We would be myriad replicas of Sisyphus, forever pushing our boulders uphill to nowhere, only to be rebuffed. We would be like ants in a colony, faithfully working away; for nothing.

Hope is our apprehension on earth of the heavenly light, made possible by the energy of forgiveness. Hope is the only means we have of seeing our way around this muddled earth with all its dark corners. Without hope we live in a state of endless terror, of the fear of what is round corners, behind walls, out of our eye line. To be without hope is like playing a lifelong computer game, assaulted by demons.

Hope is our human entitlement as children of God but for so long, living in the shadow of Adam, we lost hope. It is being restored now, as we stand by the Cross.

I am a thief: I have stolen ideas, I have stolen a reputation, I have stolen office supplies. Perhaps my punishment is harsh; but I bring myself to admit that I have stolen. I beg forgiveness and my Saviour says to me that I am forgiven and that in dying I may be illumined by the light of hope shining from a distant place, light that is created by the wonderful, mysterious encounter between the Creator and the created, by the insubstantiation of those who have been saved into the being of the Creator.

Yet there are those who walk in our Saviour's Church of Hope with a list in their hands of tariffs for light; if we pay them so much in torment and treasure, if we perform a modern day variation on the Medieval theme of indulgences, we will be assured all the light we need here on earth which will draw us safely into the light of our Creator.

But human pride obscures light so that we have to move our position, to evade the obstacle, to be in a permanent state of flex and flux to keep an open channel between ourselves and the light. It is ironic that those who claim to be the most faithful inheritors of Luther should be the most ardent sellers of contemporary indulgences, armed with the price list for heaven.

There is a paradox in our approach to hope which we need to grasp. On the one hand, hope is less clear cut than the transaction model just mentioned; we simply do not know the price of our entry into the light of our Creator; but, secondly, the terms we are being offered are much more generous than any tariff that humanity will ever devise. It is in the nature of humanity that it forms power relations, and the Church of our Saviour is no exception. The tariff model is based on a power structure where some people put themselves in charge, make the list and then tell us how we should pay; but God has no need of power relations because we are not in the same category as God. So, just as there are no meaningful power relations between a human being and a grain of sand, there are no power relations between God and humanity.

Once we see that hope is not related to power we need not be frightened of the earth. Instead of seeing our lives through the occluding glasses of earthly vanity, so that we are always frightened of other people, we can live in the innocence of heavenly light. Earthly fear, of losing out to the competition, of not being able to keep up appearances, of being less physically strong or beautiful than our peers, of being made a fool of, all this fear is undergone because we have misunderstood the purpose of being here. We are not here to compete, we are here to strive, individually and collectively, to reach the heavenly light.

Even in the gloom of Good Friday, as we stand at the foot of the Cross, as we see the thief turn to Jesus and admit his sin and beg for forgiveness, even now, the scene is still lit by that distant heavenly light because at the moment of his own greatest agony Jesus turns his mind and that of the thief towards heaven. If we are just a little cynical we can see why the thief might have been so anxious; after all, he was near to death and had nothing to lose; so he asked for forgiveness and was shown the hope of the heavenly kingdom? Is that the sort of game we play? Do we regard being here now, standing at the foot of the Cross, as filing our insurance policy with the almighty? Is it a coincidence that the older we are the more likely we are to be in church? Does religious conviction uncannily mirror concern for a comfortable transition from earthly gloom to heavenly light? Is it simply a prudential punt? I fear we are all a little too apt to file our insurance but claim higher motives.

I have to wonder why my prayers were perfunctory in my 20s, brisk in my 30s, solid in my 40s and now substantial in my 50s. Have I really grown in the knowledge and love of our Saviour or am I conscious of time passing?

Our eyes may grow dim as we ponder the approaching end of earthly life, but the heavenly light never dims. Here on earth we only see it faintly, in the same way that we see the sun in the light of the moon; but it is still the true light that we see, the true light in a moon that has emerged from the eclipse of Adam's sin. We may not know the substance, the true meaning, of our insubstantiation into the life of God, but, through our doubt, we may glimpse its reality. The imprecision of hope does not arise because of the "whether" but only the "how".

God knows our weakness, knows if we are filing an insurance policy while pretending to act in love. God knows the games we play with ourselves and with God. There are no places into which the heavenly light does not penetrate; no walls too thick, no scheme too dense, no sin too great. Our sin is not thinking that we are worthy of heaven, our sin is thinking that God's mercy is as shallow and narrow as our own.

"This day," says our Saviour to the thief, "You will be with me in Paradise." But if we take our worldly glasses off and see the world as God created it, we will see that we are already in paradise; a paradise which sin has defaced but which our Saviour will make radiant.

Look steadily, straight at the Cross; behind it, past the gloom, there is a glimmer of the heavenly dawn.

## Prayer

Lord Jesus, as you hang upon the Cross promising paradise to the repentant thief, forgive us for abandoning heavenly hope and cowering in earthly fear; may we struggle towards the Cross, creeping from the darkness of our own devices towards its shadow from where we shall see the light of the heavenly dawn. Amen.

## v. Dependence

*I thirst*

***John 19:28***

Dependence is a word which we all hate. We think of people who cannot feed themselves, of children that cannot walk, of disabled people who cannot hear or see, of scroungers and misfits, of the poor and the poorly, of the bruised and battered, of the helpless and the hopeless. Our images of dependence are a warning to our sense of integrity; but for the Grace of God, we say, go I.

It is such a strange idea that it is the Grace of God that keeps us independent. Many people think it is the other way round, that the Grace of God is what we depend upon; but perhaps that is too technical a debate for this sad and solemn time when we ought to concentrate more closely on the human condition as it relates to our dying Saviour instead of worrying about theological metaphors.

Hanging on the Cross, dying, Jesus is sick, disabled, poor, bruised, battered, despised, outcast; and he is thirsty; and he cannot get himself a drink but has to ask for help. And when the drink comes it is horrible and he cannot take it.

Millions of times every day this happens to people all over the world: to people in wheelchairs who wait to be loaded into vans; to starving peasants who watch helplessly as their crops are washed away; to refugees in camps; to people not five miles from here trapped in the welfare state. All over the world there are millions, hundreds of millions, of people, consciously or unconsciously, living their lives, day after day, in the imitation of our dying Saviour. Instead of respecting them, of seeing their union with Jesus, of seeing him in them and them in him, we want to separate ourselves, to be proud of our independence. We worship choice: free to drive wherever we like in our cars; free to choose from 50 different flavours of ice cream; free to choose from hundreds of varieties of wine, beer and whiskey; free to fly the world. This, as we now know, has disastrous ecological consequences but what should concern us today, as we stand at the foot of the Cross, is the damage it does to our understanding of who we are. The essence of our existence is the simple, though not easy, choice of loving or not loving God; the other choices by which we set so much store are incidental.

Yet there are some Christians who walk in our Saviour's Church of Dependence with a list in their hands of the marks of Godly approbation, who say that prosperity, the freedom to choose earthly things, is a sign of our Saviour's love, inferring that the poor are less loved. There are lists of skills which indicate divine favour; there are physical characteristics, there are mental characteristics, all humanly defined, which are supposed to illustrate closeness to God.

We have already thought about the false distinction between virtue and vice based on external appearance; and we also have to get away from drawing any spiritual conclusions from lifestyle options and choices, flexing our analysis to see that matters are not so simple. But, having said that, we should remember that Jesus came to earth as a baby of poor parents in an occupied land; and through all of his mission he kept warning how dangerous this world was for the rich and how its rewards would make it more difficult for them to go to heaven; and he kept saying how heaven was prepared for the sinners, for the poor and the weak. Nonetheless, the symmetry between earthly fortune and heavenly prospects is fixed so firmly in our minds that we cannot shake it off.

If we only stop to pray, we know that earthly dependence is an illusion, a poor shadow of the dependence on our Saviour. In the terrible twentieth century we learned to understand the idea of the suffering Saviour who kept company with the imprisoned, the tortured and the condemned. We came to understand that the Passion and death which he suffered fitted him uniquely for the mission of consolation. It does not matter how often and how vehemently Jesus is claimed by the rich and the powerful, he will not be bought. It is incredible to think that he who has everything can be bought when his mission is to give, to enrich the poor; not only the economically poor but the poor that we are.

Jesus can give nothing to us if we do not learn to take. If we are not prepared to be dependent upon Divine love expressed through human loving, how are we to live lives of Christian discipleship? To be a witness of Christ is to give in love but it is also to take in love. We are very adept with our accountancy model. We can add up all the good we have done, all the things we have given, all the virtue we have shown; and then, on the other side of the ledger, we can add up all the self-denial, all the gifts refused, all the pleasures foregone.

I say when I insist on giving and will not take, when I glow with the superiority of my generosity, when I think my neighbour too mean to give me anything, I am not being virtuous, I am being proud; I am not learning to live like my Saviour.

Some people, aware of the dangers of power and the need to cultivate dependency, took up the monastic life; but most of us never will; and so we have to try to live out our lives of dependency in a fiercely competitive world. This is terribly difficult. Perhaps the temptation we should fear most is that of power. We may think that we only have power in relatively small things but the routine exercise of power and choice are so seductive, particularly if we think we are exercising power and choice in the name of the good.

By the time we are so helpless that we cannot function without others, when we rage against the dying of the light, when our active minds are frustrated by our feeble bodies, it is too late. The rage only shows how badly we have lived our Christian lives. Instead of disciplining ourselves in humility, in subjection, in gratitude, we are trained in assertiveness, in choice, in the exercise of power. When our Saviour came to earth he emptied himself of all his divine power and became like us; lived less well than us, spent his whole mission on the road dependent on others for food and drink; and then, at the end he needed a drink as we, close to death, might need a drink and be too weak or confined to stretch out and grasp it for ourselves. But the purpose of coming to grips with future incapacity is not so that we will be prepared in a functional way; we are to learn dependence because that is our true state. Any power we have comes from God and so it is agency not power; any power we have is illusory.

Jesus is thirsty. We may give him something to drink; but only if we will also take the drink he offers in the shape of our neighbour.

Take and drink; the taste is bitter. Say nothing.

**Prayer**

Lord Jesus, as you hang upon the Cross dependent on the few friends who remain to give you a cup of bitterness to drink, we are sorry that we have so often fled and only returned to you with a bitter cup. May we struggle towards the Cross exchanging assurance for dependence on your Grace which is the only true freedom. Amen.

## vi. Love

*He said to his mother: "Woman, behold your son" then*
*he said to the Disciple: "Behold your mother".*

**John 26:27**

There is no word more abused than "love"; it is the human talent for corrupting the divine that can take its most sacred word and turn it into selfishness. I love chocolate means I want chocolate; I love a girl means I lust after her; I love you means I want something you have; I am doing this out of love means that you must be more like me.

We have got it completely wrong. If ever a word has been turned upside down and inside out, if ever a glass has been fractured, if ever a picture has been blurred, if ever a candle has been blown out, it is love.

Love is not something that we do to other people, love is making space where people can do what they want without precondition. It is that simple; and that difficult. How else could we understand it?

I am born to choose to love or not to love; I perform a variety of acts of preference and denial; I form friendships and break them; I marry and divorce and marry again; I try to love my children but sometimes I am speechless and indifferent; sometimes I cannot express how deeply I feel and sometimes I too readily say how deeply I feel when it would be better to say nothing; and yet, through all of this thicket of small torments and triumphs, Jesus loves me.

Do I think Jesus loves me for what I have done or not done? How can my actions and words, my restraint and silence, be worthy of the love of my Saviour? How can I think that there is some correspondence between what I do and how Jesus relates to me?

Of course there is no correspondence. There is no way of describing the relationship between the love of Jesus and the way I behave; they are not relational in any way we understand; and for that reason, for that state of being, I live in a judgment-free space, a space of love, which God has created for me and in which I live and move and have my being. Jesus meets me in this space which God has made; he meets me on earthly ground which God has made, he meets me by a lake and in the city, he meets me on a mountain and in a market town; he meets me wherever I am but he never pushes or pulls, he never makes a face or drops a hint; he never passes a comment on what I have done or on what I intend to do. He inhabits my space when I let him and sometimes when I do not, thanks to the zeal of the Holy Spirit. But he lets me know that it is my space. I am not living in his space; for God lives in God's own kind of space quite separate from mine.

Here he is now, living in earthly space, ready to die so that we may continue to live in space created by his love; here he is commending his mother to a friend and the friend to his mother. He has no other instructions; he does not lecture them on what love might mean; he seems not to be interested in obedience.

Yet there are Christians walking in our Saviour's Church of Love with a list in their hands of the components of love, who think that love is a form of obedience. They carry lists of what love requires, of actions, words and attitudes which will indicate whether we are loving or not loving. They have rules for who can love who and who cannot, they have rules for what is good love and not good love; they have honed love down to a set of proofs that Euclid would recognise; there are propositions, working out and proof statements; there is a whole subculture of love theorems which have been devised to circumscribe, to keep people in confined spaces, to ensure that love does not get out of control. In an act of supreme arrogance, divine love is modelled in human love, divine enterprise is modelled in human enterprise; but, worst of all, divine space is cramped into human ecologies. There are supreme moments in our lives when we know how to love outside the walls but we grow frightened; we do not flex, we wither.

Jesus is a terrible disappointment to the Pharisees and to contemporary Christian leaders. He sits with sinners and enjoys a meal and he says nothing about their bad behaviour. He disrupts a perfectly proper trial of a prostitute and sends the prosecution packing. He forgives sins without ever wanting to know what the sins were. He spends a lot of his time telling the law makers that their laws are not divine at all but a human invention. He seems to like the outcast Samaritans, he has a soft spot for the Prodigal Son, he empathises with the Publican at the back who thinks himself not worthy to pray, he tells Peter that he will deny him but seems to think that recognition of the denial by Peter will be punishment enough; he even seems to have no complaint against Pilate.

Looked at objectively, Jesus is a discredit to contemporary Christianity; he refuses to judge, all he wants to do is to love.

We, as we watch the final minutes of his life, as we see Mary and John bravely approaching the foot of the Cross, where do we stand in the argument between love and judgment? Are we prepared to take the risk of love, of creating space where others might do things we would prefer them not to do, or are we content to be Pharisees, defining everything that must happen and must not happen in earthly space? Are we prepared to take the risk of love and then ask our Saviour for the strength, when we have taken that first step, not to judge when we feel that the space we have created has been violated, that we have been let down.

What we so often mean when we think this way is that our love has not been returned; that we are, in love terms, in debit. But if we think that love is a matter of debit and credit we have misunderstood. Love is a valve, it is one way, it is not a boomerang, it goes and it goes and it goes; for its own sake. That is why parents who expect their children to return love are fatally deluded. It goes and it goes and it goes. But of course the more of it you give away the more of it you have; the more space you make the more capacity you have for making space.

No wonder people worry about love and the space it creates; love is the greatest risk of all; but that risk is under-written by the King of Love who hangs before us now.

Jesus, surveying the desolation of Calvary, with his dying breaths is still God's child of love, still making space for others to love.

The mystery of love is that the closer we come to our Saviour, the more space we have.

**Prayer**

Lord Jesus, as you hang upon the Cross with no thought but love for those who are faithful, forgive us for a love that pinches and encircles; may we struggle towards the Cross, freed from the desire to control to live in your openness, learning to make space for all our sisters and brothers as the vessels of your love. Amen.

# vii. Responsibility

*It is finished*

**John 19:30**

From the beginning of time, when we were given the freedom to love and not to love, this death was inevitable, bearing within itself divine and human responsibility. From the sin of Adam to the proclamation of John the Baptist via the dramatic history of the Chosen People, it has come to this. The sacrifice by the faithful Abraham of his son, averted by God's intervention, confronts the grandeur of David and Solomon. All the fear and hope of the prophets has come to this. The whole activity of the whole world from beginning to end, all the good and bad choices, all the false starts, all the unfinished enterprises, all the glass that has been smeared and broken, have come to this, to this single, solitary point of flesh on a cross in occupied Palestine. All the music that has lifted us above ourselves, all the prayers, all the hands joined in supplication and raised in triumph, all the inspiration that has lifted us out of baseness into animation, all of the striving for heavenly light generated by God's Grace, flows from this point, from the reservoir of our Saviour's blood.

Last year I was walking quietly up a flight of steps. I passed through a narrow doorway and Father John said: "We are here." I crawled on my knees the few feet to the place where the Cross stood, and thought: "It all comes down to this. To this tiny, physical space; everything comes down to this."

"It is finished." At the simplest level, the life of Jesus is finished. The life of a man who walked the land of Palestine for three years, preaching a Gospel of Love, is finished. The enterprise of fellowship which he built has almost disintegrated. The man who was the friend of everyone, even—particularly—sinners, has been abandoned. Jesus knows this. His statement, at the simplest level, is obvious.

"It is finished." At a deeper level the history of the Chosen People from Adam to Jesus is finished. There is no genealogy past the Cross. The line of faithfulness and faltering has ended at this gruesome place. There is a final act to come but Jesus does not know this. The most he could know was that he had acted in obedience to his father for the forgiveness of sins and that Adam's debt, in some mysterious way, had been paid.

"It is finished", at its deepest level, encompasses the ultimate act of forgiveness. The purpose of the Incarnation has been worked out in the Crucifixion. At the deepest level, everything human and divine is concentrated in this battered human frame.

At the root of our thought, of our ability to grasp what is going on, there is a paradox of failure and success, of tragedy and triumph which we try to deal with through our earthly expressiveness. There is nothing more haunting than a cross made of gold, nothing more poignant than blood celebrated in rubies. There is so much that we want to say and we have so few means to say what we want. The love of gold and rubies which killed our Saviour celebrates his death.

Why is this important, now, at this minute? Because if we only do this now, once in a year, we have to flex ourselves out of thinking of this moment as the end of a story and flex ourselves into the story. This story is not about the relationship between our Saviour and us, it is the story of our Saviour and us. We are a part of the story as murderers and, mysteriously, we are part of the story as captives freed. If only once a year, now, we need to bring ourselves to feel ourselves as both of these things and then to fuse them into one wholeness in our hearts. We are not simply to think of murder and not simply to think of freedom, we are to think of the freedom granted to murderers, to us.

Our means are slight; and often when we try to think, our minds are crowded with two thousand years of culture, of music and painting, of meditations and narratives, of proverbs and prayers. All the images take us away from enactment; we think we are watching when we are doing. We need to understand our freedom and responsibility and where they have led, to this single point in space and time.

Let us stop for a few moments and focus on the fused idea of ourselves as murderers freed.

One of the reasons why this is so difficult for us is that we cannot hide from ourselves what was hidden from the dying Jesus. Stretching for the future, before he has been placed in the tomb, we see him in the middle distance, rising.

But that is our strength and our weakness; we are not satisfied with the present.

Yet to survive the perils of earthly life, to bloom now and again, to reach that heavenly light, we should live in the shadow of the Cross. For the more bitter the soil with blood, the more rich and frequent the bloom; the deeper the shadow, the brighter the light. For our soul's sake, for our survival's sake, we need to look as deeply into ourselves as we can to recognise the divine conditions which have made us human and the human condition which makes us divine. The hinge of this human/divine symmetry is the Cross on which hangs the dead Jesus who took human flesh and put aside his Godhead so that we might know not just intellectually and theologically, that we have been saved; but to know it in our hearts, in our blood, in our pain.

Let the noise of the crowd fade. Let the turmoil of the past week settle. Let the terrible torment come to an end. There is nothing more to be done now. There are many things we could have done better; but there is nothing to be done now. It is time to stand still. If we know how to—and it is never easy—it is time to pray.

The minutes go by and, as the final drops of blood fall to the ground, as the lance pierces his side to produce a tiny drop of blood and a weeping of water, it is easy to be melodramatic; but the drama is too great for that. This is no time for sentimentality, it is the time for seeing death and salvation with the clear eyes of responsibility and freedom. The whole world, from the beginning to the end of time, is narrowed down to this single point; and so must our lives be. We were born to stand at the Cross, to choose to stand at the Cross because sometimes we make wrong choices. We stand for ourselves and, as part of the mystery of the Body of Christ, we stand on behalf of the world's wrong choices. We are privileged to suffer; we bear the Christian responsibility of being here on behalf of all those who are not here. For just a fraction of time we have to bear the weight of this sorry death.

For now, for just a moment, there is nowhere else to go. For just a moment as we stand with Mary, Jesus is our dead child.

**Prayer**

Lord Jesus, as you hang upon the Cross at the end of your incarnational mission, we are sorry that we have lived irresponsibly as if you were not among us; may we remain at the foot of the Cross so that we, nourished by your blood as the reservoir from which all Grace flows, be true disciples worthy to join you in your heavenly home. Amen.

# Epilogue

When I was writing a Crucifixion scene for 2007, I kept thinking of an image, no doubt a composite of vaguely remembered paintings and churchware, of a Crucifix with a Jesus in glittering gold set in the rubies of his blood. Apart from the incongruity of the materials, given his incarnational mission to the poor, what struck me was how this image represented the radical transformation from realism to a form of decorousness, almost decoratedness.

For my writing, of course, I had to concentrate on the language rather than the image but they share this reluctance to come to terms with reality.

Ever since I have been able to understand churchy language I have thought of Jesus not beaten so that the skin was roughly torn from his back but scourged. I have thought of Jesus not being cruelly assaulted with a thicket of wicked thorns but crowned. I have thought of Jesus not pulverised with coarse bolts but nailed by his hands and feet; and, oh, that final mercy of not having his legs broken, nor being stabbed in the side with a blunt dagger or sword, but being pierced with a lance. This last, at least, foretold so beautifully in the words of Jeremiah and Simeon, as if the narrative continuity, the inevitability of the cruel events, somehow made them better, as if the nobility of Jesus and the drama of his death somehow raises it above the physical pain that the Cross involved.

When I came to buy my own cross so that it would always be close to my heart, I chose a simple design with no figure. I was not sure then why I did not want a graven image of Jesus; but I know now. It is more than fifty years since I began to live with the story of Christ Crucified, lived in churches and museums, in picture books and Bibles, in spectacular movies and Passion plays, in Stations of the Cross and Seven Last Words, in painting and sculpture, in Bach and most recently in the rock re-telling in Manchester last Good Friday, annually focused on Holy Week but never far away. It was only when I went to Calvary last year that I realised how the reality had slowly lost its real life. The conclusion I drew for myself, not for anybody else, is that this murder in which I am complicit will die as a reality in me unless I can escape from all the reverential baggage and re-tell the story to myself so that the account makes me wince.

So when I started to think about the death of Jesus as it might take place this Good Friday, I thought about torture, about broken glass, glowing cigarette ends and sulphuric acid; and I began to think about humiliation, crouching figures dressed in orange jump suits, isolation cells and sleepless nights, extra-rendition; and all the means of humiliation and torture we have developed as the physical manifestations of our complicity in the murder of all murders.

But, other than recognising and being sorry for our complicity, there isn't much point in bringing ourselves to a pitch of private, unbearable pain unless we are simultaneously, in the great mystery of the world's existence, on the watch for the new dawn of the Resurrection.

There is a liturgical convention, perhaps to keep us aware of our sinfulness, perhaps to pile on the agony, perhaps simply as an acknowledgment of the way our culture worked before the breach of the dramatic unities, that we don't mention the Resurrection on Good Friday; but I can't help it. For me there is always a faint glimmer of the new dawn on the distant horizon behind the Cross, making its outline yet more sharp and black.

And, like the cultural accretion that surrounds the Crucifixion, the Resurrection imagery and language almost totally lack immediacy. Only John's half line about Mary Magdalene mistaking Jesus for the gardener (a phrase frequently omitted from the Easter Day reading) and the Emmaus episode in Luke have any dynamism. It is as if the real link is between the Crucifixion and Pentecost when the Holy Spirit gets cracking. As for the images, I can't take seriously—and therefore cannot rejoice through—the fussily androgynous angels, the dazzling napery, the European pastoral verdure and the general air of Olympian frolics and Holman Huntism.

As for the significance of the event, we can surely understand the somewhat flat-footed reactions of the disciples and the women—I doubt we would do any better—but in our language today, with almost two thousand years to think about it, Jesus has not torn a massive post-incarnational hole in the fabric of human time, he has risen; Jesus has not smashed the forces of evil and made an irreversible promise of salvation to all humanity, he has achieved a victory o'er the grave; Jesus has not lived the greatest transformational event in world history, he has risen indeed. Alleluia.

As a quid pro quo for acknowledging on Good Friday the glimmer of light behind the Cross to sharpen its impact, I would burn palm crosses in the fire of the Easter Vigil, the palms of fickleness which ultimately form the foundation of our penitential act on Ash Wednesday. After the Light of Christ is brought into church and the Exultet has been sung, we slowly climb towards our greatest joy, beginning with the creation and tracing the history of our salvation; O how easily we have forgotten the Cross as if we have had too much of it in Holy Week. Perhaps seen from the radically different liturgical angle of the Vigil, the Cross might regain its true meaning.

We renew our Baptismal vows with St Paul reminding us that in the Cross we have all died and in Baptism we are all brought into a new life. But as long as we are so full of the reverential baggage of history, art, literature and ceremony, it won't be much of a new life, just another personal metaphor dressed in corporate liturgy. For surely the point of the Easter Vigil is to remind us all of our life and death story in terms that will make us, like Jesus, suffer and die—and live again. Alleluia!

# 4. Men of the World

*2008*

## i. "What Is Truth?"

I am the documentary man. I am making a fly-on-the-wall documentary about Roman justice, watching Pilate manoeuvring his way through the minefield of Jewish religious politics, land rites, taxation and military infractions. The crew is somewhat irritable because as we were packing up for the festival, an emergency case came up. There's this B list celebrity called Jesus who has made a bit of a splash in town this week and got the authorities rather annoyed. They want Pilate to sanction his execution. Pilate is worried; you can see it as he keeps going out to talk to the leaders and coming in again; it isn't that he's reluctant to execute people, far from it, it's just that there isn't really a charge and that makes it difficult. There is a suggestion—and it's really no more than that—that this Jesus wants to overthrow the Government; which is a bit odd because earlier in the week when the Pharisees tried to tempt him to insult the Emperor he publicly supported imperial taxation which, for a Jew, is quite something. Pilate is talking to Jesus in an unusually quiet and intense way about his aspirations; he says he's some sort of king but nothing to do with the world; a kind of superpriest, I suppose you could say, except that he doesn't seem very keen on priests.

While Pilate goes out yet again, picked up by the external cameras, we mull over the angles: Jesus is a mental case worth a flogging which Pilate can reasonably administer without causing any problems; or he is a vague threat, in which case he can be put into prison until after the Passover break; or he's a real danger and Pilate knows something we don't know, probably picked up from that snitch, Herod's intelligence service. On the other hand, it could simply be that Pilate wants to do the Jewish leaders a favour, though we can't figure out why; or he's frightened, as he often is (in fact he's at his cruellest when he's most uncertain). It's that last option that seems most likely as he shuttles to and fro between Jesus and the people outside; he doesn't want to kill Jesus because there's no charge; but he's frightened.

Although we are aware of the huge noise outside, it is really quiet in here as Jesus talks to Pilate. He is strangely calm, even serene, in spite of his bruised and bloody face; he is relaxed in his beaten up body. It is not the incongruity but the apparent normality that makes it such good footage; ordinary people doing ordinary things never become boring; it's the forced incongruities of drama, the clever cuts, the obsession with the extreme, that become boring. Pornography and violence are the hallmarks of second rate film makers. This man is, well, ordinary but different. You can't take the camera off his face. It's a trick that you see pulled off but not so well as this by successful political leaders; he's looking at everyone intensely but you feel that he's actually only looking at you.

Jesus says he has come into the world to tell people what is true; and then Pilate, right out of the blue, asks: "What is truth?"

It's not the sort of question that Pilate usually asks; he usually wants to find out what the truth is of a given situation; Romans aren't very good at abstraction; and, I have to admit that all too often it's not the sort of question that documentary makers ask either. What is truth? It's a question that gets blown away by the hysteria, the pressure of deadlines and Pilate's mounting fear. Truth is what usually ends up on the cutting room floor. But this time, when we come to edit the film, it's there; it's the most compelling piece of footage; and we don't know what to do with it. The only thing we can do, given that Jesus does not answer, is to go back and look at his life and his teaching to see if that gives any clue to the answer he would have given. It's a bit hackneyed but a flashback might be effective at this point.

What are we to do with Pilate's question, as we stand outside, at the end of the interview, trying to sort out what it means? We have ready access to all the teaching and miracles, the kindnesses and the warnings, so how will we proceed? Well, the art of the film maker is to create an elegant, coherent piece of narrative architecture out of a welter of material. You know how it goes. A scene is set up and if it does not quite work, you order another "take" until that piece is just how you want it. This is difficult because everything has to come together: the words delivered properly, the right facial expressions, elegant picture composition and a sense of continuity, or disruption, with the preceding and succeeding shots. You can see how all this piecing together can make abstract truth a bit, well, abstract. And when you have got all the pieces you want and put them into some kind of order, throwing huge amounts of material away, you decide that the architecture you had thought of isn't quite right; so you throw some of the carefully edited material onto the floor and you go away and re-write bits of the script and then do some more filming until your stamina or your money runs out. Everything has to be in its neat and tidy place; it is the most contrived form of art.

Handling this flashback is so easy because there is very little choice. There are pictures of Jesus opening his arms to everyone, healing people, making people smile, handing out bread and fish. There's a fair amount of homespun truth about being good to your neighbour and, because he's a Jew, a lot about loving God. We've cut the tricky stuff about Jesus and God as his Father as the audience would find that obscurantist; but the lakeside flashback is simple enough in its impact. But it doesn't answer Pilate's question. In the end, if you go along with Jesus, it's what you do that answers the question, not what you say.

As we review the Good Friday shots, it becomes more difficult to work out what to do. Our usual technique of taking and re-taking, of editing and re-editing, is being called into question. We increasingly feel the need just to run the whole thing. We began, as usual, by wanting to present our version of Jesus but that is becoming more difficult. Of course, the difference in Jesus movies is quite natural, it's an inevitable result of our natural inability to handle perfection. Look at Jesus the Movie showing at your nearest church and you will see that each editor has a different take.

- There is Jesus the castigator who spends all his time complaining about Jewish society and the bad behaviour of the rich and poor alike, of the priests and the peasants.

- Then there is Jesus the empathiser who just lets it all happen, man, who doesn't really mind what people do as long as their heart is in the right place. They just have to feel it, like, in their soul and everything will be all right.

- Then there is Jesus the revolutionary, who came to turn the political world upside down and was murdered by the authorities for being too radical, the man who overturned international capitalism in the Temple court.

- There is Jesus the choreographer, who loves liturgy. He likes the right number of candles and the right number of backward steps and genuflections and he thinks that this choreography should be entirely male.

- And then there is Jesus the comfortable, who spends all his time cuddling children, feeding animals and generally keeping everything neat and tidy; everything and everybody in their place, the Jesus of Suburbia, or, rather, middle-class Suburbia.

Now it seems to me as a film maker that there are two things we can do here. The first, the old-fashioned, high art, approach is to take pieces from each of these sets of perceptions and put them together into a multi-faceted Jesus; lots of sharp editing for contrast. The more modern and risky approach is to forget all the characterisation and go back to the original footage and just run it.

While we are weighing up the options, let's take a look at the material for editing. The Jesus of Suburbia is being squeezed out by two much more powerful versions, Jesus the castigator and Jesus the Choreographer; there is hardly any room for a gentle word or a smile of encouragement. How strange and sad it is that we have resorted to the art of film, resorted to making and re-making. No wonder Pilate isn't sure what truth is. He can't properly get a fix on it. He is so worried by administrative matters that he finds it difficult to sleep and he watches a lot of late night movies and recently they have all been different cuts of Jesus the Movie. He is becoming ever more confused.

Unlike Pilate, we don't watch all these movies; we have made our own and we are very pleased with it. The Jesus of Suburbia has become an old friend; and, like all old friends, he changes over the years but never beyond recognition. The Jesus who was sympathetic to rebels steadily becomes the Jesus of the solid state and comforter of the elderly. The Jesus of frugality effortlessly morphs into the Jesus of modest comfort. Now and again as the world shakes and shudders, we bring in a new scene of Jesus the Third World prophet and Jesus the protector of the great whale, but the overall shape transforms itself slowly with our lives in such an artless metamorphosis that we do not notice.

We all suffer from this self-centred view of Jesus. This might be rather a harsh judgment on ourselves but we have to ask whether we still retain the wonder, the sense of drama, in our relationship with him, whether it informs our days and comforts us at night; whether it infuses our kindness and our passions. Conversely, we have to ask whether Jesus has simply become a rather dull, academic documentary, whether he has been taken captive by the militia who bombard each other with Creeds and Confessions, Articles and Covenants. We have to ask ourselves whether, using our own version of Jesus, we could answer Pilate's question.

As an experienced maker of documentaries, I know you have your own particular problems making honest films, so here is the secret. I will tell you what happened when we were trying to edit our fly-on-the wall documentary of the Roman Justice system. We fiddled around with all the footage except what we had taken of Jesus; somehow you couldn't cut it, you just had to let it run. It was natural and graceful, it was eloquent and economical, it never over-stated or under-stated; you had to take each word, each sentence, each gesture, each scene, for what it was. I know that there might be differences of interpretation but these are not very great if you look carefully at the face, if you listen carefully to the words, if you bring yourself to remember what he did and what he taught. It's difficult if you're an artist but the trick is to try to take yourself out of the equation. It isn't a movie about my view of Jesus, it's a movie about Jesus. As he would have put it, God isn't a concept invented by humanity, humanity is a reality created by God.

This is not the day for re-making but for knowing that there is only one way. Watch with me now, watch Jesus the Movie; uncut.

**Prayer**

Heavenly Father, who sent your Son to live among us so that we might better learn the truth of your goodness; as he stands humiliated before us, help us, through Jesus, to recognise the magnificent truth of your goodness and our shortcomings in being worthy of it. Amen.

## ii. "Behold the Man"

I am the practical man. I am a trader in spices, caught up in the drama. After the sleepy backwater of my home town there is always something dramatic going on in Jerusalem, and I have to admit that this is more dramatic than anything I have seen on other visits.

There was, for example, a moment of supreme drama just a few seconds ago, more complete in its way than any other scene so far in the sorry story of the trial of Jesus, when Pilate produced Jesus. We see him now, being paraded before us, looking like a failed gladiator who has lost a fight but somehow hasn't died or killed himself; and although he retains the trappings of power, Pilate might be a beaten gladiator himself, offering Jesus to us as if we can do anything about it. He says: "Behold, the man!" and for the very first time I begin to wonder whether that is all there is to it; it is the very use of the word "man" that somehow does not work for me, does not encapsulate the whole of what I can see in the face of Jesus as I stand, slightly behind the rest of the crowd, trying to summon up the courage simply to watch, to detach myself from the hysteria. This is hardly heroic but at the moment it is the best I can do. You have to start somewhere, and detaching yourself from the mob, driven by self-indulgence and fashion, is a good place to begin.

I don't know what I am doing here, anyway, a foreigner, a Gentile, a slave who bought my freedom, a trader in spices.

Let us, then, consider Jesus together; behold the man. Since I came here there has been talk of little else. This man, whose picture I will still see, even though he has been taken away by the soldiers, has performed miracles, he has made fun of the rather mad, old-fashioned laws that the Jews stick to so fanatically; but it's not that. It's the smile behind the pain, the sense that what he is going through, well, was meant to be.

As we stand at the back of the crowd, waiting for Jesus to re-emerge, to be goaded up the hill to Calvary, what do we think about the man? How do we behold him?

In two thousand years of distancing and dispute, some of us have almost forgotten. We can remember the lovely little baby and a teacher in parables, and a risen phenomenon; but the man is more difficult. Perhaps that is why Dan Brown's book, *The Da Vinci Code*, is so successful because it talks about a man who loved a woman and had children. Is it partly because our society is so sexualised that we are not really human unless we are having a sexual relationship? Well, partly, but perhaps it is more a matter of cultural heritage. At the beginning of the unceasing re-appraisal, there were a great many followers of Jesus who tended to be gnostic, who thought that substance, the earth, bodies were basically and irretrievably evil; how they squared that with the God of creation is a difficult question. But the incarnational forces in the church gained the upper hand which explains the rather particular nature of the Nicene Creed. Then, at the Reformation, there was another bout of anti-materialism from which we have never really recovered. We associate being religious with being other-worldly; and some of us associate being truly religious with being celibate.

What we know, but Pilate could not, is that this man whom we behold is the Creator's injection of self into creation. Until then there was the Creator and creatures; with Jesus there is still the Creator and creatures, but one of those creatures is also the Creator. When we behold this man we also behold our God. Yet in recognising this supreme mystery we must not, in awe of God, forget the man.

This man is us; we are this man. Because he bridges the gap between Creator and creature, brings God to earth, we are full of the energy which this has released; Jesus lives in us through the power of what we call the Holy Spirit. These are massive doctrinal ideas but at root we have a man, someone with whom we can identify, who laughed and cried, became bored and irritable, and who ate and drank with all manner of people. His perfection condemned him to an inevitable death. Wherever and whenever a Jesus had been sent to us he would have been killed; that is the underlying, collective guilt from which we cannot escape as long as we are on earth, it is what not being with God means; but none of this makes any sense at all unless we behold the man.

I have travelled far with my spices, I have seen all manner of peoples; but I will never forget this one man. What was he trying to do? From the story I have heard he said that he was specially sent by God to recover the world for God. Some people say that he is the Messiah who is supposed to restore Israel to worldly greatness but that seems to be a minority view; most people who know anything about it know that Israel has never been that great compared, say, with the Assyrians, Persians, Greeks and, of course, the Romans. The Jews set great store by David and Solomon but the extent of their magnificence and territory are greatly exaggerated. A very few people say that he says that he is somehow the Son of God which is difficult for the Jews but not much of a problem for people like me, accustomed as I am to many religious and philosophical ideas. Most people, it seems, just wanted him for what they could get out of him, a spectacular piece of magic, healing powers. They weren't very bothered by the theology; they were only interested in what they saw, heard and heard about. But what was he really trying to do? I think he was trying to bring something back that had been lost. I often think that humanity's greatest fault is to make simple things complicated. Everywhere you look there are people making simple things complicated and it becomes so involved that you then need somebody with a clear vision to get rid of all the tangles so that we can start again. But you have to travel far from the conventional and the safe to see that this simplification is necessary.

We, too, have travelled far to be here. We have come from Baptism to the Cross; from that moment when we died to sin and were re-born in Christ we have been on a journey. Sometimes it seems that the journey is a perpetual climb up this hill towards the place where Jesus is about to die. At other times it is a puzzle that we can't solve, but whenever the journey seems too arduous or the puzzle too difficult, we need to start again with the man because the man is our way to God. For all the complexities of the way in which we try to understand our relationship with the Creator, Jesus himself has taught us always to start with him as he is the great intercessor, through him, through the unique channel of his incarnate self, we can establish a relationship with God.

If we are to do that, we need to use our imagination, to find a way of living alongside the Jesus who healed and taught; and the Jesus who suffers and is about to die. As he stands, bruised and bleeding, scorned and scarred, scandalously dressed and searingly crowned, let us remember what he told us. The man we are looking at was born to bring us the good news of the kingdom; he uniquely articulates a Gospel of love as he came to live the meaning of God as love rather than as power or judgment. As he stands here, resigned to taking up his cross, he does not stop loving. He never stops loving. He never will stop loving. He does not blame us for colluding in his death. He wants us to know that we can kill God and still be folded back into the Creator, to leave the "guilt" of our "collusion" behind.

Pilate is washing his hands. It's all over. They are going to kill this sweet tempered man. As usual, after the drama of the verdict, most people are already losing interest. What is another crucifixion, after all, to people who see too many? They have grown hard; perhaps that is why it is so easy to shout for punishment. Where I come from the people are more relaxed. I think Jesus would have done well in my home country where people are less rule-bound. Our philosophers say that you can relate the way people behave to the kind of climate in which they live and there is something to be said for that; but I think that it takes so long for people to get over fear, to think about things that are more constructive. It seems to me that in any struggle between love and fear, the fear is always stronger, the love more tentative, more at risk, more vulnerable.

That's the idea I have been looking for when I think of him! Vulnerable. He has given himself to his mission, he has laid himself open, he attracts violence in a way that only the virtuous can attract violence.

If he is a god—and there is no reason why he should not be—you still have to start with the man to see the god; there's no other way. To that extent at least, Pilate was right. He didn't say: "Behold the God!" You can't find the god a man is, or represents, unless you study the man. I've watched all kinds of faces; and the face I know best, because of my trade, is the face of the bargainer, the face of the man who shows no emotion when the dice stop rolling, the man who wants you to believe that he has nothing when he has more than you. I can't see any of that in this face. If this is the face of God, then God is a simple fellow after all, constructive and loving; and constructing out of love, the way people make things just for the sheer joy of the figure emerging from the stone.

We who roll the dice and keep our faces straight, we who know how to say one thing and mean something, not precisely opposite but slightly different, we who exercise power without thinking about it, find the idea of vulnerability deeply troubling. Yet, as we watch him now, let us to try to reverence that vulnerability, the kenosis, the sacrifice of control, the setting aside of power. We who see our incarnate Saviour about to die should carry this picture of him as the one above all others which we need in order to live faithful lives.

We have seen the arbitrary power of Pilate and the unbroken love of Jesus demonstrated in his vulnerability. We are to choose. As long as God is abstract, somewhere else, omnipotent but unreachable, there is some excuse for us to choose power and control, to see our lives as purely earthly, for we know none other; but the reality of the Incarnation, God in history, destroys the defence that God is so difficult, distant and complicated that we might as well just get on with our earthly lives.

He had some followers, I know, but they all seem to have run away. I wonder if his movement will last. Vulnerability doesn't seem like a good core value; love sounds better but without vulnerability what is love?

Later, we will need to answer that question of the trader in spices. Without vulnerability, what is love? But for now, behold the man; and then hold him until death.

## Prayer

Heavenly Father, you sent your blessed son to take flesh among us so that we might better learn the indivisibility of the human and divine; as he stands condemned before us, help us to imitate the perfection of the humanity of Jesus and aspire to be enfolded into the perfection of your divinity. Amen.

### iii. "Today You Will Be With Me in Heaven"

Soldiers are the scum of the earth but where would you be without them? You're ready enough to hang medals round the necks of our commanders but treat us little better than slaves, doing society's dirty work. You want quiet streets, to keep the barbarians out, to get criminals despatched; send for the soldiers! As you can see, I am here on your collective behalf, nailing three men to crosses. The first one is an easy enough case; he's a danger to society and isn't sorry for what he's done. The second is a bit of a wimp; he says he is sorry and deserves what he's getting. But the third one, the one in the middle, is a basket case and should have been sent home to his mother. If you put Jewish scruple and Roman ruthlessness together you get harsh decisions but this is one of the worst I've ever seen. But I'm only a soldier, not a judge, sent to align the cross beam, knock in the nails and then just hang about until it's all over.

They all take it differently. I think if I was nailed up there I would want to think long and hard about how it happened and whether it could have been different; but these three start talking. The first man is wasting his time, just foul mouthed; but the second one, who is still going on about getting what he deserves, asks the middle one for forgiveness. The middle one simply says: "You will be with me in heaven before the day is out." I don't know what that means but forgiving people, particularly when you're in such a mess yourself, seems noble to me, the sort of thing that we learned about in the stories of the Republic before the Empire. After that, they went quiet and all I have to do now is wait until it's over.

Here we are, soldiers of Christ, waiting at the foot of the Cross, waiting until it is over. Not for the first time today, we are in a compromised position because we have knocked in the nails but continue to claim that we are soldiers of Christ. This is the supreme paradox of the death of Jesus and trying to untangle it has led his followers into some of their most convoluted and subtle thinking, so let us go back, as the soldier would say, to the training manual. Jesus, condemned to die, suffering immense physical pain, was born so that he might connect the Creator with creatures, with humanity. The way that some Christians describe this is to say that Jesus came to redeem us, or to save us, or to take away our sins. But these statements do not make sense on their own. Why did Jesus have to do any of these things? Surely not because the Creator was a demented accountant or a mad judge who wanted justice, who wanted somebody to pay. The clue is in the mysterious story in Genesis 3. The version of the story which we most often hear, runs something like this: the serpent, the craftiest of creatures, whose identification with Satan began in Persia and was transferred by the Book of Revelation into Mediaeval iconography, this serpent lures humanity—no, better still, a woman—into trying to be God and in order that this serpent should be crushed, God must punish himself in the form of the mutilated Jesus. An alternative and more plausible understanding of the story is that the serpent, the symbol of wisdom, beckons all of humanity to abandon the naive idyll in utopia and to fulfil our role as God's special creatures by learning how to exercise freedom of choice. The reason why this freedom is so important is because without it there is no such thing as love. God is love and we have the awesome privilege of choosing to love, a choice which we often misuse. It is the freedom to choose not to love that explains why we are here now.

How bad could it get, we have to ask ourselves. Well, in the Old Testament it got so bad that God regretted what he had done and almost wiped out humanity; but this version only makes sense if we think of God in relationship rather than as an impassive force. Throughout the Old Testament the Chosen People underwent or forged, depending upon your point of view, a fearful oscillation between faithfulness and disaster as they struggled with a God they could hardly grasp. The Incarnation provides the means by which we can grasp the idea of God but something else needed to happen to avoid the oscillation, to sustain us in some kind of journey, to give life and history a forward trajectory. In the Crucifixion we are not only forgiven, we are told that there is nothing that will not be forgiven and nobody who will not be forgiven. Sometimes this has been taken to mean that it does not matter what we do because Jesus will put it right through his death; but the converse is true. Because he died to demonstrate the indestructibility of God's love for all humanity, everything we do in the exercise of the choice for which we were created counts enormously. It is so important that we should love out of love and not out of fear that everything that we do is significant.

Sitting here watching people die makes me wonder about what we are here for. One minute you are enjoying a drink with your friends and the next minute a goblet goes flying and before you know where you are, you are dead or arrested for murder. One minute you are enjoying a mild joke at the Emperor's expense and the next minute you are being sent to the top of this hill to be killed. It makes me value the little things. I might be a soldier but I'm also a human being. I notice the landscape, the flowers, the smiles on faces, the taste of a grape. Since I started this duty I think I have become kinder. I know that there is so much roughness and retribution in this world that we must cultivate kindness; we must be meticulous in everything that we do to celebrate the gift of life. I, who have taken life to make my living, value it more now perhaps than those who stay at home. Sometimes what we have to do is difficult and distasteful which is why I love doing something for its own sake, because it's the right thing to do, whether or not anybody notices or knows.

As soldiers of Christ our celebration of nature and life is more directive; we do not simply enjoy what we experience, we know who deserves the praise. Yet, praising God in a judicious sort of way, giving credit where credit is due, is not enough. Our form of celebrating the wonders of creation should be to live lives of celebration where everything we do counts significantly towards a kingdom of love on earth. When Jesus forgives it is not because our wrong choices do not matter but because it is vital for our being that we become unfettered from our mistakes so that we can continue to choose to love. If we think that human beings are fundamentally wicked, this is an impossibly risky strategy because it leaves the way open for unlimited infraction; if we are given a moral inch we will take a mile. But if we believe that we are fundamentally creatures of love, the need to retain sorrow without guilt is overwhelming for our mission.

So many Christians who believe that we are fundamentally wicked have got themselves into hopeless muddles over what we are watching and it is easy to understand why. We are watching God's own self in the form of a human being, suffering horribly; we know he is going to die. We have to work out why. It is impossible to take this in. It is a stupendous sacrifice and an equally stupendous scandal. The obvious conclusion is that it is the direct result of human wickedness. But the only way to make sense of it is to go back to the basic manual and re-learn that we have to understand everything in the context of love; not some sentimental attachment, but something difficult and dangerous and ultimately steadfast. Thinking of the effect of the Crucifixion in terms of atonement, ransom, redemption is to understand it from our own perspective, to think of it in terms of human justice and judgment. But the Crucifixion is an act of God so it has to be thought of in God-like terms; and the only thing that we know about God is that God is love. Every time we stray from this central focus to our own anthropocentric understanding, we go wrong. If we are sorry because of what Jesus did we have missed the point; the reason we need to be sorry for where he is now is not because of what he did but because of what he is. His love has taken the form of suffering because our love did not fulfil its promise.

Our lives are lived on two levels: on one level we struggle to fulfil our promise and on another we mourn the love that has failed. We are part of a pilgrimage of lifelong spiritual *schadenfreude*. We say sorry and perform some kind of act of sorrow, but to be sorry is a permanent corollary of being created to love; it is part of our necessary imperfection. Whenever we are not sorry we have lost touch with ourselves and with the beloved; that is why penitence is turning back to God, it is putting us back in touch with ourselves as creatures and therefore back in touch with the Creator. The reverse of this is that the permanent state of sorrow is assuaged by a permanent state of forgiveness. As we were created for one thing and one thing only what appear to be episodes in our lives are simply tangential symptoms; the real meaning of our lives never changes.

It's all grind; I can't see an end to it; but if you watch people like this Jesus it all begins to make some sense. He may be a bit of a basket case—I was probably exaggerating when I started talking about him—but where would any of us be without forgiveness? Nobody's perfect; so no matter how hard we try to love other people we need forgiveness; and we need to know it's always there. How could you be happily married if you never knew when you got home a bit drunk, whether you would be forgiven or not? Because you know it will always be there you don't take advantage of it. Let's face it, this Jesus had nothing to gain by saying what he did to the repentant one; he forgave because it seems like part of his very being. Perhaps one way of thinking about people like Jesus is that we think they are mad just because they are good all through, they always forgive. But you need people like that. They help you to see that human beings are basically good, that most of them don't take advantage and that when they do they are sorry. I see criminals like these brought for punishment; I see people who join the army because they enjoy being cruel; I see people who think burning houses down is a bit of a lark; I see the appalling misuse of power. Yet, when you look at the faces of people you cannot help thinking that they were made to do good.

Jesus was always clear about forgiveness as he walked through Palestine but when we are enfolded back into the Creator we will no doubt still be shocked to find that the whole world is there with us. The whole world, the soldier and both thieves.

**Prayer**

Heavenly Father, you sent your son to bring us courage when we fail so that we might better discern the unfathomable depths of your love; as he hangs before us now at the point of death, help us to turn again to Jesus when we wrongly choose not to love so that we may be one with you in Paradise. Amen.

## iv. Silence

Jesus has said his last words; and now there is silence. The historian has nothing more to record than the actual time of death. The film maker has one last shot to get right and only one chance of getting it. The seller of spices is standing in the middle distance, still looking at the man. The soldiers have stopped gambling. Jesus said something but it was so indistinct that nobody understood what he was saying. He will say no more. There is silence.

To understand this silence we need to remember that from the time of the arrest of Jesus up until his Crucifixion there has been nothing but noise. We are so used to background noise from traffic and machinery, computers and phones, radios and televisions that we have forgotten what real noise is like. When we walk in the mountains or bathe in a distant lagoon, we hear the noise of the train or aeroplane that brought us. We have lost the noise that contrasts with silence because we have lost silence. Because we have lost the silence we have lost the noise.

Yet there is more to silence than physical silence. There is the silence of self-denial, the refusal to make a noise, the refusal to speak. George Steiner famously wrote in the mid-1960s that after Hitler's mass murder of Jews it was impossible to use language with integrity; it could not, he said, adequately report what had happened with the degree of intensity that was required; in which case it was better to say nothing. Because the SS had listened to Schubert we had to ask what the culture was worth and whether going into the permanent mourning of silence might not be better. He was not, of course, thinking about such trivia as asking somebody to pass the salt; he was thinking about the way we use language to convey significance.

Whether Steiner was right or wrong, we are now burbling our way out of significance, murdering our language through the traditional cruelties of forced labour and malnutrition. Even if Steiner were wrong, we make part of his point for him by hurling accusations of Nazi at trivial infractors and tiny political factions that call themselves Nazis. This makes it ever more difficult to understand what it meant to be a Nazi under the control of Hitler; the word becomes devalued. Almost every day of our lives we hear life's little misfortunes described as "a nightmare", "a shambles" or a "disaster". We have stopped using hyperbole as hyperbole. Yet, like fast food and pop music, there is a kind of noise that becomes addictive, that becomes part of the backdrop of our being or, to put it negatively, it is the kind of noise that stops us from feeling lonely. We might ask, on the other hand, whether we are most lonely when we are surrounded by people and noise and things; and most at peace with ourselves when we can find silence.

Here, now, after all the noise of the trial and the climb, we are at the end of the journey.

Talking about silence is one of life's unavoidable paradoxes. What kind of talk about silence is germane to where we are now?

In this silence, as Jesus has finished talking, we need to review all that he has said. For the greatest man who ever lived it is a slim collection. After all, between a third and a quarter of each Gospel is an account of his death which, incidentally, tells us of its importance for the earliest Christians. Then there are the passages that repeat. But what distinguishes the Gospels from the books that never received Canonical status is that the Gospels were all about a man who preached the kingdom of love on earth, whereas the books that were ruled out were only interested in a kingdom of love in the sky and neither were they were interested in the death of Jesus. We have tried to connect the kingdom of love on earth with the significance of the death of Jesus and so there is room for only one more thought: if Jesus had been born both divine and human, as he was, and proclaimed the same Gospel, and had ascended into heaven, without the kind of death he is dying now, what would we think? What would we know and what would we not know?

In this silence we need to review our own way of talking to ourselves and to each other about Jesus. Part of the way we talk slipped into our way of witnessing in the second half of the last century. Until then, we had thought of God as impassible, of never changing. We were apt to slide over Old Testament remarks about God changing his mind or being sorry for what he had done, reflected in the story of Noah. We were caught up in the doctrinal cat's cradle; if we let go of one loop of string the whole lot would collapse; which doesn't show much real faith in the Jesus enterprise. Then came the horrors of the twentieth century, made real by the mass media; and we began to think that Jesus, the incarnate God, had a passable aspect, that he was not somewhere in the sky watching us suffer but that he was suffering with us. It is as if we have come to realise that God through Jesus understood the imposition of creation and would not change it for anything, but saw how difficult was the mandate created for us. And it is difficult. So difficult that when social conformity was relaxed in the twentieth century, most people stopped trying to live the life we try to live.

Because the life we live is both difficult and precious we need to mind our language. We need to retain two things: first, we must always remember that "God talk" is hopelessly inadequate; but, secondly, we must ensure that our "God talk" is earthly talk, talk of the here and now, of the kingdom of love on earth.

As we stand here in the moments before the death of Jesus, between his last word and his last breath, what might we say to ourselves? Jesus has shown his love; that he has lived out for us the imperfection of our love; that we can now without doubt understand the degree of difference and the fundamental identity, consubstantiality, of his love and ours. For love is undifferentiated; God is love, we were created to love; our roles are different as creator and creatures but love is our only concern. As we stand we may think of the indescribable triumph of love in Jesus or the all too describable failure of love in us; but even if we have put him up there on a cross, he is still down here standing with us.

There is a time for theology and a time for silence. There is a point at which words fail in the face of mystery, just as they fail in the face of a beloved. The mystery of Jesus the beloved draws words out of us in the way that the earthly beloved draws words out of the lover. We are caught between words and wonder, between skill and silence. That is where we almost always need to be, caught in the middle, alive to both our human gift and our human failing, between God's human form and mysterious being. Just as there are times when we instinctively feel it is better to say nothing than to say anything, no matter how beautiful or loving, this is the time when we are moving, inexorably, towards silence, towards a contemplation of a mystery that has eluded all our words. This man who is there, above us, is also down here, with us, watching himself. In a way that words will never master, he is helping us to bear his Passion.

We need to ask ourselves what it is that we are bearing. Is it a feeling that we ought to be sorry because it is the kind of event that evokes sorrow? Is it a feeling that we are somehow complicit and that if we had acted differently things would have turned out differently? Or is it the sorrow of the steady state of our relationship as creatures with the Creator? Is it the sorrow of our condition rather than of our individual behaviour? I like to think that our sorrow is of this last kind because I like to think that Jesus is with us now, sharing the sorrow of La Condition Humaine because we are what we are and he is who he is. The febrile accountancy of good and bad added up, of guilt apportioned and debts written off, seems to me to be a totally alien set of transactions from what is happening now as we stand together with Jesus, up there and down here.

What, finally, might we say about silence? We need to give ourselves mental and emotional space to come to terms with the mystery of God's love and our terrible transgression. Today we have thought about the murderous treatment of the Jews and other groups and tribes that the Nazis wanted to eliminate; we have seen genocide in faraway places like Cambodia and central and East Africa; and as near as the Balkans; and as we stand here now, countless people are being killed in the Sudan. There is plenty to make us protest and plenty to keep us silent. Whenever we are in danger we must stop shouting with the crowd and cross the empty ground to Jesus as he stands condemned. And we must never forget, as we stand by him, that we once shouted in the crowd.

We need to be careful with the truth that we tell ourselves. The relationship we have with God through Jesus in the power of the Spirit must not resemble the truth of the film maker who packages elegance and architecture, who creates the kind of reality which makes the complex simple and which provides us with a route to escape. We need to keep ourselves grounded in our untidy dialogue with God. We must not be persuaded by easy words either to sell out or to think that we have overcome our difficulties in establishing a relationship with God. If we think that we will never communicate again then we should look at Jesus as he hangs now, in silence. If we think that our communication is smoothly effective then we are deluding ourselves. If we want to know how difficult it is, we can think of the lives of the saints; or, better still, watch the life of Jesus uncut.

More often than not we are like the seller of spices; we take small steps towards God and away from God; our life is not one of heroic gestures but of constant, tiny efforts. Such striving can be exhausting and even we, faint heroes, need time to recover, to say nothing. To look carefully at the man, to look and never stop looking, to behold and never stop holding.

As soldiers of Christ who knocked in the nails, we must remember that everything is forgiven, even this, not because Jesus paid some kind of supernatural debt but because without unfailing forgiveness the human purpose of choosing to love is too much to ask. We must remember that our crime and our suffering are a common element of our humanity; we are soldiers, not here to judge but to do the will of our Commander as best we can, our Commander the King of Love.

## Prayer

Heavenly Father, you sent your son to suffer with us so that we might better feel the strength of your compassion; as he lingers between his last word and his last breath, help us to love Jesus in joy and in silence until the very end. Amen.

# 5. The Paradox of Violence

*2009*

## i. The Scourging—Casual Violence

The starting point for any meditations on the Passion and death of Jesus must be our attempt to hold his humanity and divinity in reflective tension. This is the Son of God who died for us but he is also a human being like us. The familiar tableaux of sacred art which most memorably represent the events of Good Friday should not deceive us. If we are tempted, we might better look at more contemporary representations informed by our intimate knowledge of the mass, state-sponsored violence of the twentieth century, of gas in the trenches, of concentration camps, of Hiroshima and Nagasaki, of Agent Orange and Extraordinary Rendition. Not that there had not been mass violence and torture before—our story today connects with the most sustained military dictatorship in history—but the scale of twentieth century violence was such that it permeated all levels of society in a way that was viscerally explicit; and, through newspapers, cinema and television, it made us complicit. We could no longer plough our furrow and sit by our hearth, disturbed only by the occasional story of a boy who didn't come home.

At the heart of our social narrative there is a deep paradox about violence. In the past 100 years the parallel developments in medicine and militarism have been enormous; a massive fall in infant mortality was the precursor to the slaughter of the First World War. It was almost as if we had saved the babies so that they could die at Paschendale. Social reform took children out of factories and mines, out of chimney sweeping and prostitution, but the next generation of legislators sent millions to the front and the next generation sanctioned the carpet bombing of civilians.

When we read the Passion accounts, one salient characteristic is how the violence is so casual: in all four gospels (Matthew 27.26; Mark 15.15; Luke 23.16, 22; John 19.1) Pilate's order to scourge Jesus is just a casual afterthought with no purpose except, perhaps, to please his accusers. It is neither an act of torture intended to elicit a confession nor a punishment; it is simply an arbitrary exercise of sadistic power. We later see this again in Acts and the Epistles of Paul where scourging is simply a commonplace of the exercise of military power.

Violence is almost always wrong but there is something peculiarly nasty about gratuitous violence. While we may not approve of calculated aggression we can see the point of neo-Darwinian, competitive aggression; we can see the cause of violence born of extreme exasperation. We understand because of the way we are how stress, bewilderment or impotence can lead us to lash out; but the violence against Jesus was none of these. There might be an argument that his silence or enigmatic statements might have provoked anger but by the time he was scourged, his death was inevitable, he was a victim inside a well-organised system. Everyone knew, after the release of Barabbas, that he was going to be crucified, so what was the point other than to assert a petty, disgusting rite?

The central theme of these meditations is our complicitness in the pain and death inflicted on Jesus by the fanatical religious and barbaric secular authorities and we can recognise that complicitness in the contemporary world of casual violence. I hardly need remind us of the gratuitous cruelty of dictators, the connivance of democracies, the pointless acts of gangs and individual criminals and the myriad acts of cruelty which infect our society. Often, like Pilate, we wash our hands; but more often we simply grumble. How often do we complain, write letters to our leaders, support Amnesty International and similar organisations? This links with a second perspective of our meditations, how we, like the crowds watching Jesus suffer and die, just stood by. We could argue that they had good reason, that they were subject to arbitrary power which would punish them for their bravery; and we could argue that the same constraint applies to would-be protesters living in contemporary dictatorships which lack due process. It would be a very brave person who would protest against the cruelty of cynical military regimes; but we cannot argue such extenuation for ourselves. There is not much point in struggling for centuries to secure democracy only to let it wither on the vine.

The scourging of Jesus looks pointless; but behind the cruelty, there is evidence of fear. Pilate, even though he was a Roman Governor, seems to have been frightened; and fear leads to disproportionate assertiveness, seen at its most vivid in the bully. The deficit in self-esteem or self-assurance is made up through violence. This is the kind of explanation which modern psychology would understand but to explain is not to condone; and we too easily make that jump: "He had no alternative," we say; "He was driven to it"; "It was either the victim or him." If we reach this point we have sold out to the logic of fear. Our media is full of such explanations which ultimately lead to tacit justification. We are all in danger of buying in to this anti-salvation agenda.

Here we meet the paradox of the Passion which inhabits the whole of our Christian life. Jesus suffered this violence in the act of saving us, presenting us with the gift of salvation which frees us in two ways pertinent to cruelty: first, it gives us an alternative narrative to that of inflicting cruelty to try to secure self-esteem or reduce fear; and, secondly, at the root of that new narrative is the centrality of love as an alternative to competition.

In this year of Charles Darwin (2009), the radio and television have been full of wonderful programmes about the way in which he developed his theory of the *Origin of the Species through Natural Selection* whose breadth and elegance is truly breath-taking; but we must never forget that it is a description of the evolution of plants and animals which optimised their fit with the environment. The idea of the "survival of the fittest" did not mean those with the greatest physical prowess but those which best fitted their ecology. Our mistake has been to transfer this evolutionary explanation of "passive fitness" into a rule which applies to human competition. We have leaped from Tennyson's "Nature red in tooth and claw" to humanity so that evolution is no longer a simple explanation of how we arrived where we are but is transformed into an explanation of, and even a justification for, aggression. In spite of all the wickedness for which organised religion is responsible, Richard Dawkins is still as wrong as a human can be when he exalts the Darwinian paradigm of natural selection above the imperative of love, underlined in the meekness of our Saviour.

In order to learn as best we can from the suffering of Jesus we need to think of it in two, totally inter-dependent ways: first, Jesus the man suffered terribly; we must never forget this or we will be swept into sentimentalism; secondly, the meekness under the pressure of pain was faultless. This is not, however, a story which we happened to learn, of the infliction of pain behind high walls; Jesus was behaving as he did as a public demonstration of the reality of love in the face of aggression. It is the stark contrast of meaningless violence and loving purpose. The extent to which the Gospel narratives are taken up with descriptions of the Passion and death of Jesus is no accident. Indeed, one of the ways in which the New Testament came to be what it is was that supposed Gospels which down-played the events of Maundy Thursday and Good Friday were deemed non-canonical. We are supposed to imagine ourselves as far as we can into the mindless infliction of pain and the conscientious response of love.

Let us now look at gratuitous violence from three points of view: the victim, the perpetrator and the spectator. Without wishing to exaggerate our own, personal sufferings, we will be very lucky—or perhaps unlucky—if we go through life without suffering. It is part of our condition, it is part of being a creature, it is the necessary price we pay for exercising conscience, of freely choosing to love; for an intrinsic part of any deep love is the willingness to make sacrifices. Our love of Jesus calls for this response just as his love for us called for it; but although his response was public it was, nonetheless, uncomplaining. Just as it is inappropriate to ask for love, so it is to complain to others about our suffering; it is between us and Jesus. The Psalmists complained to God and, in the privacy of our own prayer or in collective generalisations where we share the sentiment but spare each other the detail, it is proper to bemoan our fate; it is difficult to be imperfect as part of our condition; but using this as a form of competitive virtue or victimhood is unhelpful.

From the perspective of the perpetrator, violence is only effective in a superficial, short-term way. It gets the lion his food but it gets humanity nowhere. We are, therefore, not only to reject violence because it is wicked but also because it is ineffective. There is, however, a third consideration. Violence coarsens our self-understanding such that it is easy to become indifferent to it. How often have we heard the comment that the first act of violence is the most difficult but after that it becomes progressively easier?

From the standpoint of the spectator that last point also applies. It is difficult to be indifferent the first time but it becomes progressively easier; before we know where we are—literally—we add revulsion fatigue to compassion fatigue. Jesus never allowed himself to be blighted by humanity fatigue; he never stopped loving us through our agents of torture and death. He never stopped praying for us; and he carried through his purpose. On this point the Gospels are economically eloquent. Whether you take each word and incident literally or whether you think that the Evangelists chose their material in the power of the Holy Spirit to illustrate the truth of Jesus as they saw it, the accounts of the Passion and death of Jesus starkly contrast the gratuitous violence of act and expression with an economy of response which gives us a model for our own, brokenness.

After all the dissection of the different roles of victim, perpetrator and spectator, after the dramatic contrast between the perpetrator and the victim, we are confronted with the central mystery of humanity: that we are all three types. Our imperfection offers us the opportunity to suffer for Christ; but, conversely, it offers us the opportunity to turn away, to turn our backs, or even to be participants in cruelty. It is our three-fold being in this sad, sacred drama which gives it a poignancy, a plangency which is never dulled or mellowed.

Here is our best chance, as we imagine ourselves into the moment when the skin is flayed from our Saviour's back, to recognise the extreme ambiguity of our existence, so often standing at a point between walking away from or towards Jesus or just standing still, refusing to look at what confronts us. For 2,000 years we have wondered at the mystery of how Jesus could be both divine and human; but the mystery is how our response is so fraught yet so fulfilling.

**Prayer**

Lord Jesus, it is only at this point of contact between the thongs of the
whip and your sacred back that we can bring ourselves to shudder at
what we have done and what we have failed to do; for we, who were given
flesh, took your flesh. May we learn from your love, articulate in silence,
suffering and sacrifice, how we may love you; and grant us the Grace
to see ourselves as fellows in your suffering, as well as perpetrators and
spectators so that we might know truly who we are. Amen.

## ii. Thorns—Nature Subverted

We are all familiar with the changed attitude of Christianity to slavery
and race, to corporal punishment and the treatment of children, to
genocide and banking; but how aware are we of the continuing tension
in Christianity about the treatment of the world's resources?

When the Bible was written its world possessed more resources than
people. St Paul and St Luke might have had some inkling of the city
of Rome's dependence upon Egyptian grain imports but that was the
startling exception to the general rule that the earth's abundance seemed
limitless. The Chosen People were required to multiply and use the earth's
resources to sustain themselves. At the beginning of the twenty-first
century, five decades after the first serious warnings about overpopulation
and the depletion of resources, our idea of stewardship of God's creation
is much less assertive; but we need to remember that there is still a very
strong strand of Christian thinking that says that humanity, as superior
to all nature, must express that superiority in exploiting earthly resources.
There is a strand that says that we can judge how much God loves us
according to how wealthy and powerful we are, and while it might be
clear to us that this is a case of cynically manipulating religion to justify
selfish behaviour, we need to acknowledge its virulence and its dangers.

The relationship between Jesus and nature is theologically neutral. He
was remarkably subject to its forces and he only exercised power over

them in order to convey the power of his Creator parent. He was born in a poor place in poor weather; he was tested in the wilderness; he was tossed on the waters of the Sea of Galilee; and now, here, he is assaulted by thorns and will soon be murdered by fixation to a tree.

In our culture the purpose of thorns is to protect the beautiful or the precious, the flower and the fruit. There are places, like sub-Saharan Africa or Mexico, where thorns appear to exist for their own sake, to protect nothing; but in our consciousness it is not easy to escape the association of the rose and the thorn, to think that the thorn is the price of the rose. Here, the role of the thorn is radically reversed so that it is not used to protect the beautiful and the precious but to assault it. The use of the thorns to torture Jesus (Matthew 27.29; Mark 15.18; John 19.2) is depicted as a parody of earthly power, for they are twisted into a primitive crown; the most exalted headgear is inverted into being a humiliating gesture. Jesus' assertion of his own kind of kingship is subverted into a claim of earthly power which is then ridiculed. Not for the first time, he is deliberately misunderstood. He is being punished for his meekness. Were he claiming to be an earthly king the conclusion would no doubt have been the same but the foreplay would have been very different. Claiming to be a king in the imperial empire was a serious claim; but we can see that at no point did anybody take Jesus' claim seriously: the religious authorities were quite properly frightened of Jesus' miraculous powers and they were confused by his claim of relationship with the Father but they did not take him seriously as a secular ruler or a Messiah. Herod, quixotic to a fault, veered between respect and mockery, just as he had never reached a settled view of John the Baptist and Pilate, frightened though he was of the religious authorities, was not in the least frightened of Jesus. So the crown of thorns was a pretext for cruelty and parody.

Perhaps, too, we think of Jesus using the thorn as a metaphor for human ambition in his story of the sower (Matthew 13.22; Mark 4.18–19; Luke 8.14). Here is the quintessential, non-acquisitive person being punished by thorns, representing the worldly threat that he has resisted, to the Word of God. In the parable, the thorns choke; in real death they pierce, drawing blood which makes a mockery of the finery in which Jesus is dressed, in a purple, scarlet or simply gorgeous robe, depending on the translation and evangelist (Matthew 27.28; Mark 15.17; Luke 12.11; John 19.2, 5).

But in this era of ecological awareness, the thorn which punishes takes on a completely different aspect; for in seeing something that was created by God Our Parent being used to inflict pain on the Son, we see the wider picture of nature subverted for ignoble ends. For us, living now, any sensitivity we have moves outwards from the particularity of the power politics of Jerusalem and Rome, to a world of receding glaciers, evaporating lakes, endangered species and threatened livelihoods. We see the thorn subverted magnified in nature subverted. What was particular in Jesus becomes general in our stewardship; and that opening out reinforces the point that the whole process can be reversed. Our general failure of stewardship is particularised into the crowning of Jesus, illustrating yet again how we must see ourselves as complicit in the Passion and death of our Saviour.

There are, essentially, four charges against us as stewards: that we are indifferent, ruthless, unjust and sentimental; and we can see immediately how these attitudes to the environment so closely mirror the way in which the authorities and the crowds, as our representatives, treated Jesus. Perhaps indifference is too light a word for the crowds and is certainly too light a word for the followers who deserted him, but the correspondence is close enough. There is no doubt that the authorities were ruthless; they had a very selfish objective and did not mind what steps they needed to take to achieve it; and one of those steps was the indifference to justice. As for the sentimentality, it is so easy for us to distance ourselves in a chocolate box kind of reverence, from the real pain.

On the wider issue of our stewardship, there is no doubt that many of us are indifferent, just hoping that we can go on driving our cars, taking cheap flights, over-purchasing and wasting, land-filling our rubbish, wishfully thinking that climate change will go away. Our ruthlessness in pursuit of material comfort and our voracious desires are the causes of injustice, both in respect of poor people in developing countries and our own but, more worryingly still, in respect of our descendants. Our consumption is materially damaging the prospects of our children and grandchildren. All this grabbing and gouging, mining and mangling, fishing and foraging, pesticiding and poisoning, travelling and trashing has not freed us from our sentimentalism about nature: it is there for us, it brings joy, it will always be there, no matter what we do.

There is a lure in our dealings with nature, a kind of super-sentimentalism which is summed up for me in the idea of the thorn-less rose. The perfection of symmetry in beauty and protection, in the flower and the thorn, is replaced by an overbalancing of ease and an artificially exaggerated prettiness; we are always in danger of escaping from beauty into prettiness; but, to parody Keats, whereas truth is beauty, prettiness is ephemeral. This descent into the pretty is an intrinsic part of our escape from the reality of the power and danger, the life-threatening and life-enhancing properties of beauty; the idea of beauty as challenge and risk. It is this effeteness of perception which can so easily turn us away from the horrors of the world, all concentrated in the Passion and death of Jesus. By this I do not mean that Jesus in some way bore all our sins, or cancelled them, or performed the grotesque act of what is called "Penal Substitution"; what I mean is that in spite of universal complicitness in the Passion and death, the culmination of all the wrong choices the human race has ever made and will ever make, we keep our emotional, and sometimes even our penitential, distance. Just as we are fastidious in the face of poverty and degradation, so we may be in the face of what is before us. Yet the risk of beauty is before us in horror and wonder; for not only are we, collectively, the perpetrators of what is before us, represented by those people some two thousand years ago, we are also the beneficiaries. Our benefit lies in this; that from this time we know that there is nothing that Jesus will not do for us; and we know too that this commitment of him to us will survive no matter what we do to him. The real significance of his Passion and death is not that he in some way died *for* our sins but that he died *of* our sins; but that made no difference to his divine love for us.

And such a poor king! Those who pressed the crown of thorns into the head of Jesus thought they were making a marvellous joke at his expense, taunting him with his failed ambition. It was as if they could not believe that he did not really want to be a king in spite of everything they had heard; for Jerusalem was a small, claustrophobic, multilingual place and almost everyone must have heard of the final few days of the mission of Jesus. Surely he wanted to be king. Everybody wants to be king, don't they?

Well not, of course, in the old-fashioned, literal sense of the word. We don't want to live in a palace and be a head of state and we certainly don't want to go out onto a battlefield and fight for our kingdom. We want our kingship easy; in the spirit of the times, we really want it unearned. In a fascinating transition from a dictatorial monarchy to a democracy, we all want our own way; we are consumers and our central value is choice; we all want to be monarchs of all we survey. For us, too, there is the added dimension of who we are and how we exercise power over other people. Not only do we have the power of the consumer to buy blackberries from Mexico, trainers from Taiwan, flowers from Kenya and cars from South Korea, but we also have other powers that we take for granted. We are intellectual pace-setters, exercising a moral and cultural superiority without thinking about it so that we feel shock and resentment when leaders in the Third World accuse us of decadence; and we wield power over our own little corner of society, in committees and unofficial power bases.

The central point of this meditation is that to look at behaviour between humans is not enough. The drama of Maundy Thursday and Good Friday has been understood for almost two thousand years as a human drama; and our tradition has understood this as a fundamentally significant event in salvation history. Whatever our explanation for the Passion and death of Jesus it has always involved the behaviour between humans and the choices they make to love or not to love the Creator as creatures. Only now, as the temperature rises, as the scientists become more insistent, as politicians prevaricate, can we see that our obligation to God Our Parent is not only a matter of the way we treat humanity, it is a matter of the way in which we treat creation.

We can see the crown of thorns as an icon of the natural wrenched from its place and deployed for vicious human ends, as a means of denying the Creator. Icons will come and go as our circumstances change but for now, the crown of thorns is an emblem of nature subverted.

**Prayer**

Lord Jesus, it is only at this point of contact between the thorns and your sacred head that we can bring ourselves to shudder at what we have done and what we have failed to do; for we, who were given creation, have subverted creation. May we learn from your love, beautiful and terrible in its poignant repose, how we may love creation; and grant us the Grace to see ourselves as fellows in your power, not venal spectators or perpetrators, so that we might be honest stewards of creation. Amen.

# iii. Mockery—Just Joking

There is a wonderfully powerful sketch in *Monty Python's Flying Circus* where the physical violence of a terrorising gang, a parody of the Kray Brothers, is belittled in comparison with sarcasm; and in the *Monty Python* film *The Life of Brian*, in the spectacularly ironic parody of the Passion, a queue of condemned men are offered crucifixion or an alternative; and one first volunteers for crucifixion but then turns round and says: "Just joking." The idea that anybody might be killed on a cross was just a bit of a laugh; and to those inured to state-inflicted violence, that is what it was, a bit of a laugh, in the same way that dysfunctional people today commit violence "for fun".

Never was there a dafter rhyme, a kind of whistling in the light, than the expression "sticks and stones may break my bones but words will never hurt me". It is a platitude that defies all the evidence. We are living in an age where words are losing their grace and sharpness and are becoming ever blunter, brutal weapons of assault. The whole purpose of language is to strengthen and enhance the possibilities of human co-operation but it seems increasingly the case that words are deployed to deceive or to demean. At the height of the frenzy over the disappearance of Madeleine McCann, newspapers which could not gain a new angle on the story simply cast nasty aspersions on the grieving parents. The power of a good deal of what we, rather strangely, call "reality television" rests on the appetite of the public for seeing the inadequate exalted and then humbled. Our culture has adopted cruelty as a key media selling point. The use of cruelty is so ubiquitous that we hardly notice it until it is applied to us; until that apparently casual, throw-away line which we think will not—or should not—affect somebody else, is thrown at us. Anybody and everybody seems to think themselves entitled, as a matter of common freedom, to express any view about anything, no matter how ignorant and negative. We have come to see restraint not as a virtue but as a bar to linguistic indulgence; our cheapening and coarsening of language, of discourse, of sentiment, of sensibility, of feeling, parallels our crude materialism. Although we have this erroneous "sticks and stones" platitude running in the background, we know that it is the word that counts. Brutality usually follows a self-deluding justification or the barking of an order, acts of mass exploitation are usually supported by spurious theories, personal spite is honed to sharpness; the man boasts his strength and woman her beauty; but the clever use their words, not to clear minefields but as ammunition to assault the other or otherness. The dangers are summed up in the Letter of James (ch. 3): the bit in the mouth of a horse is tiny but it turns the whole animal; the rudder of a ship is tiny but it turns the whole ship; the tongue is likewise tiny but it makes great boasts, like a spark it sets light to a forest, it alters the whole of our lives.

The Passion of Jesus is shot through with mockery: the mocking kiss and address of Judas; the sham proceedings before the High Priest; the antics of King Herod seeking a sign; the strange, almost surreal, mockery of Pilate which suddenly breaks out into "Behold, your king!"; the mockery of the thieves, softened in Luke; the dice playing of the soldiers; the taunt that Jesus can save himself if he is the Messiah. From beginning to end there is a narrative of superiority and cynicism, of the abuse of process and its victim.

Both major misuses of language—deception and cruelty—feature in our narratives. As we have seen, Judas in what is, admittedly, a very shallow piece of deception, betrays Jesus with a soft greeting and a kiss. False witnesses, again, in a rather shallow way, are brought forward to convict Jesus; and there are numerous uses of cruel language on the part of the crowd and the authorities.

But in many ways the more besetting vices of language are cynicism and abdication: Caiaphas thinks it better that one man should die for the whole people; the disciples run away; Peter denies Jesus; and Pilate washes his hands.

We are so used to these forms of behaviour that we hardly notice: we expect politicians and journalists to lie to such an extent that the only lies we really resent are those from the clergy and the police. Perpetrators and victims console themselves with the thought that most deceptions are shallow; we are all grown-ups; we know how necessary it is to say one thing and mean another; because we see through the deception it is not serious. Before long we are not sure. When is a false statement false and when is it a joke? How many layers of irony can we withstand before we lose our bearings? In a wonderful poem about perception, entitled *Carnal Knowledge*, the poet Thom Gunn ended his verses alternately: "I know you know I know you know I know" and "You know I know you know I know you know".

But our kind of deception is not the straight, shocking, blatant lie; we are much too clever for that. As a natural reflection of our contemporary social mores, language reflects the flaking of solid accountability: just as we have moved in administration from leadership to the Gilbert & Sullivan situation where everybody is somebody and so nobody is anybody so, in our language, we have gone from the active: "I hit Jim" to the passive: "Jim was hit". In both cases Jim doubtless sustained some discomfort but in the second sentence there is a degree of coyness about causality; it is subtlety that entwines us rather than brutality that assaults us.

Paradoxically, although our deception may be becoming more subtle, our linguistic cruelty seems to be ever more blatant and virulent. The deceptively neutral ideas of "extending the envelope" and "testing the boundary" deceive no-one. What was once unsayable becomes "challenging" or "edgy"; the kind of cattiness which was a part of teenage rivalry is a commonplace of entertainment; silly and defenceless people are encouraged to stand up so that they can be pilloried; cheques are signed, consumers chuckle, knowingly; lives are wrecked.

In this we are all more or less complicit. No doubt we occasionally deceive through subtlety; and no doubt we occasionally say something and then wish we had not said it, seeing pain spread across the face of a colleague or friend, showing us that the burst of cleverness was a betrayal of vulnerability; but it is what we consume or let pass that condemns us, not what we do. In a highly inter-dependent world, these failures are two sides of the same coin. Because we consume cynical, cruel or deceptive language, paying the authors and publishers for their infliction of damage to our social capital, they receive a return on their investment and re-invest; and, like a drug addiction, the more we consume, the bigger the hit we need to be satisfied. The cruelty increases, the violence increases, the sexual coarseness increases, the degradation increases. I have so often heard it said that there is nothing we can do; that the market is too big; that we would dearly love to protect our children and grandchildren but the peer pressure is too great; the somebody elses next door or down the street are more powerful than we are.

At quite a different level, as educated and powerful people, even if we do not consume, even if we are sceptical about everything we hear, we too often wash our hands, live in a state of denial, run away. It is too much trouble. We will grumble at the back of church or in the pub but we won't do anything about it; things have gone too far to turn around; the good old days will never return; somebody or other has betrayed us and the values we stood for; we are victims of a huge, linguistic and aesthetic conspiracy.

But the point of the Cross is that we are not victims; we have made choices which have led us here to stand before the world's most unjustified but inevitable victim. The significance of the Cross is that it stands for all choices; it is, literally, a symbol of our freedom. It tells us that the greatest betrayal we can undertake is to portray ourselves as victims and not perpetrators; Christ is the victim; we are the perpetrators and perhaps the aspect of life in which we most often make wrong choices is in the way we talk and the way we stay silent.

The mockery of the crown of thorns and the purple robe might lead us to think that the inscription over the head of Jesus is the final joke: this broken man is proclaimed King of the Jews. When the religious authorities tell Pilate that he should write, "He said he was the King of the Jews", they are surely missing the point. This is not only Pilate's joke at the expense of Jesus—there can be nothing more obvious than that this dying man is no king—but it is also a joke at the expense of the Jews who are given this pathetic leader, and at the expense of the authorities who are, in effect, told that this is the only king they will get. As jokes go it works well because it hurts everyone; Pilate's revenge is bitter/sweet.

Let us project ourselves forward. The self-importance and the mockery came to nothing. The failure of the Jewish religious authorities to see what had come and what was coming proved fatal to their power and position; the Roman Empire was conquered by the Cross; the man who was tortured, mocked and murdered became our King. In this we should take comfort and the strength to be brave. We are not torturers and murderers; it is our mockery and our complicit silence that have brought us here, to the spectacle of unmitigated disaster and defeat, to a remembrance of the Letter of James, of the tongue that is a spark; restrained, it brings warmth, light and comfort; unrestrained, it destroys everything in its path, as we have seen recently in Victoria. We never know when we toss the verbal equivalent of a cigarette butt carelessly out of a car window what damage it will do. We speed away, oblivious and later, when we read about the fire, we wonder whether we started it, shrug, and move on. There are so many trivial incidents that could have caused it; it can hardly have been us. Then something in us, a perverse pride, a feeling of guilt, changes our outlook and we begin to watch the flames with a possessive, perverted pleasure. Whoever it was had it coming; it was going to happen to them sooner or later; if it wasn't me it would have been somebody else.

Suddenly we say to someone, because we can't hold it in any longer, "I started that fire, you know," but when we see the horror with which the admission is greeted, we check ourselves and say with a half laugh: "Just joking!"

## Prayer

Lord Jesus, it is only at this point of contact between the tongues of the mockers and your sacred heart that we can bring ourselves to wonder at what we have said and what we have failed to say; for we, who were given language have almost killed it. May we learn from your love, vivid in everything you said, how we may love you; and grant us the Grace to see ourselves as fellows in your mockery, as well as mockers and cowards, so that we may be truthful in all we say. Amen.

## iv. Nails—The Point Is

"The point is" and "What is the point?" are two ideas at opposite ends of the spectrum. By the time we reach "the point is", we have made up our mind and are trying to persuade others; if we ask "what is the point?" we are on the verge of stopping something or deciding not to start it. A point is a highly focused idea, intellectually and physically; we have crossing points and turning points, points of view and points of contact, points on salary scales and points for sports scores. Because a point in geometry has no area, occupies no space but is simply a notion, we expect any point to be tiny and, if it is given physical expression, in a knife, a needle or a nail, we expect it to be sharp. But the nails used to crucify Jesus were probably not sharp at all. Our only Gospel evidence for Jesus being nailed to the Cross comes from John (20.24–29), and then only in a post-Resurrection scene where Jesus invites the doubting Thomas to inspect his wounds. Those wounds are often represented as rather neat and tidy but the crude nails used for common criminals were shattering rather than piercing; murder was not a work of art; it was a common, civic necessity.

I was brought up in a deeply ideological world, as a Roman Catholic socialist in the days of Aneurin Bevan and Pope Pius XII. The only real difference between politics and religion were the buildings; the Knights of St Columba walked as a body from St Joseph's to the Weaver's Institute. The atmosphere was tribal, the arguments circular; the "left" was as hostile to its nearly "own" as was one Christian denomination to another. I continued to live in this strange world right through university; books were making my mind ever more open and flexible but the real world was harsh and combative. For the record, I was always hostile to "far left" groups, was uncomfortable about strikes and demonstrations but regretted the need for them more than the events themselves. I never believed that ideological politics would work: then there was Prague, then the miners' strike, then the Berlin wall came tumbling down; and Francis Fukuyama famously and, prematurely as it turned out, wrote about the end of history. Then there were twenty golden years of unbridled, unideological exuberance; then there was the internet bubble, the credit crunch and the banking collapse. The use of the term "unideological" is, of course, ironic. One ideology had simply triumphed over another.

Ideologies are intellectual and religious nails used to secure objects; they are used, literally, to nail things down. Jesus was killed by the twin ideologies of conservative Judaism and military imperialism: no seminar, no debate, no room for manoeuvre; just nails.

Today, our ideologies are less blatant and perhaps more subtle but we have ideologies of education, child rearing (most applied to the children of other people), immigration, punishment, social worth and the distribution of the fruits of an intensively inter-dependent society. But we must be careful because no matter how reasonable we think our stance may be on any issue it can so easily become difficult to see past ideology to people. Just think about the way in which ideologies supposed to secure greater human happiness have killed millions of people; what is the point of an ideology that uses cruel means for a benign end?

The crucial point is that the exaltation of an ideology over loving our neighbour is the strongest possible symptom of psychosis. Jesus was fundamentally non-ideological; he would not judge; and where he was confronted by harshness for the sake of ideology, he condemned it. That is not to say that he did not have core values, that he did not have very deep beliefs, but his belief centred on the ultimate indispensability of God and the primacy of love. Contrary to popular prejudice, love is not a matter of doing things to people, of spreading a kind of personal ideology through assertion, it is valuing other people for what they are in themselves and allowing them to express themselves; love is getting out of the way; of emptying the ego, of learning how to take.

Ultimately, this difference of approach, of cultural and moral temperament, brought Jesus into cosmic conflict with humanity. Jesus was content to explain, to understand, to see everything in terms of the ultimate essence of God's love but we, made to choose, could never accept any maxim so simple. Because we are made to choose we weigh options and look for patterns; and when we find a pattern that fits our

temperament and our times we take security in it and exalt it above our
own selfishness by calling it a belief, an ideology, a code. It is not the
actual code that matters all that much; there is less difference than we
would like to think between Nazism and Stalinism, between socialism and
capitalism, between Christianity and Islam; we are all marching around
with our hammers and nails: a poster here; an opinion there; a judicious
piece of patronage; a paragraph in the papers; a smile or a frown. We all
make thousands of decisions and without some kind of framework we
would find this impossible; and so would other people who want to know
in advance how we will react to proposals or pressure. Again, the problem
is not the pattern or the predictability but the divorcement of the pattern
or process from people; and the irrational intensity of faith in the pattern.

We can see the fundamental difference between the perfect humanity
of Jesus and our humanity; we cannot survive without a measure of
ideology but as a necessary adjunct to our createdness as imperfect
creatures, we should simply see that as a tool for dealing with complexity
and shock, not as a something more important than the Creator out of
pure love.

I am, of course, asking for the impossible; but not really. When I was
getting ready, as the first ever member of my family to go to university,
my grandfather, the Catholic socialist par excellence, told me that the
world had quite enough clever people but not enough good ones. We can
afford to take the risk, to take people as we find them, to love them freely,
to create space for our neighbour and the world will not fall apart; there
will still be enough grafters out there. We might be laughed at and even
insulted but those are tiny inconveniences compared with what Jesus
suffered for who he was. It is too easy for us to adopt a mid-way position
in our religion, somewhere between the Pharisees and Jesus; on the one
hand, they were extreme, on the other, Jesus is just too good to be true.
Yes, we know that God is love—it says so at the beginning of the Marriage
Service—but we have to temper love with judgment; we have to temper
mercy with justice; we have to be cruel to be kind; if we spare the rod
we will spoil the child. But the mistake we keep making is introducing
necessary civic measures, necessary simply because we are imperfect and
liable to do things which harm our neighbour, into the religious sphere.
Nobody doubts that we need policemen and judges but that does not

mean that God is a judge in command of a host of clerical policemen. Every time there is a prospect of a new openness to love, a sense of untidiness, or things "getting out of hand" we need our hammer to find the offending loose end and nail it down. There is a proverb which says "cleanliness is next to godliness" but I often think the more dangerous assumption is that "tidiness is next to godliness". All our major theological disputes are between the tidy and the powerful, on the one hand, and the approximate and not so powerful, on the other; and that is an interesting set of antitheses because Jesus was, in the world's terms, neither tidy nor powerful; and the saints who break open the idea of love and scatter new seed are suspected by the tidy and the powerful. Because we need patterns, we value tidiness; but there is surely something fundamentally untidy about love because it is permissive rather than assertive; if love is creating space in which others can operate freely, the last thing that we would want to do is to give the receiving space a sharply defined shape, for that would defeat the object of allowing freedom. Put another way, the major debates in the history of Christianity might be seen as conflicts between love and power. Love says: "I want to let Jesus into my heart"; but power says: "But to do that you need to have a set of characteristics which I will define for you."

It is no coincidence that the Cross is our logo; it is very sharp and very simple; but we have precisely inverted the brand values of the logo. The ultimate brand value of the Cross is human weakness, the vulnerability which is a necessary precondition for love. If there is any triumph in this it is a paradoxical triumph, the triumph of the non-triumphant, the victory of the anti-king. The metaphor we like to use is that in his Crucifixion, Jesus saved us from our sins but I would rather put it that he saved our capacity to love by showing that it was possible to love, no matter what odds there are against it; and that conflict of the capacity to love and the odds against it are both factors in each of us. This is not a war between the wicked and the loving; it is a war within ourselves. It is a war that is timeless. It afflicted and enhanced the Jews just as it afflicts and enhances us; and the reason why we need to be here today, I suspect, is that we know that if we had been there when Jesus lived that things would have turned out no different. We would have stuck to the ideology, voted for tidiness, been frightened of tomorrow, been over-faced or out-faced by the simple, living, non-judgmental person that told us to cast the first stone.

I think that that line of Jesus was his killer. There must have been two people taken in adultery but the man was let off and the woman was framed; and then the processes, built on centuries of misogyny and prejudice, were ridiculed by this man from Galilee. In the films of Frank Capra such heroism always won through; in the real world of Jesus it led to the nails which secured him to the Cross.

There is a widening of human flourishing which is made possible by the adventure of love, by the movement of the hand and the heart to open; in the essence of our imperfection it is not pattern seeking that is wrong—as I have said, it is necessary—but it is only the open mind, the open heart, that can see new patterns that broaden our understanding. Jesus was not denying the paradigm of Judaism, he simply wanted to put it into a wider context, into a new pattern; and we are surely called upon to do the same. It is time to put away the nails, to live, against our inclinations and convenience, with a great deal more untidiness; only then will there be the freedom in which each of us can find new ways to live, new ways to be more like Jesus.

## Prayer

Lord Jesus, it is only at this point of contact between the nails and your sacred hands and feet that we can bring ourselves to shudder at what we have done and what we have failed to do; when we, who were given free will, have become slaves to prejudice and ideology. May we learn from your love, generous and particular in its constancy, how we may love each other; and grant us the Grace to see ourselves as fellows in your suffering, as well as those who drove in the nails or watched them being driven in, so that we may be true creatures of our Creator. Amen.

## v. The Lance—The Turning Point

Does it matter if Jesus' bones are broken or his side pierced? After all, from the soldier's point of view, Jesus is dead or very nearly. Yet for us the pathos is overwhelming because the piercing recalls the Old Testament (Zechariah 12.10) and because the drops of blood and water pattern Baptism and the Eucharist. In one gesture we take in the history of Word and Sacrament.

"History" might sound like an odd word but the whole point of Christianity is that incarnation is part of our earthly history; we worship the Creator, the timeless God, but we worship the Jesus of history. This is why there are occasions, on the one hand, when the Old Testament can look unnervingly out of focus. "What," we might ask ourselves, "has all the regulation in Leviticus, Numbers and Deuteronomy got to do with us?" The answer is that the Old Testament is the record of the struggle of the Chosen People to come to terms with God the Creator with very little to go on. There is a deeply puzzling issue concerning the operation of the Holy Spirit prior to the Incarnation which can be partially solved by the idea that the Holy Spirit is, in essence, our incarnational perception, the aspect of God which allows us to understand the essence of Jesus.

On the other hand, there are occasions when the Old Testament is unnervingly prescient which explains the tendency of some to see its pronouncements as foretelling the future; "They looked upon him they pierced", the whole burden of Psalm 22 and passages from Jeremiah and Isaiah, bring us up short; these are, however, less startling if we see the life and mission of Jesus growing out of the Old Testament, of fulfilling its hope, rather than fulfilling its detailed specifications.

This is a moment in our salvation history which began when the world began but which was given particular, concrete form in the historical Incarnation of Jesus; and the more we look at this final scene, the more unlikely is this climax of a human life. If we were to write an account of a divine visitation to our planet it could hardly end like this. The soldier of an occupying power, in an act of perverse health and safety box-ticking, will not break the bones of the murdered divinity but will pierce the body with a lance; for nothing; for no-one. Yet, because of the echo of Zechariah and the Psalms, we are left with the sharpness of the whole narrative of struggle, of faithlessness, repentance, setback and liberation which comprises the Old Testament. The incident also sums up the story so far in the New Testament; the narratives of the Evangelists all describe the same trajectory from hope to despair; the history of Jesus Christ, God made man, is over.

But, of course, it is not over. The Sacramental life also has a history represented in the blood and water which issues from the still warm corpse of Jesus, the history of Baptism and the Eucharist; and here, again, we are not left to live through the history, we are living in the power of the Spirit who not only gives us incarnational perception but also the capacity, as humans, to behave sacramentally. There is a lively debate in Acts about the Holy Ghost in Baptism but there is something altogether more settled about the status of the Eucharist; our capacity to live in sustained sacramentality through time attests the Spirit.

The link we most easily make is between the Eucharist and the Crucifixion which we describe as one and the same sacrifice. How can we do this? There is the conventional explanation of sacramentality, that what we say and do, what we execute in word and in gesture, gives effect to the reality of what we are invoking. That clearly works in an understanding of the Institution of the Eucharist but could we properly understand that Eucharist without the Crucifixion? Could Jesus simply have said: "This is my body . . . This is my blood . . . given for you"? Well, to the extent that he is God, he could have said or done anything; but the point is that, without the Crucifixion, the meaning of the Sacrament would be obscure. Baptism we can almost intuitively understand, but the giving of a body in sacrifice makes no sense simply in the context of the Last Supper. The story of the Passion and death is searingly illustrative of the gift we are being given; that it is a gift given at extreme human cost; that it is, literally, priceless, that it is given in the teeth of the most outrageous human provocation not to give it. This is not simply a variant of the theme of sacrifice running through the Old Testament; as the Epistle to the Hebrews makes clear, this new dispensation is made in supreme love, over-riding all other considerations. There is a paradox in the language, of course, because love, being unlimited openness to possibility, does not actually conquer anything, but this love, if you like, clears away all the obstacles between God and us so that we live in the open space of love and apprehend it well enough to try to replicate the space in the way we deal with each other. This sacrifice is the only way we could know how unequivocally God loves us. The significance of the Cross is that it tells us that we can do nothing that will in any way inhibit God's unlimited love for us; that is the ultimate mystery and wonder of it, more wonderful, more embracing, more generous, than the mechanics of Penal substitution or of celestial accountancy.

The Eucharist tells us that the God who is with us, literally within us, cannot fail and that, therefore, we will not fail. The Crucifixion, considered simply as an ultimate confirmation of our fallenness, of our brokenness, could only say to us that we are helpless in the face of choice, that we are ciphers, that it simply put right what was wrong; but this is not reconcilable with the reality that we were created in love, to choose to love. We are broken, it is part of our condition; but in the brokenness of Jesus, in the bread and on the Cross, in the cup and in the blood and water, we experience the solidarity of our divine and human brother with us. For to say that we are recipients of the Grace of God is not enough; nor is there any grounds for saying that the Cross is a gift for the Elect. What the Cross says to us, in its historical starkness and in its sacramental beauty, is that we are all—every one, everyone who has ever lived—we are all partners in our own salvation. There is no point in pilgrims whose salvific faith is predetermined; there is no point in pilgrims who are either the passive recipients of Grace, or not; there is no point in a pilgrimage where stewards are in place to choose who may journey and who may not; such an arrangement would put the stewards in the place of God.

The key point is that the Eucharist is not a symbol of Grace, an esoteric metaphor, it is our food for the journey; and because we take this food, the very body and blood of God, in the full knowledge of the Passion and death, we are clear about what we are taking. We are clear about the pain and the loneliness, the sacrifice and the squalor, the promise of love and the utter hopelessness of ever living up to our aspirations.

But brokenness is our life's condition. The terrible heresy of those who believe in "the Fall" and the essential corruption of humanity, is that they presume to compare us with the perfect God instead of celebrating our createdness as seekers after God.

There is something deeply symbolic in the almost empty stage when Jesus dies and just afterwards. I like to think of the women standing nearby and the young Apostle John. I like to think of the soldiers, clearly in a hurry, who wanted everything to be over. It had been a hard and nerve-racking day. There had been a series of portents and strange happenings, the Roman and Jewish authorities had been very edgy; there was something preposterous in the use of the death penalty to deal with this lovely man. Now the women are quiet and the soldiers hurry away; and there is an empty space which is the ultimate symbol of love.

Which brings us back to the beginning of our meditations, to the thought that this broken body was broken in Sacrament and in human suffering, for us all. It is preposterous for us to presume to say for whom it was not broken; moreover, we can infer the precise opposite from the life and teaching of Jesus. This body was broken in Eucharist and on Calvary precisely for those who would appear, in human logic, to be beyond redemption.

But the thought goes further than this. The brokenness of Jesus is particularly congruent with the brokenness of the tortured and the exiled, the abused and the incomplete. Good Friday is the festival of brokenness, it is the affirmation of the incomplete; it is the day when pride falters, when language thins, when the comfortable orientation of human endeavour seems fragile. We are all weak; and so this day is for us; it speaks to the brotherhood of Jesus; how could we think we were anything but weak beside his weakness? He has come from the stable to this; from the manger to the Cross, from the straw to the thorn; it is the day of the weak, the day of the broken.

We shall understand this best if we understand our own brokenness and its necessity. Today is indeed the festival of our brokenness but it sits between the festival of our nourishment and the proclamation of universal salvation. To live on Good Friday is a microcosm of living in the pilgrim world, nourished for the journey but still in want of the ultimate prize, that Resurrection of the body or the proclamation of the kingdom here on earth.

The language thins into nothing, like a tune that has broken up on the wind and left a slight, shrill note behind. The light, which has been uncertain all through the day, hovers between its recently lurid renaissance after a period of unaccustomed darkness and the onset of night. We are living in a twilight zone between the promise and the realisation, between the hope and the fulfilment.

The light thins and the sound thins; the density of the Old Testament thins to this one moment of ultimate truth, the hinge on which all Word and Sacrament turns. We have now reached the point of ultimate simplicity, the fulcrum of history and divinity; we have finally reached a point of silence, the silence which better honours love than a torrent of words, the silence of love which speaks eloquently of how we have failed and how we cannot fail; of how we have chosen not to love but cannot fail to love; of how we have planned so many fences but how the Lord has torn them down. This death loves our brokenness and scorns the pride of our completeness. What we see when we look up at the Cross is a sacramental declaration by Jesus of human brokenness, grounded in the Word and alive until the end of time in the Eucharist.

**Prayer**

Lord Jesus, it is only at this point of contact between the soldier's lance and your sacred corpse that we can bring ourselves to shudder at what we have done to you and what you have done for us; give us the Grace to live in Word and Sacrament so that we may live holy lives in our imperfection. Amen.

# Epilogue

If the story of the Passion and death of Jesus is one of casual violence, torture, mockery and dogmatism, the Resurrection is a story of awesome power, affirmation, gentleness and particularity. We can become so preoccupied with the mystery of the presence of Jesus with us after his resurrection that we can easily overlook the simple things such as the conversations between Jesus, God's angels and humanity, the assurance

Jesus gives to his followers, the achingly affirming dialogue with Mary Magdalene and the discourse of the traveller on the road to Emmaus where what was Instituted at the Last Supper is confirmed at this first post-Resurrection breaking of the bread.

Viewed in the long perspective of the salvation history of the Old Testament and the Sacramental history of the New Testament and beyond, to our own day, the eight days from Palm Sunday to the "First day of the week" are so dense and dramatic that they can take on a disproportionate significance. They begin with the doomed Jesus riding into Jerusalem and end with the risen Jesus walking out of it; they are packed with resonances of the Prophets and the promise of Sacrament; and in a fuller way than Penal Substitution can articulate, timeless scores are settled. Because of the way that we are, it is the first half of the antitheses that tend to stick in our minds: the entry rather than the exit from Jerusalem; the man whom they pierced, not the Lord whose feet they embraced; the conquest of sin rather than the triumph of love. Important as is the Institution of the Eucharist at the Last Supper, the most important thing for us is its re-enactment in a post-Resurrection context. Easter is the celebration of the Lord's triumph over death and the triumph of love; but it is equally the celebration of our triumph over death and the triumph of our love; if it were not, what would it be for?

The story of Emmaus acts as a welcome counterbalance to the Apostolic kerfuffle first in Jerusalem, and later in Galilee. Its quiet coherence contrasts starkly with most of the other post-Resurrection incidents in the Gospels. We can think of the story as the pattern for our Christian lives: we are travelling; we are joined by Jesus but, in our earthly condition, we find it difficult to see him; we are instructed in word; we offer him hospitality; and he rewards us with Sacrament. There is much of the spirit of this story in Acts where there are references to the domestic faith of Dorcas, Cornelius, Lydia and to house churches; so when I use the word "triumph" I am thinking of the Christianity of Jesus not the triumph of the dogmatic Christianity of subsequent churches. As I write, as the world economy shudders, with unknown consequences for us all—but particularly for the poorest in our country and the poorest countries in the world—there is already a growing sense in some quarters of Christian triumphalism, that the wicked plutocrats have got what they deserved, that the age of greed and permissiveness is coming to an end. Well, unless the Holy Spirit has behaved in an unaccountably obscurantist way—which, of course, she is entitled to do—this terrible downfall is neither the result of our mission nor our virtue. Simply to say that we have been complicit, that we have enjoyed the dizzy rise in our own prosperity, not entirely regardless of, but neither entirely aware of, its cost to others, is an inadequate response. In thinking about the contemporary significance of the crown of thorns I suggest that we have been in pursuit of the prettiness of the thornless rose instead of admiring the natural and complex beauty of the rose protected by its thorns. Paradoxically, Christianity has found the twentieth century difficult simply because it was summer time and the living was easy. Today there are endless statistical comparisons between the current economic situation and this of 1929–31 but of course the statistics hide the immense difference between now and then and between that depression and its predecessor in the 1860s. The statistics might be superficially similar but there is no real comparison. If the current down-turn continues it is not triumphalism that we should concentrate on but compassion. Viewed from another perspective, the story of Holy Week begins in the Temple and ends in a private house.

# 6. Roads to Golgotha

*2011*

## i. Everyman

These rich people who walk round the Temple scowling at us poor people—hardly people at all to them—who can barely afford a pair of turtle doves, have no idea. They just don't understand. You would think that meat eating was an everyday occurrence.

What they don't understand is that life for the poor consists of two almost unbearably heavy yokes: daily manual work from dawn to dusk except on the Sabbath and Feast days; and the sheer tedium of life, only broken up by a birth, marriage or funeral. Of course you work in the hope that all the back-breaking, joint-grinding, skin-burning work will somehow make life more bearable, so that the second yoke gets lighter; but it never does. Or you could try it the other way round, taking your ease and hoping that, somehow, the family will get fed; but that doesn't work either.

Now some of you may think that I'm standing here on this Friday afternoon because I went for the second option and left everything behind; it just wasn't like that. I know when I first saw him that I wanted to stop work and let everything go hang but the temptation soon passed. I listened to him preaching from a boat moored just off shore and I thought I could listen to him forever but common sense soon prevailed; and that's how it might have stayed but for what happened when he came to our village a few days later.

You've never seen anything like it. There is this old bloke, Soli, who's a bit, well, yonderly, you know, a bit unusual; goes up and down the village making unpleasant remarks and unpleasant gestures but everybody knows what to expect, so you just have to get on with it. Well, Jeshua met Soli right at the edge of the village and took him by the arm and said: "You show me round. You know everything there is to know here, don't you?" And the old man, meek as a lamb, just nodded and walked down the street, pointing at houses and naming names. No, it was a bit more than that. He actually said nice things about people like: "The woman who lives alone in that house is very poor but she's very generous and she's helped me out more than once, even though I frighten her a bit"; and: "the family who live in that house behave really well but people look down on them because the woman doesn't come from round here so they think she's somehow tainted; but she always seems very nice to me."

By the time they got to the middle of the village they were at the front of an untidy procession of all those who lived in the West and people were rushing in from the other three quarters. It was partly the reputation of this Jeshua and also partly because of the way he'd calmed down Soli.

Then a mother with a new-born baby walked right up to him, even though she hadn't gone through the purification, right up to him and made as if to thrust the baby into his arms and he stood stock still, looking straight at her, and instead of doing anything drastic, she just put her left hand—yes, her left hand—on his shoulder while cradling the tiny baby in her right arm and she said: "You can cure him, can't you?" And he said: "Do you really think I can?" And she said: "Yes. Why not? He'll die if you don't save him." And Jeshua looked at her, didn't even touch the baby, and said: "Faith is a wonderful thing, a gift from my dad. The baby—what is his name, by the way?—will be fine." And she said: "Jacob." And he said: "Well, he may turn out to be a wrestler", and people laughed.

As you will have guessed by now, knowing what you know, a not very orderly queue was forming behind the woman and people were tugging at him this way and that begging him to visit people who were too sick to move. That's another thing rich people don't understand, with their Greek doctors and Egyptian wizards, they don't understand how easy it is to be struck down and die. If it isn't the stone in the grain that ruins our teeth it's the bad food in our stomach and the bad water and the skin diseases and the insect bites. I'm told that you can go to some parts of Jerusalem, the nice parts where there's a bit of breeze, and you can see hundreds of people and none of them sick; but not in our village. More or less everybody is more or less sick, so to have this man come in and clear it all up within an evening was just amazing.

I was all right. I didn't need curing of anything in particular; I got so carried away with the whole thing that I became the head steward, organising the queue and lifting the heaviest people—though God knows our village doesn't have heavy people like the ones you see at Jerusalem festivals—and bringing them to him. Then when that had all been sorted out Soli, who went on acting as his escort, took him to all the houses where there were people who couldn't be moved. By this time a couple of the leaders from the Synagogue started moaning about him touching unclean people but he just smiled and said: "Well, whatever they were before—and I never ask, you know—they're all clean now."

When he'd finished he went to the local tavern, not much of a place, really—not like the posh places you see in Jerusalem—and he sat right in the middle of a crowd of the worst people in the village, the ones who steal to get money to sit and drink instead of doing an honest day's work. They were like a hedge around him, keeping respectable people out, and he went along with it as if he'd had enough of cleaning everything up and just wanted to enjoy himself. There had been a lot of shouting and praising when he was doing his healing but this was now drowned out by laughing and singing. You would have thought that he knew that when somebody bought him a drink it was with stolen money but he just laughed at the jokes and sang the songs.

When the evening was just about blown out, he thanked his companions and said he was going for a bit of a walk up the hill and as he passed me he said: "You did a good job tonight. I'm sure we could use you. The wages aren't much, very basic really, but there will be a lot to see; and it will do you good, broaden your outlook. See that man over there? That's Simon. He's the leader of my gang and he'll show you the ropes."

So I introduced myself to Simon and said that I'd just nip home to sort things out; but Simon said I wasn't to worry because Jeshua wouldn't be leaving until he came down from the hill in the morning. At home it was easier than I'd feared because everybody was so lively and well and my dad said that with this new lease of life they'd manage the small holding all right and, anyway, it was rough justice if I followed the man who had made them all well.

During the next few months it went from wild to miraculous, to ecstatic. I'd only just got used to the healing when he started doing miracles with food; and I'd only just got used to that when there were rumours that he'd conjured up Moses and Elijah, which had blown away his inner circle. They were wonderful days but you could see that it wouldn't last. If you live in the kind of place I was brought up in you know that nothing good ever lasts. He said he had to do something really important in Jerusalem. Well, that's hardly a surprise. People think that the only place you can do anything important is in Jerusalem and its inhabitants think that nothing important happens anywhere else. Anyway, he said he had to go there and that times would get very tough.

It looked all right at first. We had decided to give him a bit of a lift as he came into Jerusalem by cheering and telling him how wonderful he was. The "Son of David" chant might have been a bit over the top but it had been a hard journey and it was nice to get to our final destination. Did I say "nice"? Well, it felt nice, but only for a couple of hours. I thought that the riot in the Temple when he pushed over some trestle tables and harried all the traders until they left was a bit of a lark but the authorities took a very dim view indeed. During the next few days there was a lot of verbal fencing, with some of the cleverest people trying to trap Jeshua, but he knew his Scripture too well for that and scored some very neat points; but he might have been better off losing the odd point because the more he won, the angrier they all got.

I was still acting as head porter, carrying people to him and watching them run home; but somehow the joy had gone out of it. I wasn't taking anything for granted—I don't think you could ever get tired of all the joy he brought; and you could never get tired of him; never—but in Jerusalem it all got so heavy and conspiratorial. You never knew who was hiding around a corner or behind a wall but you knew that somebody always was. Even booking the place for Passover involved some secret dealings which I was party to because I had to organise all the deliveries, including the lamb.

I was sorting out the waste disposal when Andrew ran past shouting, "Jeshua, he's been arrested by the Temple Police." I thought of running after him but decided it was best to tidy everything up; there was nothing I could do that his key followers couldn't do better, except for Peter who was always terrible in a crisis. He flapped every time something happened without proper warning. I found that right at the beginning when he couldn't handle unplanned departures and arrivals. He wanted everything to be straightforward and it never was, so I'd asked to be transferred to John, which was a bit bumpy in other ways because he and his brother had pretty strong tempers, but they just got on with things.

So I cleared up all the major items after the meal and was thinking of finding somebody who could tell me about the arrest when a couple of the outer circle arrived, looking terrible, and said that Jeshua had been betrayed by one of his chief officers, Judas, the Treasurer; and that he might even be put to death.

Well, I'm sorry to say—but peasants like me can't help it—when I'd heard the news I was very sad but I sat in a corner and fell asleep. It had been a long, hard day and I was sure he'd forgive me.

The next morning a couple more stragglers came in with the worst news of all, so I decided to see for myself. I've seen some gruesome things in my time—the Romans aren't squeamish by any means—but I wasn't prepared for what I was seeing now, looking across a filthy waste land to three crosses with Jeshua on the middle one. I can see most of his followers keeping their distance and there is a knot of officials, looking nervous and disgusted at the same time. The only people who seem to be comfortable are the soldiers who are playing dice and waiting for the end.

I don't want you to think that I'm cynical because I'm not. I worked for Jeshua happily and would have liked to go on working for him but I always knew that it wouldn't last. As I said, nothing good ever does. He made all kinds of promises but I knew they couldn't come true. I'll wait here because I'm loyal, because that's what I'm like, because I like to see a job finished properly, so I'll help his followers sort out and clear up; but I'm already thinking about what it will be like when I get home and start working on the land again.

The Jeshua story was a wonderful, dream-like interlude, but it wasn't real life.

## ii. Caiaphas

. . . I know; I know we don't have a legal leg to stand on; I know. But we've got to do something. We can't go on like this.

Yes, I know it was only one man that he brought back to life but we don't know where it will end. I said last week that, if necessary, one man would have to die for the people, and it's worse now than it was then. I mean, if he'd decided to revive some Galilean peasant—there's a rumour he did that in Nain—we might have managed but Lazarus cuts a bit of a dash, doesn't he, with his fine clothes and his grand house in Bethany? And so many people there when Jeshua brought him out of the tomb! And then there was the disgraceful disruption of Temple life which has cost us thousands of shekels; and then there was the insolent way he handled our questions. Too clever by half; and a Galilean!

Look, I'm not stupid! But I don't really take all that "Son of David" stuff very seriously. And on a donkey, too, what a jester. Made a complete fool of himself; but of course I said we were taking it seriously to put the wind up his followers. I know the difference between a serious rebel and a holy man; and this man is holy in a strange way; that's our problem.

You see, the real trouble is that we just don't know what will happen next . . .

The Romans! . . .

I know; I know we no longer have the power to put people to death. More's the pity so, yes, we will have to rely on the Romans but Pilate's frightened enough as it is after a whole series of bad calls on security matters. We only have to threaten to report him to Rome and he'll cave in. He never has understood the relationship between us and him; he has soldiers, we have rhetoric; but you would think it was the other way round, the way he caves in to pressure. So the plan is this:

We get one of his own people to hand him over; it looks better that way; and I think I've found a weak link in Judas: you know, the one who hands out the money to the poor. Well, I'm told by our security people that he's getting fed up with all the soft talk and wants some action from Jeshua and we'll tell him that he can have all the action he wants if we secure the person of Jeshua to spearhead our campaign for freedom.

. . . I know; I know there won't be any such campaign! What do you take me for? But Judas wants to believe that Jeshua has come to save us; and, in these circumstances, who is going to argue?

So we get Judas to hand him over; and we rough him up a bit to knock any gloss off that Galilean baby-face; and then we take him to Pilate and say that if he doesn't condemn Jeshua to death we'll use our Herodian channels to Tiberias. There's some sort of disgusting history between those two that you wouldn't want me to go into; but Pilate knows that we can get at Tiberias through Herod; and that's the main thing.

. . . Why are we going to such lengths to get rid of a peasant from up North? Look, I would have thought it was obvious, but let me just go over it again!

We have a deal with the Romans that they will leave us more or less alone as long as things stay quiet. All they want is safe roads to get their goods up from Egypt; and taxes. They don't mind a bit of brutality on our part as long as it doesn't challenge their monopoly on serious brutality. They don't like us and they don't like our law very much but they infinitely prefer our law to no law. They're not at all like the Greeks, you know. Greeks like all sorts of airy-fairy ideas but Romans just like no-nonsense law and, in a strange sort of way, that's what we give them; and that's what we're going to go on giving them.

But the problem with Jeshua is that he's now a widely admired figure, because of his undoubted healing powers, who is going around discrediting the law. He doesn't seem worried by adultery, if that scene with the woman we caught is anything to go by; and he actually said—you heard him say it last week—that he doesn't hold with our marriage laws which allow divorces; and he isn't keen, to say the least, on the Temple economy and the time-honoured sacrificial rituals; and the times he's broken the hygiene laws are countless. Ugh! All those beggars and peasants and prostitutes and lepers.

No, I don't think so. They're all very well in their way when the sun's out; but they won't put up any resistance by moonlight. They're fishermen, for goodness sake, except for a couple of them. Their chief, Simon, might lash out—I'm told by our people that he's a bit of a hot-head—but it won't amount to much.

And we have to hurry. Time is of the essence. We want all this cleared up before Passover.

. . . All right; all right! I know it's a bit flimsy—now you be careful; one of our people saw you sneaking out of the house he was staying in—but we're not really putting him on trial for the past; we're putting him on trial for the future.

How do you think we will survive? How do you think our ancient traditions will survive? How do you think that stability will survive, if we allow love to become more important than the law?

This man is on trial for loving; you just can't have order, civilisation, comfort, if this sort of thing runs wild. We need to know where we are; we need to know where we're going. You can't do that once love breaks out.

You never know what love might ask you to do.

This man is on trial for loving.

### iii. Peter

People get me wrong. It's been happening since I was three. It's the first thing I can clearly remember. We were playing a game and the rest of the boys kept on pushing Andrew out of the circle so, without thinking about it, I shoved the boys on either side of me to make room for him and one of them fell over and banged his head. I was punished for being aggressive.

Every time I make a spontaneous gesture I'm accused of being impetuous and even bad tempered. He wasn't like that—well, only once—which is why I wanted to follow him from the very first time I saw him. Some people say it was the miracle of the fish but I'd made up my mind before that. I just wanted a good catch to leave behind for the family so they would not mind so much if I left for a while. When the net almost broke we all laughed but it was still important to get the fish in. I might not be the world's most elegant talker but I do know how to fish; and he appreciated that. He said that I'd have to be a fisher of people and I liked that.

From the beginning he was clear that I was second in command. I thought this was a bit rash of him. After all, young John was much cleverer than me and James was much more passionate about it all; but he said that I was a rock, that I could be depended on. I can't see why he was so constant when I fell short so often. Still, he never told me off—except that once—and when I was impetuous he would laugh with me rather than at me. He had a way of slowing me down just a little when I was about to go over the top. He would say: "My dad and I know how anxious you are to please; you don't have to prove anything to us." But it wasn't a matter of proving anything. It wasn't showing off, or anything calculated like that; I just did things because it seemed to me that they needed doing.

But he couldn't mind me all of the time so I did get myself into a mess now and again. The first really embarrassing incident was when he seemed to be walking on the lake and he called out my name and, you've got it, without thinking I just jumped out of the boat to go to him. It was all right till I thought about it; and then I began to sink and had to get back to the boat before I went under. I know some people will think that I was a bit of an idiot but he just said how nice it was that I'd ventured out and how funny I looked trying to stay upright.

Those were the days, those days in Galilee, when he taught the people in between fishing to keep the family going. He was often quite difficult to fathom because of the way he said things; but we all loved him. We would do anything for him. And that was before the really big miracles started. It was wild enough when he turned the water into wine—he did like a glass of wine, unlike the holy men they tell you about in the synagogue—but when he started performing mass feedings we just couldn't believe it. He even held a major feeding event for Gentiles; but by then we were so awestruck that we couldn't argue, even if we wanted to. We thought, for the first time in our lives, that something good was never going to end. We should have known better. Nothing good ever lasts if you're poor.

It all changed when he started talking about going to Jerusalem. That was when we had our only real row, when I tried to stop him coming here and he told me not to tempt him; it was difficult enough, he said, facing up to what was going to happen to him, without his best friend trying to hold him back. You see, although he told me off it was softened by him calling me his best friend. He said he would have to come to Jerusalem and die; and that was it; and I would have to accept it, so I did. Well, almost.

It was all going so well, in spite of his gloomy prophesies, until a few hours ago. The arrival in Jerusalem went like clockwork and we put on a really good show. I wasn't sure about the bust-up with the Temple traders but it was only a bit of knock-about. Not like him at all; but he was under a lot of pressure.

After we arrived he was being hard pressed during the day with Pharisees, Sadducees, lawyers and officials trying to get him to say something silly or damning but, as you would expect, he kept his head; you should have seen their faces when he told them to be faithful to God and pay their taxes! The pressure might have been building up but he was on top form. And we got him off to Bethany every evening where he could get a good rest.

The arrangements for the big meal all went well, even though the owner of the building was a bit odd: I mean, when have you ever seen a man carrying a pitcher of water? Jeshua was still saying some ominous things but I must say I was getting used to the mood music. To be honest, we were all getting used to his rather gloomy moods. He didn't laugh so much as he did back in Galilee but who would hold that against him? Jerusalem is a grim place. My job, as I saw it, was to make sure he had everything he needed and I felt almost calm after the meal when we went to the olive grove. Something odd had been going on with Judas but I didn't take much notice as he was always a bit odd. I should have spotted something but I didn't. So we went to the olive grove after a really inspirational meal where he talked for a long time about going away; but we didn't really follow and his smile was so reassuring.

But something must have affected him when he was praying just a short distance from us because he came over to us a couple of times looking, well, distracted. The wine we'd all had at the meal didn't help and we were all a bit drowsy which meant that he looked a bit frightening when he came over to say that he felt something terrible was going to happen. And then it did. I blame myself for not being ready. I should have been more careful with the wine but he never commented on things like that. When Judas came with a bunch of Temple officials and guards all I could remember was my promise to defend him, so I lashed out. He looked at me and just said: "Come on now. There's no need for that. If I needed that kind of help my dad would see me right", which I should have remembered he would. So Jeshua fixed the servant's ear; and winked at me, as if to say: "We won't mention this again."

Before I could recover my composure, the guards were marching him off and the others had disappeared into the night. I blame myself for not organising things better. We should have had a contingency plan for this kind of situation. After all, the authorities had been making enough fuss but we all thought he would somehow sort everything out. He talked about dying because the prophets said that it had to be that way; but we still thought he would fix everything. Since the beginning I might have been some sort of organiser but he was really the one who was in control.

Anyway, I was just wondering what to do when the moon came from behind a cloud and I saw John loping off. He was the brightest so I thought I would be wise to stick with him. "What will they do?" I asked him when I caught up. "It's difficult to say," he said. "It could be anything from a bit of a ticking off for preaching in the Temple to as much as a flogging, just to get the point across. But the only way to find out is to follow him. They're taking him to the High Priest's house and I know someone there who will let us into the courtyard where we can wait to see what happens."

We hurried into the city centre and John got us admitted to the courtyard and we stood round a fire to keep warm. John had gone away to find out what was going on and I felt isolated and a bit threatened. The runners for the high officials were standing in a knot saying nasty things about Jeshua; they said he was a fraud, just a bumped-up peasant from Galilee. I was about to go over and put them straight when a servant girl, looking really frightened—she must have seen the threat in my face—asked if I was really one of the followers of Jeshua and to sooth her I just said: "No. Don't worry. I won't do anything rash." I was trying to stay calm, right out of character, but I really was. Then somebody else asked and to keep consistent I said the same thing. And again, the same thing. Then I heard a cock crow and I remembered what he said. I shouldn't have pretended I wasn't one of his followers. I should have allowed myself to be my usual self and let them have it; but in being too careful to do the right thing, I did the wrong thing.

Not that I've had much time to reflect. Since then it's gone from bad, to worse, to despair. When we heard that they had condemned Jeshua to crucifixion, we could hardly believe it. How could they condemn him just for some rather provocative preaching? John said he couldn't believe it, that they had broken the law; but what does that matter to powerful people from Jerusalem dealing with a humble preacher from Galilee?

As soon as we heard the news we all decided to go to Golgotha together, to support each other. And here we are. Desperate, helpless, trying not to cry. John and Mary have gone close because he seemed to want them for something; and I don't mind really. I am his best friend but John has his job to do as the record keeper.

I've seen enough violence in my time but nothing like this. I mean, you can see from the faces of the ones either side of him that they're a bit rough and probably deserve what's coming to them; but my Lord and Master? What has he done? He's challenged the authorities and he did say that really holy people and the authorities were always in conflict and that he'd be caught up in it. But crucifixion! You can hardly believe it. We're used to rough treatment but this is out of order.

I want to lash out again at some of the officials who are walking past, taking a sadistic look; but there are Roman soldiers over there and I just have to put up with it.

You might think that I am heartless because I'm thinking about what to do next. But you have to. There are scores of his followers, mostly from Galilee, and we have to keep together until we can make arrangements for going home. Apart from the fact that it's far too dangerous for us to stay here, it's also too expensive. Judas and his moneybag have both disappeared, so here we are.

Look, the only way I can love him is by doing something. I can't find nice words or make a speech. I can go on organising his followers until there's no more need for it; and then I will have to go back to fishing. I'll make sure, for his sake—that's what he would want me to do—that everybody is all right.

John and Mary are coming back and he's shouting something. I can't bear it. I will have to try and hear what he's saying. Poor Master; such nice hands for a builder, such a beautiful face covered in blood, such laughing eyes grown dull. He is looking at me now but he's stopped shouting. His breathing is heavy and slow. "It won't be long now, Master. You'll soon be back with your dad."

### iv. Mary

I suppose there must be a mother somewhere who rears and loves a child without pain; but I don't know one. I don't mean the kind of pain that comes and goes, like labour pain, but the chronic, nagging pain, the pain that reminds you that you love the child so much you can hardly bear it.

That's how I felt from the beginning, from the moment I knew that I was carrying a special child. Naturally there was a fuss when the word got out but I almost didn't care; the love pain had already set in and it has never left me since. I'm not complaining. It's the best kind of sensation you can ever have; it shows you how alive you are; but there are limits; and I'm reaching mine now.

I should have known from the start. The conception was unusual enough but it seemed natural at the time. When God asks, you say "yes".

Then there was the trip to see Elizabeth which was strange because she was also experiencing the strange ways of the Lord. As soon as I got through the door she was praising me to the highest heavens and I responded with my own sublime joy; but she deferred to me all the time which was extremely embarrassing; at least I was useful and it kept me out of harm's way while Joseph was calming everyone down in Nazareth. It was strange, too, how John turned out in the end, given that Elizabeth and Zechariah were so old-fashioned; at least my Jeshua had better manners than her John who was, I am sorry to say, noisy and scruffy.

When I got back from Elizabeth's, Joseph had calmed most people down but the joy of the remaining months of pregnancy were marred by family and supposed friends who couldn't resist a dig; but I was the only person who knew what had really happened to me, except for Joseph who couldn't feel it but who had had an extremely vivid dream about Jeshua.

It was almost time for me to give birth when we had to go on a stupid trip to Bethlehem to fulfil some kind of legal requirement; but in some ways it was better to give birth in a noisy inn, attended by strange women, than in the family home where they didn't know whether to be pleased or angry. By contrast, Jeshua had hardly been born when we were visited by a noisy gang of shepherds saying that angels had told them to come and worship Jeshua. It all sounded pretty improbable but by then I could believe anything. And then, after we had settled down nicely, we had a visit from what you might call a delegation of soothsayers who talked about planetary motions which aren't the kinds of things that good Jews are supposed to take any notice of. But they were very generous!

The incident that really settled everything was at his Presentation. The lovely old man said Jeshua was going to be a saviour but he also warned me that I would have a tough life, as if he knew something, although I did not need to be told. But it was Annah who left her mark when she said: "Whatever happens, never lose faith; it will all come right in the end. This isn't a silly old woman's optimism, it's the power of the Spirit that moved in you and is moving in me." I wonder what she would say now; and I can't quite set aside her promise, even now.

Jeshua was, on the whole, a good boy. I don't mean just in the usual way of toilet training and table manners, but in his infinite capacity for kindness and consideration; and then there were his practical jokes and his wonderful sense of humour. He wasn't perfect—not even a Messiah could be that—and sometimes he was impatient and he would speak out of turn when he wanted to right a wrong when he was too young to know how complicated the world is; but I suppose all young people suffer from that. At least he acted from the best of motives but he did get us into trouble with all the important people in Nazareth and so they never let us forget the "unusual" circumstances of his birth.

I thought he would leave home earlier than he did but he kept saying that his time had not yet come and we were grateful for what he brought in with so many mouths to feed; and he showed no real signs of getting married. Then, one day just after his 30th birthday, shortly after the winter rains had finished, he said he was going to live in Capernaum and do his father's work, by which he meant our heavenly Lord. It took some getting used to but who was I to quibble when Joseph took it so calmly.

It was all rather sudden but he soon came back, asking for help with domestic arrangements; and before long I found myself going backward and forward between Nazareth and Capernaum on a fairly regular basis. He could depend on Simon's family for most of what he needed, paid for in the usual way by people who welcomed his teaching, but he was so used to me being around that he couldn't really do without me; so I spent as much time with him as I could as he walked the length and breadth of the land preaching God's kingdom, healing people and performing amazing acts. I was overawed; I knew it was God's power within him; but I couldn't help it, I was so proud of him!

You might have thought that I became the chief organiser of the itinerant routine but I kept well out of the way. Simon managed all the heavy work and had a close working relationship with Zebedee's sons and mother. They were rather intemperate, but well meaning, and she was—how shall I put it?—a bit above herself but she meant well and worked hard. My job was to keep out of the daily round of tasks and squabbles so that I could be really useful when serious disagreements broke out, which they frequently did, over everything from the best route to take to the meaning of the law and the nature of the kingdom. Even for me, with my unusual background, it was difficult to become used to the fact that Jeshua's point of view was radically unorthodox, that he thought that much of the law was redundant and that, like the prophets, he thought that living a holy life was more important than living a law-observing life. That was what got him into such trouble. it didn't matter how much good he did, his opponents wouldn't stop nagging him about the law.

The thing that marked him out most was his absolute tolerance of disagreement. He didn't mind who said what; he never took it personally; he went on smiling—and even laughing in his nice way—and everybody was always friends at the end of it. He would be having a serious dispute with a Pharisee one minute and pouring him a drink the next. And he had such a huge stock of stories and jokes that he could always find the right thing to say in an awkward situation, although he also said a lot of things that we didn't fully understand.

What struck me most—as a mother, it would—was how happy he made people. Wherever he appeared there were big crowds and lively teaching sessions and, what the people really wanted, healings. I tried to keep some kind of score but I lost count, particularly as he did a lot of his healing quietly, when nobody was looking. It's typical of him that he started his mission, as he called it, overcoming the wine shortage at a wedding and ended his mission at a fellowship meal. In between there were all kinds of strange meals but he never noticed that anything was strange.

It was hard work but I loved the Galilee days. Then he said his fate lay in Jerusalem. I agreed with Peter that it was a bad idea to go to Jerusalem but, as usual, as was his right, he pleased himself. I had never liked it, but I came to hate the place after we lost him there, and I had found all sorts of good reasons to avoid the regular pilgrimages; but that was where he was going and I knew I would have to go with him.

As usual, I stayed well out of the way as he made his grand entry into Jerusalem and as the reports of events grew darker and darker. He was exhausted every evening when he came in; and although our hosts were always hospitable, after the Lazarus event things were always a bit highly charged and I had to cool things down and make sure that he had some home cooking as well as the posh Judean dishes.

Even I was surprised when he washed the feet of his followers before the Passover meal; but he was in a very strange, sombre mood that night and excited at the same time, as if he knew what was coming and he wanted to get on with it. As we cleared away he got involved in an immensely long discussion with his followers but at last they went out for a night prayer on the mountain—he loved praying at the tops of hills and mountains—and that is when everything went wrong.

I don't know all the ins and outs of what happened at the High Priest's house, or the Governor's, or Herod's town house—and they haven't really told me because they don't seem to know much themselves, except for John—but you would assume that Jeshua made some huge miscalculation but, then, he had been making some morbid statements on the way up to Jerusalem, so this looked like a self-fulfilling prophesy. I knew nothing until the final verdict and then I gathered the stragglers, the men who had run away, and we women shamed them into pulling themselves together so that we could see what happened and whether there was anything we could do. After all, powerful people can be capricious and they might have become suddenly lenient with the festival.

But, no. That is why I say that the pain has almost reached my limit. I know that he is suffering more pain than I am—and if he's like he usually is he will be suffering mine as well as his own—but I am suffering his as well as mine. I don't suppose I would mind so much if he had been rough and outspoken like dear John who had a horrible death (though at least it was quick and private) but Jeshua's way of being outspoken was usually so gentle and even humorous: that mouth that laughed and smiled, so stretched now, in pain; that beautiful calm brow, so wise and serene, raked by thorns; that lovely hair he was so proud of, matted with blood. The eyes so bright and lively, never still, always looking round to see what was happening, to see that everyone was all right. But the worst thing is the hands, oh the hands! The hands that touched so gently, the hands that healed, the hands that blessed, the hands through which all his love flowed, now broken.

There must be some limit to how much pain we can both take; but you never know your limit until you are challenged. If people told you as a teenager what you could put up with you would never believe them; and as he is being brave for me I must be brave for him.

Yes, John, we must go over to him; I can manage that now you are back.

Yes, my son, I know he will look after me. Yes. I will look after him too. Have you any other messages for us?

Oh God!

Haven't they done enough to disfigure him? Why would they want to break his precious bones? Please, although he is dead, treat him gently; he can do no harm now!

Just a drop of blood and a little water; and the end.

But I am still his mother; and he is still my son; and although the worst fate ever to befall a mother is to survive the death of her children; I must perform in the office of a mother.

O Annah! Annah! I still believe what you said. But it is so hard!

## v. Jeshua

Is this a big thing, or a small thing? Does it make any difference, or no difference on earth and in heaven? Is what is happening now the end of the old, or the triumph of the old? These are the questions I have always wanted my dad to answer but these are precisely the questions on which he's kept silence, up until now. I know he wants me to be where I am now. He knows I would never let him down; but I just wish I knew what it was all for!

It has always been difficult to sort out precisely what I know and what I don't know. My earthly father, saintly Joseph, managed to keep himself on an even keel by being self-contained and just getting on with things; but my mother told me the stories of my conception, birth and Presentation in the Temple. As a child she constantly reminded me that I was special. She said that ordinary synagogue attendance was not good enough; and she begged a local Pharisee to give me Scripture lessons. She reminded me to pray until I needed no reminding, until it was part of life's fabric. When I grew up my mother went on telling me I was special, particularly when I felt depressed by my inability to convince people that what I was saying and doing was critical to their lives.

All through my 20s I kept asking myself: "What is all this preparation for? I'll die before I do anything." I wanted to believe that I was a child of the Spirit but I would have to wait. So I waited.

Then my mother told me that cousin John, who had been living as a hermit since his Bar Mitzvah, had suddenly burst out of the wilderness and was storming around with the power of Elijah, in the clothes of Elisha. It was just too good to miss, so I went down to the Jordan to watch him perform; and it was at that moment that the Spirit came into me. John was telling people to repent but the Spirit in me knew that there had to be more to it than that, that people were created in such a way that it was in their nature to do good and it was denying their nature when they did wrong. I think John thought that doing wrong was natural. We didn't really argue about it because we had so much in common but it sometimes caused friction. I knew then, at the Jordan, that my mission had begun and that I would spend the rest of my life spreading the idea that God's children were made to love.

It wasn't easy. No sooner had I decided that I was a child of the Spirit than doubts set in. Was I really cut out to be a wandering preacher or did I want to be a great leader? Improbable questions, you might think; but it is so easy when you become involved in spiritual issues to suffer from delusions of grandeur.

When I got through the crisis I was ready for action but from the start I came up against the suffocation of rules and regulations; people, particularly my fellow Pharisees, thought that we were created by God simply to obey a complex set of often redundant rules. The rules had got in the way and, without wanting to be, I was cast in the role of a prophet in conflict with the establishment. This was sad because I was not hostile to the establishment; I just wanted to encourage it to put more emphasis on people being and doing good, going the extra mile. There is a role for regulation which helps people to develop self-restraint; but the trouble arises when people think that they do good simply by obeying the regulations, that they don't have to do anything else!

So what started out as a lovely, gentle mission by the lake began to assume a darker tone as it became clear that I couldn't talk about love without other people thinking that this was not a gift from God but a threat. I tried to keep it light, I pulled out all the stops, I exercised all the charm that I had learned from my mother and all the self-restraint I had learned from Joseph; but nothing was good enough. My plan was simply to preach, building on what John had started, by calling people to turn back to themselves, to their good nature, to their status as creatures, and to see each other as God's children. But it didn't take long to learn that preaching was never going to be enough; I had to tell stories and then I had to be in my own stories. It was never part of the plan to annoy people by eating with notorious sinners; it just turned out that way. I needed to show the respectable people that there was no such thing as a right to enter my dad's kingdom; and also that there was no such thing as a lost cause, that nobody could condemn anybody because only God knows what gifts people have been given and what hardships they face in using them. To show how God loved everyone I spent time with everyone but it wasn't political or provocative; they had simply left me with no alternative. They weren't bad people, just narrow and frightened; and, when you look at it, all the human evils of the world come down to fear, the inability to trust God enough to let God be and to let each other be. I never could get people to see, not even my closest followers, that it was vulnerability to god that counted, not handing out bread, unless that was, in itself, an expression of vulnerability, of emptying oneself out.

But this was such a revolutionary message, even though it was not supposed to trigger any political revolution, that it was hard for my poor followers to bear. All they could think of was showing and doing. It isn't surprising because the whole of the scriptures is about showing and doing; there's no sense of simply being there for other people. My mother understood because she saw that love was as much a matter of acceptance as assertion. But Simon and the rest thought that our success could only be measured in miracles and followers.

I was trying to be rather than to do which I suppose is why we found ourselves on the journey to Jerusalem. I didn't plan to end up crucified but events took on their own shape, their own inevitability, and all the time I could feel the Spirit within me. I knew, in a way, that I couldn't articulate that when I died the Spirit would leave me and somehow inhabit all my followers. So I wasn't quite swept along but I was pulled along; and it didn't matter what Simon and the others said, there was no stopping it.

That is why there was no way of setting aside the big question of what this was all for. Was it my dad's call to me simply to lead a good, generous and holy life or was there more to it? I frequently found myself saying things which sounded more important than I meant them to be. I would be talking quite normally and then my speech would turn grave and I would find myself quoting the Scriptures as if they were about me. It was confusing for my listeners and I tried my best to explain; but people had such a narrow, old-fashioned view of God that it was difficult to build a new, a more generous and gentle picture.

Then there was the healing. There is a strong tradition of travelling preachers and healers in Galilee but what happened through me was spectacular compared with them. At first I was embarrassed by it and had to get away to calm down and put things into perspective—delusions of grandeur again!—but the spirit within me kept saying that I just had to trust the moment and be obedient to God's will. Healing was part of my emptying out of God's goodness into the world, as was the case with the other, more spectacular events such as the mass feedings. They took on a life of their own and I just had to let things happen, as another kind of emptying out.

It was when I was praying alone at night, alone with my dad, that the questions were most acute and also when I got closest to answers. What was I here for? How special is special? We are all children of God but am I a child of God in a different way? Every time I went home there were reminders of my conception; every time I went to Bethlehem there were memories of my birth in the inn; and every time I went to Jerusalem my mother would remind me of Simeon and Annah. All I wanted to do was to lead a good life and be useful; but the pressures, from inside me and outside me, were for me to be more than that.

Matters came to a head yesterday. There was something very special about our final meal. I was filled with the absolute conviction that I was a special Son of God and that what I stood for, the emptying out of myself in love, would live on through my followers. I wanted to leave them something of myself, not just until the mist cleared and they saw what my life was all about, but forever.

I was still feeling this immense power for now and for the future when I was arrested. That is why the trials, when they came, were so futile. I didn't know myself whether I was a kind of spiritual king. I knew I was a leader of a modest band of followers; and I felt the Spirit's presence very strongly within me, which is why I found myself, well, speaking on his behalf. I caught myself saying that my kingdom was not of this world; and then wondered what I meant by "kingdom". If the idea was to change the way people live, I have made a very small dent, a few small victories for love.

As I stood in front of these important people, it was difficult to understand what it was all about. Granted, I did go a bit far when they tried to catch me out over the woman accused of adultery—men always get defensive about adultery—and the nice little trap about obligations to Caesar; and I probably should have preached to the traders in the Temple rather than getting angry; but they were relatively small things. I know the Romans kill for minor offences but there's a terrible irony in the adherents to the Jewish law breaking their own law to kill me, who called that law into question.

There is no place for irony now. It won't be long before the pain overwhelms me.

And I still don't know; and I might never know. Is obedience to my dad enough? Is that what it's all about? Is emptying yourself into a state of as utter humility as you can manage, enough?

I am being killed for love. It's too much for these poor people to bear, all that love. They say they want it but it's too embarrassing because they are frightened that they can't return it and they become overwhelmed. I am also being killed for love because my death will show that there is nothing that humanity can do, even killing me, which will impair my love.

Yes. I forgive you. And you can stand for all the other people, seen and unseen, whom my father will forgive because they don't know what they are doing. Yes. I will never leave you. From today you will always be with me. Oh, and I forgive you too, even if you don't want to be forgiven.

Mother! I wish I could spare you. John will look after you until we are re-united. It won't be long, I promise.

Dad! Why have you gone away? Why aren't you here now when I need you most? I know it's almost over; but I'm so lonely.

Oh, yes. I should have seen it, shouldn't I? It's only in complete vulnerability, in complete emptiness that we truly give.

I've done it!

Yes. I can see now that my life really was important and that I will make a difference.

I am empty.


## vi. Everyman

What do you mean, I shouted insults at him? Well, yes, I suppose I did! But you can't be too careful these days. It doesn't do to stand out from the crowd. It's bad for trade and it can be dangerous. People don't want to be associated with outsiders.

Yes, Yes! I know I was there when he came into Jerusalem but I got a bit carried away and probably said some things that are better forgotten, about him being a king. But you didn't see any of his miracles, did you? I was there at the beginning so I know what I'm talking about; but there's so much trouble these days. You have to be really careful. There are Roman rules and our own law and ingrained working practices, and tribal traditions and family customs and going against any of these gets you into trouble so there's an awful lot of trouble to stay out of.

Jeshua? Well, don't be stupid! Of course he was a good man. I didn't say he wasn't, did I? I mean you can't say that healers aren't good people. He did a lot of good and he was an engaging teacher. But he got carried away. He started to ask for too much, from the people, from the religious authorities, from the politicians. You can't go round, even if you're a healer, waving goodness in people's face; they don't like it.

Yes, yes, I keep on telling you that I thought he was good. How many times do I have to say it? But he went too far. He was upsetting people. And if you're an ordinary man, like he was—and from Galilee—you can't go round upsetting people.

True, true. It would be very nice if there was some kind of reform of the law; but it's impossible. You can't change the law of Moses no matter how holy you are; that's why holy people get unpopular; they want to put themselves above the law; and you can't do that. It might be a bit onerous but at least you know where you are. Jeshua seemed to want an impossible degree of goodness. Well, we're only human.

Yes, I know, I was with him for a long time; that's why I know what he was all about; but it's not sensible to be linked with somebody who's been executed as a criminal. I've got the family to think about. I am going to need a new job.

They were good days. But all good things come to an end.

Yes, I can see his mother and his close followers standing together over there. I wonder what they will do?

## vii. Cleopas

Downhill. It's all downhill from now on. Down from Golgotha, down from the tomb, down from the upper room, down from the city to the country. It was a struggle going the other way, up the hill from the country to the city, to the upper room, to Golgotha and the tomb; but this is much worse.

There was so much hope, so much promise, we hardly dared to believe in it. As we got higher, nearer to the city, he said that we must fear for the worst but, like the best of climbs, the end would be glorious, giving us a new outlook over the troubled world. We didn't know precisely what he meant; but he always kept his promises, always. You expect really holy people to be just a little obscure; they see things we can't see and it isn't always easy to find the words to make the connection between their way of seeing and ours. And because he always kept his promises, we must have misunderstood.

There's no need to go over the events of that terrible night and day again.

Shalom. Good afternoon. We're not very good company but please walk with us.

No, it's not having to go back to work or trouble at home, although both those things are realities to be faced—and we've been away for quite a long time—it's more profound than that, connected with the dreadful events in Jerusalem.

Surely you know? You must be the only person who doesn't. Never mind; I didn't mean to be sharp. Forgive us if we're tense. It's just that we have spent the last year following a wonderful teacher and healer, Jeshua. We think he said he was the Messiah but, in any case, he preached a message of love, he healed the sick, he brought joy to everyone he met except the religious authorities; and that was the problem. Somehow his goodness came into conflict with their interests—we don't know why it couldn't be sorted out—and he was falsely accused of blasphemy and—not to put too fine a point on it—judicially murdered by the Romans on behalf of the High Priest and the religious authorities. Crucified like a common criminal. Our hopes were buried with him. But—and here's the last of it—there are now rumours that the tomb we put him in is empty and it can't have been a robbery because his grave clothes were still there and only the body had gone. We were determined to go home and make a new start—but then this—and we can't make the new start.

Perhaps he was the new start? Well, that's what he said he was. But it's all over now.

Yes, if it helps. You can tell us the sequence and if you leave something out we can put it in. As you say, you are a Rabbi and we need some help. I will repeat what you say, in a summary, so that we are clear.

At the creation, Adam and Eve couldn't cope with the perfection of the Garden of Eden, so they ate of the tree of the knowledge of good and evil and their eyes were opened to the reality of human imperfection. The Holy One chose Abraham to be the Father of Israel; his people were enslaved in Egypt but he liberated us; and gave us the law as a covenant between him and us that we would never abandon us. But we went on abandoning him in spite of our promise.

Yes, except for what you say about imperfection, that is reasonably straightforward.

All right, yes, we'll leave out the Judges and the Kings if you say they really don't matter.

The prophets were important but looked at from this distance it's difficult to work out all they have to say; so much of it is bound up with politics and the exile. But you're right. It didn't matter what we did, YHWH stuck with us; and when we turned back to him he never let us down.

We're sorry. We are doing our best but it's difficult to see a narrative thread except for faithfulness and unfaithfulness and you are right to say that there are hints of better times, what we call the Messiah and Jeshua, well, hinted that he was the Messiah but it's a strange sort of saviour that is condemned to death and crucified.

We are only too happy to try . . . Isaiah, yes, the greatest of the prophets . . . The "Suffering servant? . . . the Psalms . . . like a lamb to the slaughter . . . casting lots for garments . . . Yes, we surely believe that YHWH speaks through the Scriptures . . . so YHWH was speaking to us through the Prophets and the Psalms about Jeshua! So what happens next? It can't end there, can it? I mean, if what you say is true there has to be a better ending. Something has to happen to reverse the terrible Crucifixion . . . Well, he did say something about sending the Holy Spirit to make everything clear.

I'm sorry to say, in the turmoil and despair after his terrible suffering and ignominious death, for which we blame ourselves in a way we can't quite reduce to good sense, we rather overlooked that.

Well, that makes us feel a little better but it's not on that account that we would like you to stay with us. The sun is going down and, really, you would be doing us a favour if you would stay the night with us. It will be nice to entertain someone in our home which has been desolate for so long. It's never nice returning to an empty house, is it? There's always something a bit damp about a long-deserted house, though of course we'll make everything comfortable for you. My companion will buy some grain, oil, milk, a few vegetables; they're very good round here, as you probably know. As you're a guest, we will have a little wine. There's no wine like that which grows round Emmaus.

It's a little damp, as I said, but I will build a nice fire to cheer us up and we can make some bread, you know, with the quick recipe as we don't want to keep you waiting.

As our guest we would like you to say the Grace. And here's the bread, still hot.

It's you! Master! Our Lord and our Messiah!

Gone! Look, don't you see, it's what you don't see that matters. He was here and now he's not here. It's only a heavenly being, like an angel, that can come and go like that. But it wasn't an angel, it was Jeshua! He is gone, yes, but he's here with us in the bread that he broke. That's the point. He said at the big meal that he would always be with us; just as he explained today that YHWH had promised that he would always be with us. YHWH with us, Jeshua with us and he promised something else, remember, that the Spirit would always be with us. YHWH, Jeshua and the Spirit.

Yes, we must; we must! Of course we must. Put some oil on the rest of the bread and we'll eat it on the way up.

I know it's dark but we know this road like the backs of our hands. And it's safe. The Romans are at least good for something.

Up the hill, up the hill. Climbing from the country towards the city, towards the upper room. Climbing towards glory.

Open the door! Open the door! We have seen him! We knew him in the breaking of the bread! Christ is risen! Alleluia!

# 7. Dramatis Personae

*2012*

## i. Palm Sunday

He thought he knew what was going to happen. As he came to Jerusalem driven by the Scriptures or God or political inevitability, there was every chance that he would be arrested and even executed. He was not a proud man but he grimaced wryly at the situation in which he found himself. This was a hollow triumph; and not even his poor followers could see it although he had warned them so many times.

He was riding on a donkey through a crowd on the verge of hysteria. They were shouting "Hosannah!"—"save you"—but he knew that he could not save them from the Romans and that they did not want to be saved from themselves. Everything was a blur. He hadn't slept properly for days and all he wanted was to be in Bethany, praying and getting ready for his ordeal; if there was to be an ordeal. He wasn't certain, but he thought that he would prefer knowing to not knowing. The Temple hierarchy might fly off in any direction. You never knew. One day they were ganging up with the official Roman party, traitors to everything they stood for, and the next day they were trying to ally with him in the hope of increasing their popularity.

So much of life was a matter of self-control, of saying the right thing or at least not saying the wrong thing, of saying a little prayer before pronouncing. As he became more popular they listened ever more carefully to what he said: the people wanted comfort, the priests wanted slip-ups, and the spies wanted evidence. Now he was exercising painfully taxing restraint: he wanted to slip down a side turning, dismount and melt away; but it wasn't to be. He wanted to remonstrate with the crowds who were almost out of control; but there was nothing he could have said, even if they could have heard him, even if they would have listened if they could. As with many situations on the verge of chaos, it would be worse to stop than to go on. In a strange way he was riding this donkey to save the Temple hierarchy from a complete disaster.

He had never wanted a triumph but neither had he ever wanted to ride in a sham triumph. It was like being sober at a party where everybody was drunk; but in his own way he was drunk too. He was giddy, almost out of control even of this docile young animal. He was holding on out of desperation.

The donkey was now following the route that criminals took to crucifixion. He wondered whether they would have the nerve to do it; whether they would be driven by their own need to be seen to exercise control, to haul him in for questioning; and whether they would bring themselves to make a deal with the Romans to execute a Jew known for his knowledge of the law, his healing and his holiness. And he wondered whether, if he was condemned, the crowd would be so fickle as to support the Roman execution of a Jew.

The donkey was tiring as Herod's great Temple came into view. He would teach there until they took him. His earthly fate was out of his hands. He was being drawn to where all prophets were drawn, to the place which represented everything that was good and bad about religion, the place of the proud and the humble, the priest and the publican. He did not know what would happen but God knew; and that was enough; or, rather, it would be if he could only find a little peace and quiet to pray, to get away from this religious circus and be alone with his Father.

## ii. Monday in Holy Week

She seemed to be the only one who knew he was going to die. She had known it from the moment she had set her wild eyes on him, even before he cured her of her multiple demons. He had cured her because he knew every one of the demons that racked her. They were not, as people supposed, evil spirits driving her to wickedness, they were powers of perception which allowed her to see so clearly that the workings of the inner selves of others drove her mad. Then she saw him whose inner self was the most wonderful thing she had ever seen; perfectly pure.

As she felt his calmness infuse her, she could see right into him where the light shone; and within the calm there was a cold spot that grew as the days went by. She knew he was frightened but he kept his self-control.

Of course she loved him. It had been impossible not to; not just in the manner of a grateful sufferer whose life had been saved, nor even solely in the way of a disciple. She loved him as a woman loves a man and that had caused toxic friction among his followers even though he made it clear that he could not accept her love at present, that there were more important matters on his mind; which she knew there were. But as he was going to die she wanted to be united with him if only for a moment before he was taken away.

So she took all her savings and bought the ointment. She would never need to bring anything to a marriage settlement. As the risen Lazarus looked on placidly, she opened the jar. And as her sister's face turned from irritation to horror as the room filled with a sweet odour that overcame the smell of the cooking, she knelt before him and then slowly stretched out her hands and bent her face towards his feet. The anointing—well, it wasn't as ritualistic and graceful as she would have liked—had to be hurried; she needed to finish before their passivity turned to outrage.

If only. If only things could be different. If only he would relax a bit more and enjoy himself. She wished he was not always so intense, always in such a hurry. Yet, in the intensity, he noticed her. He noticed everybody. For him everybody was special and that is what she could not handle. She knew her weakness. She wanted to be especially special.

For a brief instant she was able to wash him with her tears and embrace him with her body. She knew it would cause trouble but one moment of bliss with him was worth a lifetime of recrimination. He was so nice about it; and so gently truthful. She was preparing him for his burial. But only the two of them seemed to know it.

### iii. Tuesday in Holy Week

He was overworked, grumpy and alienated. He didn't like Jerusalem and he certainly didn't like being pestered by foreigners.

"Beware Greeks bearing gifts," he muttered to himself. He knew it was a cheap shot but they were a tricky lot. Stay-at-home Jews—even Greek Jews—might not be perfect but the ones who came in for the festival were never satisfied. They went through the rituals but their fancy clothes and jaunty steps spoke of a different agenda.

Now a group of them were hemming him in, asking for a special audience with Jesus as if he was some sort of magician. He had no alternative if he wanted to escape, so he went through the motions with Andrew but he knew that Jesus had too many other things on his mind: ever since his Hosanna entry the factions had been competing with each other to trap Jesus; and he could feel them closing in. "If they can't get him fair and square," he thought, "then will find some excuse to seize him."

He still couldn't work it out. He knew that Jesus had been a bit short with him over the feeding of the crowd but his beloved leader had never hurt anyone and his healings were countless. Why would they want to put somebody in prison for doing good?

Stay-at-home Jews weren't perfect: "and if we have a fault," he admitted to himself, "it is that we don't give people the benefit of the doubt. It's as if we want to catch people breaking the law; and I suppose that Jesus has been guilty of some technical breaches; but the people who were cured won't care about that. Although they won't be grateful either."

There he was now, talking about himself as the source of new life, about being raised up. Perhaps the main reason Jesus was becoming unpopular had nothing to do with the law. Perhaps it was just that a rigid system didn't have the capacity to handle generosity. Jesus was overflowing everywhere and there wasn't enough capacity to contain it.

Philip saw the Greeks smirking but most people couldn't get enough of him. It was obvious if you looked objectively why the Temple hierarchy were rattled. They never commanded the kind of attention Jesus got and everyone knew why. They were too interested in outward show. Jesus accused them of being hypocrites which didn't go down well; but it was the story about the vineyard that would do for him; that and the Hosanna demonstration.

How could people be so ungrateful? There was hardly anyone in that crowd born in the province who hadn't benefited from Jesus through the cure of a relative or friend, or through hearing first-hand or by word of mouth some of his beautiful and powerful teaching.

"Beware Jesus bearing gifts!" It didn't sound quite right.

## iv. Wednesday in Holy Week

He felt hot and cold at the same time. He wanted to get it over with but he could feel himself holding back. They were keeping him waiting on purpose, to test his metal but every moment they kept him he came closer to bolting. He couldn't stand delay. They would have to get on with it.

That was the trouble with Jesus. That was why he was here now. Delay was dangerous. Either Jesus should put up or shut up instead of which he dithered. One day he was riding triumphantly into Jerusalem frightening the authorities and the next day he was using clever-clever devices to fend them off. Somebody had said that Caiaphas was prepared to sacrifice Jesus for a period of peace and quiet, to get the Romans off his back, and that was what had finally prompted Judas to request a meeting.

Right from the beginning Jesus had all the attributes of a Messiah priest-king but when push came to shove he'd bottled it. Either he should have gone in for the holy man bit or he should have made his move, but instead he went one way and then the other and he didn't seem to recognise the instability he was creating.

A flunkey ushered him in to the High Priest's office. There were three of them, Caiaphas, the Treasurer and a security guard. The first two ignored him and the third got between him and the archway. "So you've come to shop Jesus?" What a stupid opening. It was as if they resented his coming, as if they were doing him a favour rather than the other way round. These people were so habitually, professionally rude that they didn't notice it. Jesus had been right about that, as he had been about so many things; but being right wasn't enough to save him; and their rudeness wasn't enough to stop him. "I have come to assist you in securing the safety of our people and your authority," he said, stiffly. "I love Jesus and in safer times he would be a luxury that we could afford but these aren't safe times. Pilate is sailing too close to the wind and it's only a matter of time before Tiberias dumps him." "Thank you. I didn't ask you here so that you could lecture me on politics. What do you want?" "I want what you want," he said, as unsure inside as his speech was sure.

"How much?" asked the Treasurer. "Nothing," he said. "I don't need any money." "Lucky you!" said the Treasurer, looking relieved. "Never mind all that," said Caiaphas. "We are not going to issue a contract so we must give him something or he will go back on his word later and deny it all. They're like that."

Still the same superciliousness. He almost didn't take the money but thought he would find a good use for it. The poor were always with us. They would arrest Jesus and he would have to testify to support a minor charge of sedition. They could safely let him out after Pentecost. It was an unpleasant business. The better of two evils.

## v. Maundy Thursday

He was the least of the Apostles. He would never go down in history because he never said anything and although he did a great deal it was all routine fetching and carrying, a man of food and drink, wood and water.

But things had happened tonight that he would never forget, which were worth all the work. He had been completely taken by surprise when

Jesus came to him first with the bowl of water: "You've been pounding up and down all afternoon carrying supplies for this evening, moving furniture, borrowing cooking pots. Here, give me those sore-looking feet of yours", so he did. He always did exactly what Jesus said. Jesus took his time. Even when he was in a hurry he seemed to take his time. It was like a soldier walking, in a hurry but unhurried. It was as if Jesus knew how to make time. The herb-infused water was lovely. He sat barefoot for the sheer pleasure of it but when Jesus came to Peter he left to bet on with his work, to avoid the scene. He hated that sort of thing. He liked the quietness of Jesus. He enjoyed it most when they were together, usually early in the morning, when he was getting ready for the day and Jesus sat quietly, cross-legged, watching the sunrise.

Then there was the meal which had taken on a mysterious and ominous significance. Jesus had been very emphatic about what they had to do in the future as if he was going away, there and then. The usual, unrestrained joy of the Passover had been somehow dampened. Unusual, that, as Jesus had such a sense of humour and loved the big occasion. Tonight he had been almost solemn, especially when Judas had nipped out on an errand. Peter was a bit jumpy but he should have known better. Judas just couldn't sit still, even at meal times. Jesus had said something about giving his body to be broken and his blood to be poured; they were to think of him as eternal food; he would bring everlasting life. He didn't understand but if that's what Jesus said then no matter how difficult it was to comprehend, that is what Jesus meant. They had all sworn to stay with him no matter what happened. Whatever did they expect? People got too worked up around the time of Passover. It would soon be over and they could get back to normal in Galilee.

In spite of the shadows and the puzzling words, something mysterious and grand had happened. He knew that Jesus planted seeds and that there would be a right time for them to flourish. The things he said would come true. Jesus seemed to be saying that once he had left them they would go on celebrating him, as well as the Passover, through sharing his life in bread and wine and that this practice would spread all over the world. He didn't see why it should but if that is what Jesus said then that is what would happen.

He had worked up a sweat during the clearing up. It was nice to be out in the cool, walking towards their favourite olive grove.

## vi. Good Friday Morning

It was preposterous. But these people were. It was just so uncivilised to take religion seriously. If you made Tiberias a god you were saying farewell to religion and a good thing too. Rome was built on solid, engineering principles, but out here it was all fanatical Jews and slippery Greeks.

It was preposterous that he had to step outside his residence to talk to them because they had the arrogance to declare that his house was unfit for them, "polluted", they said. They had followed the form and sent him a formal petition about this Jesus of Galilee and if he didn't act immediately the whole affair would have to be held over until after their ridiculous lamb slaughtering and there was something about this festival of theirs that made them mad. He knew the Moses story; but he also knew that the Romans wouldn't be as soft as the Egyptians.

There they were, with their peculiar way of shouting quietly. They wanted him to sign the death warrant and he knew, in the end, that he would; but they needed to know it was his decision. Then there was his wife telling him to be careful. It was a pity she didn't have better things to worry about but the social life here was so dull. He would have to see the prisoner.

He thought at first that the man was a simpleton but he realised that that was just his prejudice. He was going on appearances and that was never safe. The Jews had made quite a mess of him; strange how religious people could become so violent. The crown was a good touch, though; that must have been his own little Praetorian Guard. But anybody who could bear themselves as he did after so much ill-usage must be a bit special; it wasn't a simpleton's face; it was an old man's expression on a young man's face, a face of what the Greeks called wisdom!

He found himself shuttling in and out of the hall-way, defending the accused to the Jews. He was being sucked in. He was making a fool of himself. If he wasn't careful he would be ridiculed as well as hated and that was much worse. Anyway, this Jeshua said that his kingdom was not of this world and, given his reception when he was led out, it was as well that his hopes of kingship lay elsewhere.

He drew himself up and, trying to look as tall and decisive as possible, he passed the formal sentence. They weren't grateful. They observed the minimum courtesy to avoid being prosecuted for insulting the Emperor. He could see why the priests wanted this man killed but why would the mob applaud the execution of one of their own by the hated Romans? It was a nasty, though trivial, business and he just wanted to get back inside away from the noise and smell. He didn't want to catch the prisoner's eye but he was drawn in; and the man said: "I forgive you." Not at all Roman; but charming in its way.

## vii. Good Friday Afternoon

She was the other Mary. She didn't mind that: of course his mother came first; and she knew that she could not compete with the beauty and charisma of the sister of Lazarus. But she had been there from the start and she wouldn't leave until it was over, which it almost was. Jesus, thank God, did not have long to live; he was going faster than they usually did, according to what she had heard.

There were all kinds of things that she should have been doing or thinking: she should have been crying, for a start, but she would not give "them" the pleasure. She should have been holding things together, persuading the men to come nearer, but this was no time for scolding—they either would or they wouldn't; and she should have been thinking what to do next which was her job, that's what they relied on her for, but there wasn't a next. She should have been thinking back with wonder at all the healing and teaching but her memory was numb with the horror of where she was.

His mother came back from the Cross with John and stood next to her. They said nothing. The talking was over; and the dying was almost over, thank God. Killing somebody for doing good was bad enough but calculating how to cause the most pain was barbaric. If the Romans were civilised, she didn't want civilisation. He had been the personification of a love she could not have imagined, lived out at every moment, in every glance, in every gesture, in every word: he smiled; he touched; he hugged. He never asked questions about status; he didn't have any idea about clean and unclean. People were all the same to him. The holy man who never judged had been judged by men who called themselves holy.

It was one more setback in a life of struggle and disappointment but this was the worst. She could not imagine anything worse. It wasn't the injustice, it wasn't the barbarity, it wasn't even her own loss; it was the thought that even love personified, lived out, witnessed, could not triumph over the forces of calculation and cynicism. He was the only person who had made the triumph of love glow within her, like the growth of a baby in the womb. At first it was only real to her but he had persuaded—no, he had exampled—her to believe that new love would be born in the world and that it would spread out like a light from its heartland in Jerusalem to Jews and Gentiles all over the world.

But there he was. A last cry and, mercifully, dead while those who flanked him still twitched. But that light of Jerusalem had gone out. It was completely dark: in her heart and all over the city. The way she felt, there would never be light again.

## viii. Easter Vigil

Another Passover gone; well, the main event anyway. Back to work to pay off the debts. The prices they charged at festivals were ridiculous; and it wasn't much of a lamb. But they had you where they wanted you. He kicked the ground petulantly but then remembered it was his friend, it was what gave him his living. It wasn't much of a job but burial sites provided steady work.

He put his lantern down. He didn't need it any more. It was still dark but he knew every rock and every bush. He had thought of keeping the

light because there was a new body in that new tomb but he wasn't going
to allow it to worry him. Graveyards were his business. He didn't know
what it was all about, the Temple and the Romans were always squabbling
and that poor innocent man had somehow got himself mixed up in it. He
went towards the place, slowly, almost creeping, saying a garbled prayer
as he went. The Pharisees said that we would all be raised up at the end
of time but all he could think of was Sheol, the end of everything, the
body in its new linen sheets already rotting.

The thin layer of grey on the horizon showed a tinge of pink and it
warmed him. He never ceased to wonder at the way the light changed,
the way that the sun seemed suddenly to spring from nowhere. His mind
began to wander, as he looked eastwards, watching the light. He saw two
figures, white, sharp against the red-brown rock. He took a step towards
them to ask what they were doing on private land but their assurance
daunted him. He stood, rooted, not knowing whether to advance or
retreat. Out of tranquillity there was a roaring sound, like a storm out of
nowhere. The ground shook. It was an earthquake. He knew he was in
open ground so there was no immediate danger. He crouched down for
fear of falling. There was a flash of intense light, bigger and softer than
lightning. He closed his eyes.

It stopped as suddenly as it had started and he opened his eyes. All
was calm as it had been moments before. He must have been dreaming.
Everything was as it had been. Everything was as it had been. No, it wasn't.
He looked again. The tomb had been torn open so violently that there was
a vivid contrast between new, bright rock and the dull weathered rock
around the roseate wound with its bloody streaks.

He crept on his hands and knees across the sparse new grass as if he
was hiding from someone until he could support himself against the
entrance. He moved his head ever so slightly so that he could look into
the gaping hole. The two men were sitting stone still on the low stone
shelf with neatly folded sheets between them. No body! He had never
seen anything like them. He must have been dreaming after all. And then
one of them moved as if to speak.

For a moment he was paralysed; and then something gave in him and
he turned sharply, grazing his hand; and then he ran and ran and ran.

## ix. Easter Morning

She had not slept all night and now she was deadly tired but it had to be done. Like the last act of a betrothed girl whose soldier boy has been killed in a battle, like the last act of the abandoned lover, putting the keepsakes in order and hiding them, she must go through with it. She must see his face and undertake the anointing of the dead that her outrageous act of love had so unerringly pre-figured.

They were so disoriented that they had not thought about how to open the tomb until now. They took turns at pushing the barrow with its cask of embalming ointment praying that the guards would not stop them and either confiscate their cargo or solicit a bribe. They had the usual payment just in case but the soldiers were dozing. One final push up the hill, up the steep and narrow path. Then a man came hurtling round the corner, looking like death, oblivious of where he was running so that he almost pitched himself into the cart but at the last moment he swerved violently and passed them, almost knocking her over. These were strange times.

Mechanically, they set the barrow down next to an abandoned lantern and a spade and walked disconsolately towards the tomb. It was open. But it wasn't grave robbers. It looked as if there had been an earthquake. They went on as if driven, almost falling, supporting each other as they stumbled and then, as they reached the entrance, a blazing spirit guarded the doorway with another just behind; but before they could turn around and run away the spirit said in a voice whose sweetness matched his beauty: "What are you looking for?" And she just managed to say, "Jesus!" "Ah, Jesus! He is no longer here. He has done what he said he would. He has risen and will meet your brethren in Galilee. Go and tell them the good news."

There was no further occasion for talking. They bowed low and then turned and ran back down the slope and were catching their breath at the bottom when, as if out of nowhere, they saw the spirit of Jesus. "Peace be with you," it said. "Be glad." They fell to the ground and she grasped his feet, those feet she had dried with her hair and anointed with her hands and she kissed the wound in his right foot. This was no spirit! He was, as he always was, in a hurry without hurrying, no sign of impatience, enjoying their joy but urging them to share it: "Go and tell Peter and the others that I have risen. Don't be frightened. It was not," he looked up the hill to the three posts, "in vain."

He smiled that smile for her and she knew that their love had been so fulfilled that it would overflow the bounds of their personal drama, overflow the borders of Israel, overflow the edges of the known world until it filled the whole earth.

He smiled that smile and was gone.

They ran and ran, not stumbling but as if they could run forever. She knew how their message would be greeted; but it did not matter. If Jesus could overcome death, he could overcome everything.

## x. Easter Evening

He had walked the familiar places in and out of time. He had seen them running. He had seen the disbelief but what struck him was not their inability to grasp what had happened—that was understandable enough—but their weakness. Not the simple weakness of the bewildered who cannot bring themselves to act but their utter weakness without him. It was their kind of love. It was their kind of tribute. It was the best they could do. He knew, as he had always known, that in spite of the hesitation and the broken words and the broken promises, they really loved him. And he was so sorry for them. But he must be true to the Father and show himself to them as utterly the same and yet utterly transformed.

He walked across the field where poor Judas had been hurriedly buried. Poor Judas. But he, like both the thieves, were safe with his Father.

Cleopas and his wife, half dazed, made their sad farewells. They wanted to stay but there was work to be done in the garden if it was to sustain them through the year. They walked together in the silence of deep love and deep sorrow, each wishing they could carry more of the load of the other.

"Such a dream shattered," she said. "Such a promise," he said, "not broken, but wrested from us."

He could not bear it. "Father," he said, almost out of habit, as if he was still in his former state. Not needing a reply, he moved from timelessness into time and took their road.

They were far too kind to ignore a stranger even though they would have preferred to take refuge in their own woundedness. "Peace be with you," he said; and when they looked up, surprised, bravely trying to hide their brokenness, he could not help himself. "Why so sad? Be of good cheer." But they could manage nothing more than a brave, broken smile.

They told him their story and when they had finished, as the sun began to set, he told them his, from the Garden of Eden to the Garden of Gethsemane and the garden where the tomb lay empty. They wanted to believe. They so wanted to believe. But, as he knew, it was a thing too wonderful.

Even through their grief a tremor of consolation passed through them as their house came into view. They would have preferred to be alone, to try to lose their sorrow in each other's arms; but they were so good, so generous, that hospitality overcame their private feelings.

He slipped outside while they made their preparations and stole a kiss. When they called him he sat at the table and, as the guest, he took the bread and blessed it, and broke it, and gave it to them, and slipped out of time as his body in the bread now with them, was out of time; and they understood; and the news of the Father's love for him and his love for them began to break all over the world.

# 8. The World and the Cross

*2015*

*The somewhat complex titles of these reflections tell their own
story: I have tried to connect four aspects of Good Friday with
four concrete world events or phenomena from the past year
and four attributes of kingdom building. I can only hope that the
actual text of the reflections is less daunting than their titles.*

## i. When They Are Far Away: Jesus on the Cross,
## Ebola and the Nature of Vulnerability

The gaze of Jesus, hanging on the Cross in a desperate struggle for life
which his body will not give up, no matter what his spirit says, for he is
the man whose godhead has been laid aside, sees past the foreground of
rubble, past the knot of his dispirited followers, past the sneering officials
and indifferent soldiers, past the familiar landscape and over the hills to
the world outside the unremitting factionalism of Jerusalem to a world
he has never seen but knows he has lived for and will die for.

There is no reason why he should have seen that world; from the
beginning of myth, before recorded time, the message to God's Chosen
People has always been the same: they are to be the bridge between the
Creator and creation; and so it was neither partisan nor blinkered for
Jesus to teach the Jews, it was simply a continuation of what we might
euphemistically call a "divine strategy". There is the charming story of
Jesus and the Syro/Phoenician woman who, literally, out-witted Jesus
with her remark about dogs picking up crumbs from under the table but
the very peculiarity of the encounter emphasises how focused Jesus was

on his mission. The "strategy", if we may call it that, was to deepen the Jewish understanding of God's purposes for man until such time as they were ready to carry it as a light to the Gentiles.

We, with our hindsight, know what happened, although the ultimate separation of Christianity from Judaism looks more like the result of growing, mutual incomprehension, leading to a gradual widening of the gap rather than a critical break. If we look at Acts, the Letters and the subsequent writings of the early Christian Church it is impossible to say when the real break came, although Matthew is unable to hide his bitterness while John is unable wholly to curb his condescension.

Critically, although the Chosen People had come to rest all their hopes in the coming of a Messiah, they were never very clear what such a figure might be or do, and they had no discernment process for deciding if any claimant was the Messiah. The hierarchy became trapped in a hopeless, self-referential, largely uncritical understanding of God and religion which put it at the centre. The great days of the Redactors who gave Scripture its authoritative form in a spirit of self-criticism and creativity were half a millennium away; and it was only after the catastrophe of the Temple's destruction in AD 70 that a new era of self-criticism, starting with the Council of Jamnia in around AD 90, would come to flourish, too late for a reciprocally constructive dialogue with a Christian sect that was metamorphosing into a new form of life, the caterpillar transformed to the butterfly, without which it could not be.

Perhaps St Luke makes the point too sharply when he describes, time and time again, how Paul the Pharisee went first to the Synagogue, only to be turned away so that he must resort to the Gentiles; although, from what we know, piecing together the chronology of Acts and Paul's letters, he never gave up; the Letter to the Romans provides ample testimony for this persistence. But Paul is in no doubt that being in Christ and Christ's spirit being in us is a condition of self-understanding and not of race nor heritage.

As the vast, multi-racial Roman Empire, which produced Popes of many different ethnicities, declined and disintegrated, people became more ignorant of otherness and, therefore, less tolerant of it until both Western and Eastern Christianity became racially particularistic. Then, with the seafaring explorations of the late fifteenth and sixteenth centuries, Christians had to ask how far the people of the Americas or Africa could be considered equal human beings, a dilemma whose intellectual complexities, portrayed in Shakespeare's *Tempest*, were completely overwhelmed by the Christian slave trade. Ironically, perhaps, one of the major objectives of Stanley's Africa explorations in the 1870s was to thwart the Arab/Swahili slave trade. Pass on another century and we will see black Americans fighting for their rights in the fiercely Christian Southern states of the United States; and pass on again to today when the world is still largely divided between the rich, white North and the poor, black South.

Thirty years ago when I first went to Sierra Leone, it was a commonplace among the aid agencies to say that none of the Government's hospitals worked and that the only really viable outfit was the Nixon Memorial Methodist Hospital. Looking back, I am ashamed of my glibness, complacency and, worst of all, cynicism because behind the commonplace lay the assumption that the Government was beyond redemption. There is a debate to be had about how the Government's hospitals got into such a sorry state and how the blame might be apportioned between the British colonial administration and the newly independent country, a very fascinating discussion about the nature and the roots of corruption, but when I paid my last visit to Sierra Leone ten years later, we were still saying the same thing. I had been part of the development assistance establishment which did its little best and, perhaps, could not have done very much more, given the size of the problem and the size of our budgets, but we could and should have said and done more to help the Government recognise and then live up to its responsibilities. It did not need to be told it was corrupt and incompetent; it knew that. What it needed was hope.

So when the Ebola epidemic burst upon Sierra Leone last year it was not ready; and, like development assistance agencies for the last 70 years, the West pitched in with emergency assistance. But the test is whether we will now stay in Sierra Leone to build a health system capable of withstanding another epidemic without calling upon us for emergency assistance.

All of which seems a very long way, both in time and place, from Jesus hanging on the Cross; but, unlike the Crucifixion itself which took place in time, its meaning is timeless and cosmic; and, if we continue the thought which began with the mission of the Chosen People, we will see that Jesus died for all of us, throughout time and indifferent to place; that is why his gaze transcended the physical landscape, his ambitions being much broader than those for his own people.

At this point we are in severe danger of descending into platitude when I introduce the idea that, if Jesus died for us all, if we are all created in the image of God because the Spirit dwells in each of us, then we are all equal in the sight of God and should be equal in the sight of each other. I can hear the fountain pens being unscrewed in preparation for letters of protest to the *Daily Telegraph* and a chorus of "ah buts". So let us escape immediately from the territory of the platitude: to assert that we are all equal in the sight of God and should all be equal in each other's sight is neither to say that we should all be the same—which we are clearly not with our great variety of gifts and weaknesses—nor that we should possess identical life chances, income and wealth, which is clearly impossible. But when people say to me that my call for equality of concern and respect and my advocacy of vastly improving the life chances of the poor is "left wing" my reply is that what I seek is justice, to which I will return later.

In the meantime, we need to be careful how we qualify our obligations to our fellow human beings made in the image of God. Are we justified in invoking family, and then clan; is our obligation to our neighbour somehow geographically definable or is there some way in which we have to accept that our empathy has limited muscularity? How might we balance our proper prudential obligations to our family and community with the apparently insatiable demands of a corrupt and chaotic world? Is fixing what has been broken simply the responsibility of the breakers; or, if the breakers were our colonial forefathers, are we not free from the sins of our parents?

If we examine these questions—and there are many more—carefully we will see that they are all fundamentally contractual where our conduct relies upon the disposition and actions of others: our obligation to family and clan seems to be inherently contractual, something from which we cannot escape. As none of us chooses where we were born and into what conditions, all geography should be a matter of chance, the opposite of contractual, but we have made the whole world into an impenetrable fabric of contracts. As for the muscularity of our empathy, it seems not to depend on our own capacity to exercise and strengthen the muscle but on the behaviour of the object with which we are being asked to empathise. All our instincts are prudential, the survival of our family being literally in our DNA and so how reasonable is it for Jesus to call for us to make a radical break with this biology and care not for the morrow; all very well for the lilies of the field not to toil nor spin but hardly realistic. And, of course, when it comes to fixing what is broken we need proceed no further than the argument about whose fault it was in the first place.

One final note before I go on. It turns out that the help that we offered to Sierra Leone during its Ebola crisis was not so open-hearted as we might have hoped: it turns out that one of our major reasons for offering help was to ensure that the terrible disease did not reach our shores; it was, in essence, not a generous but a defensive, self-interested act.

Jesus' death, on the other hand, was not contractual. Jesus, to use approximate language, gave himself freely for us. I would not go so far as to say that he did so expecting nothing back but what he expected was, necessarily, nugatory in comparison with what he gave; it always will be; we use the common word "love" to describe the relationship between the Creator and creatures and vice versa but they are incommensurably different. Although it is difficult for us to grasp this, as I remarked in respect of the lilies of the field, if we are to be true followers of Jesus then we have to learn to live with the unconditional: there isn't a bargain to be struck; there isn't a deal to be made; there isn't a minimum set of conditions; there isn't a way of being a conditional Christian.

Which brings me to the core of this first reflection: the essence of pride is to put ourselves above God, to repeat the mistake which Adam and Eve made in the face of the serpent; it is to say that we know better, for conditionality is a sure mark of pride. What we have done is to take religion and mould it into an instrument for our own purposes rather than for God's. Our tradition is warped by the temptations of earthly power, complicity with injustice, the exercise of clerical judgment over private behaviour, the exaltation of comfort over sacrifice and the celebration of the status quo at the expense of the marginalised, particularly women. Of course the Church is a human institution subject to human error but the scale of our infraction is staggering and that is accounted for by the subtleties of pride. The devil does not wear horns and a tail; he is neatly dressed and turned out like one of us, knowing precisely how we will react to his blandishments.

By way of repentance we need to deconstruct our conditionality and come to the Cross in a state of absolute vulnerability because the only true relationship we can have with Jesus is one in which we are as vulnerable now as he is as he hangs there on the Cross for the whole world, not just vulnerable in the narrow sense of leaving ourselves totally open to the searing truth of the Cross but also in the broader sense of being open to the unconditionality of our whole existence, personal, and corporate in the Church.

Vulnerability is hardly a great public virtue; indeed, particularly among males it is supposed to be synonymous with weakness and as women, quite understandably, contest for public space and opportunity, vulnerability is part of the baby that we throw out with the bath water of prejudice; these are not the times for the vulnerable. We all know, from our own experience, that the depth of our love for one another, particularly in the context of marriage, is directly proportionate to the extent of our vulnerability. Looked at from an ideal, non-biological perspective, true love is the unconditional openness of the one to the other. We often think that the real way of expressing our love is by buying things or doing things but from this perspective, the most expressive form of love is the sound of silence.

Moving outward from our own conditionality, we can see more clearly the opacity we create with our family and community conditionality and, outward from this to the way we view society and our relationships with other societies. Looked at from this point of view we can see that we have tied ourselves down by a thousand tiny strands, the way in which the people of Lilliput tied down Gulliver. Every time there is a crisis, instead of loosening a tiny strand, we tie another one. It's strange how supposed right-wing, libertarian newspapers like the *Daily Mail* and the *Daily Telegraph* are theoretically against the "nanny state" and against the interfering bureaucrats of Brussels but as soon as something goes wrong the cry goes up: "What is the Government going to do about it?" And we offer our cry to politicians, sincere in their narrow way, who do not think that self-restraint and vulnerability can be relied upon but think that everybody will behave as badly as the worst, so they set up inspectorates and audits and targets and ever more regulation; and in doing so, they subtly shift responsibility for what we do from us as individuals to regulators. When something goes wrong today, as likely as not the regulator rather than the perpetrator will be blamed; and once we have reached that point our world is impossibly complex and divorced from personal responsibility.

As we stand at the foot of the Cross, how comfortable are we in blaming everybody else for the ills of the world? Can we honestly say that the Sierra Leoneans, or the United Nations, were responsible for Ebola? Where are we in this broken world? Are we really whole, protected and superior or are we, like Jesus, broken and vulnerable?

Jesus, the man, hangs on the Cross looking out over the whole world with very little notion of what it is like but caring for it nonetheless. We, with our newspapers, televisions and tablets know, or at least can know, precisely what the world is like: we can see the delights of creation and how we have tarnished them; we can see the state of imperfection which is our lot and which challenges our integrity; and we can see what choices we have made and their results; we can trace the connectivity between what we see and our presence in it or our absence from it. To that extent we are continually challenged and it is not surprising that we often throw our hands in the air and plead "compassion fatigue" but we cannot give up on God's world because it is difficult; that is its condition and our condition; but we will do better to act bravely and humbly than to involve ourselves in endless calculation. We may never bring ourselves to be the simple lilies of the field; we may find it impossible to be less than high maintenance, highly priced, pampered, elegant, deeply scented roses but we would do well not to lose all empathy with simplicity because the loss of simplicity is the beginning of pride.

Finally, before we come to a close there is one more related thought, and that is the apparently puzzling paradox of knowing and not knowing. There has never been a time in history when any group of people has known more about its world than we know; there has never been a time in history when there has been more further, graduate and post-graduate education; we generate unimaginable quantities of research, documentary and personal information; never was a world and its people as much photographed as our world; and yet, at the same time, we seem less secure in our notions of how to consider the crises of which we become aware; we seem to have reached a kind of individual and collective paralysis: as the crisis in Syria gets worse, the diplomacy and humanitarian aid dwindle; as evidence of climate change mounts, the measures to handle it are diluted; and with reference to the central crisis of this reflection, it took the World Health Organisation four months to react to Ebola after a warning from Medecin sans Frontiers. What is the problem? As we move away from vulnerability, from personal responsibility, from the shadow of the Cross, towards apparent self-sufficiency—and paradoxical defensiveness—and pride, we lose the foundational tool—some people would call it conscience—which enables us to speak and act in the way that followers of Jesus should speak and act; and, if we are not careful, if we do not return to a radical vulnerability in imitation of Christ, we will find that we are nominal Christians only, with the same hollow centre as our secular brothers and sisters.

Jesus hangs on the Cross for all the world, not just for each person in the world but for the corporate world which God created where we were made to love and rely upon each other, a world of fellowship and empathy, a world unafraid of itself and its responsibilities, a world full of divine Grace. We might react by going into ourselves so that there is a simple relationship between a single person and the Son of God hanging there; but surely the true lesson of the Cross is that it asks us to reach out from ourselves, not to turn in on ourselves. Over there, there is a small knot of people: the men ran away and then came back; the women never ran away but stayed quietly faithful: those who served Jesus were more grounded than those whom he had taught; the simple out-reaching bore stronger witness than the promises made at the Last Supper never to leave him. If this were a different church in a different culture—in what I suggest would be a better culture—we would, at this point, be holding hands to comfort each other rather than sheltering in our private space because the Crucifixion was not some kind of intellectual or doctrinal transaction, it was the persecution and execution of the body of Christ for which we should feel our own degree of physical pain and need what consolation we can get from each other. Jesus hangs there, looking out over the whole world and, yes, of course, that whole world includes us; but the main point is that it includes everybody else.

## ii. When They Are at the Gate: The Last Words of Jesus, *Mare Nostrum* and the Nature of Sacrifice

The end is very near. Jesus is about to say his last words before death.

Perhaps, being human, the whole of his life passes before him in a flash where everything is separate and together at the same time. What does this life amount to after all?

Albert Schweitzer, in a very famous book (*The Quest for the Historical Jesus*) opined that the life of Jesus amounted to very little; that when he says in Matthew and Mark, citing Psalm 22: "My God, my God, why have you forsaken me?" he believes he is closing a failed life. Luke, as usual, is much more positive, emphasising the close relationship between Jesus and the Father in his final, dying words: "Father, into your hands I commend my spirit" and this follows on from Jesus' dialogue with the criminals on either side of him, bearing the jibes of the one and forgiving the sins of the other and promising him eternal life, which doesn't seem like the behaviour of a man who thinks he's a failure; and the final words of Jesus in John, again typically, are triumphal: "It is accomplished."

Some people find the difference between Gospel accounts unsettling but I find the opposite. I'm not very comfortable, for example, with court proceedings where all the witnesses say exactly the same thing; it looks like a fix. Indeed, one of the primary reasons why the Gospels seem authentic to me is precisely because of their differences, even the slight variations between Mark and Matthew. At a deeper level, the differences make us think more deeply about the account we are reading; and I will come to this in my third reflection.

Meanwhile, let us go back to the question about what Jesus' life was worth. In his state of humanity, Jesus cannot have known what would happen next but in thinking about that we must not become triumphalist in hindsight. There was some kind of local, seismic event when the veil of the Temple was torn and people emerged from their graves but, in the calm light of Saturday morning, with Jesus in the tomb, there wasn't much to show for all the drama of the last week; and although as Easter children we properly concentrate on the discovery of the empty tomb and the appearances of Jesus, even the close of Acts, after so many wonderful accounts of the work of the Holy Spirit, is somewhat subdued and non-committal. To the best of our knowledge, not long after Luke's account closes, both St Peter and St Paul were executed; so it might have been the end of the brave little Jewish sect which had not yet become a separate religion. But it wasn't, and, by all accounts, what saved the word of God in Jesus Christ proclaimed and nourished in his church was the unlikely Christian reaction to persecution in the use of death as witness in itself, as if there was a perception among the followers of Jesus that just as his humiliating death had turned to triumph, so would theirs.

Strange to tell, given how often we think of our world as a place of steady progress from the dark ages, through the Renaissance and the enlightenment to our scientific nirvana, there are Christians today dying for their faith. Martyrdom has never totally disappeared from our tradition but whereas, until the invention of the telegraph, stories were told to us long after events in faraway places, we now see the demolition of the Christian churches in the Middle East as it happens and as I write this we have had the massacre of deliberately identified Christians by Al Shabab in Garissa, Kenya; in imitation of Christ, Christians are giving up their lives for what they believe.

Hopefully, we will not, in a variant of the words of the Lord's Prayer, have to face a time of ultimate trial but we should ask ourselves what sacrifice we are prepared to make in the name of the Cross.

Like much else that was crystallised in the period we call the "enlightenment", the dark and difficult ideas of the Middle Ages were supposed to be made clear and simple. Whereas the Church of the Middle Ages believed in the concept of sacrifice in imitation of the sacrifice of Jesus, new thinking tended not to think of the death of Jesus in terms of sacrifice at all; and that great economist Adam Smith described how, when everybody acted rationally on their own behalf, the "invisible hand" would put everything right. Indeed, liberal thinkers from the seventeenth century to the end of the twentieth believed that if we all behaved rationally then we would create a paradise on earth of mutual advantage. The trouble was, as Paul Khan pointed out (*Putting Liberalism in Its Place*), the only reason that our democracy survived was that millions of young men at the beginning of the twentieth century in the Great War and again, in the middle of the century, in the war against Hitler, sacrificed their health and even their lives to preserve democracy; left to the "invisible hand" there would be nothing left. I never think of the guns booming over the Somme without the memory—I have forgotten who recorded it—of the mill owners of Bradford strolling along the Brighton sea front in their silk hats, in hearing of the guns, their profits made fat by war-time procurement, never at risk of being put in danger themselves. Which, in turn, echoes the famous phrase of Sir Robert Walpole on being pushed into the "War of Jenkins Ear": "Today they are ringing their bells; tomorrow they will be wringing their hands." And, bringing ourselves right up-to-date, ask yourselves how many of the United Kingdom soldiers who have died in Afghanistan were working class, or from an ethnic minority, or both. It is easy enough to urge others to make sacrifices for the common good, as easy as spending other people's money! But however we understand the sacrifice of Jesus, he took responsibility on himself, neither shirking responsibility nor sharing it.

Interestingly, much of what we admire in sacrifice is its purpose of keeping things the same, of keeping the barbarians outside the gate, but we must remember that the sacrifice of Jesus was to make things different, as have many other sacrifices since been for freedom, democracy and justice. Which faces us with a fascinating problem: in the face of mass migration across the Mediterranean Sea, will we make sacrifices to keep out the immigrants or sacrifices to let them in?

Before we answer that question, let us look at the situation we face. It isn't appropriate here to explore whose fault it might be that we have reached our current position because no matter whose fault it is, it isn't the fault of the victims whose plight we are considering. Millions of people are being displaced from their homes by corruption, climate change, dictatorship and civil war, the worst instance of which is the four million people made refugees by the civil war in Syria. At the time of writing, the United Kingdom has knowingly admitted fewer than 100

Syrians in the four years since the civil war began. Our justification for this niggardliness is that we are leading the initiative to provide assistance for refugees from Syria in the neighbouring countries of Jordan and Lebanon; but what kind of sacrifice is this? If we are providing assistance to Syrian refugees through our overseas aid budget and that budget is fixed, we're making no sacrifice at all; the aid recipients of some other countries are making the sacrifice. But is it really either/or? Is not the strategy of providing for refugees in countries bordering Syria much the same as our helping with Ebola in Sierra Leone in case it arrives here?

But, unlike the Ebola epidemic, no human force has been able to resist the migratory tide from Asia, the Middle East and Africa across the Mediterranean to the shores of Europe, nor a similar Northward tide from Latin America into the United States.

One fundamental question is whether our making provision for this tide of refugees can be classified as a sacrifice at all? What is our entitlement compared with theirs? Is what we own by virtue of where we were born, and the life chances we have been afforded, unconditionally ours? Is our comfort justified by the accident of birth and upbringing? If a sacrifice is giving up what is rightfully ours, then, is this a sacrifice at all?

But, for the sake of argument, because this is a horribly difficult issue, let us say that what we are being asked to give up, at least in part, involves a change for the apparent worse in our circumstances. Let us try to match up our situation against the situation of those who wish to share our good fortune.

People who flee their homes, put themselves into the hands of people traffickers and set out on dangerously overloaded boats across the Mediterranean are, for a start, desperate; they will take any risk to better their lives and those of the surviving members of their family; and they know that they face the ultimate risk of losing their lives in the attempt, which many of them do.

So, what is a life worth? To Jesus, hanging on the Cross, having said his last words moments from death, to those whose boat is sinking and who know they are almost certainly breathing their last because they cannot swim and there is no rescue ship in sight, to those who have had a wonderful life and who long to meet Jesus face-to-face, to all of us life is worth everything because that is all we have got; and, therefore, to give up life, as Jesus is doing for us, is the ultimate sacrifice: "God so loved the world that he gave his only begotten son that whosoever believeth in him should not perish but have everlasting life; for God sent not his Son into the world to condemn the world but that through him the world might be saved."

Set against the ultimate sacrifice of giving up our life for our friends, what sacrifice should we be prepared to make so that others might live? To the secular philosopher this is a utilitarian question where the benefits and disadvantages can be quantified; but to the Christian the matter is neither contractual nor prudential because we are followers of the man who, at this moment, has uttered his last words and is about to die for us, making the ultimate sacrifice of his life for all his friends. What does it mean for us to be his imitators, following him without prudence or contract?

In one sense this is a hopelessly idealistic question which brings us back to those dratted lilies of the field. Does Jesus honestly expect us to give up everything we have for the poor, particularly the poor from distant lands who are crowding at our metaphorical and literal gates? Well, yes, actually, but we are not up to it. I know I'm not up to it.

So the next question is how far can we sinners bring ourselves to follow Jesus. Is it simply one less glass of wine or dessert and slightly more money in the charity box? Or will we go further and give up wine and cake altogether to swell the proceeds of the charity box? Many years ago a pugnacious Chancellor of the Exchequer, Dennis Healey, said of his austerity measures: "if they aren't hurting they aren't working" and we can at least grasp this idea in an intuitive way; if it isn't hurting, it can't really be sacrifice.

Based on what we know of the life and death of Jesus, as his followers what would we define as the nature of sacrifice? How might we apply our definition to the tide of humanity surging towards the Northern shores of the Mediterranean? Is our answer, at worst, that we should let them die rather than arrive, which we have implicitly done through abandoning support for *Mare Nostrum*? Or, paradoxically, is our response that we should save them from the sea but not let them in here?

It might be helpful to shed the original idea of sacrifice which referred to the slaughtering of animals and the offering of their blood to God, an idea that later became transferred to the Passion and death of Jesus, because this idea is all about expiation or atonement, the giving up of something earthly in order to balance the books with the almighty; that was the strict Jewish notion of sacrifice and it has sometimes been transferred uncritically to Jesus who is said to have balanced the books with the almighty on our behalf by shedding his blood—but I find this too transactional.

Rather, the ultimate sacrifice is the giving up of the self, the physical ultimate of which is giving up one's physical life as Jesus did; but this is only one aspect of the personal ultimate which is that giving up of the self, which takes us back to the idea of love as the unconditional openness of the one to the other, the lover to the beloved. The nature of the sacrifice of Jesus was that he gave himself up unconditionally not only for us as members of the human race but also to us as members of the human race who, affronted by his perfection, took his life.

We cannot equal that level of openness to all humanity but we surely can do better than sending a cheque to the Disaster Emergency Committee and letting in fewer than 100 Syrian refugees. If we are to proceed with the radical encounter with Jesus that his love for us requires, for which we were created, we have a new task from this reflection, on top of trying to behave like the lilies of the field, and that is to behave like them in the face of discomfort and danger; we are not to be frightened and we certainly are not to run away.

The proper Christian reaction to such misery as we witness cannot be to turn our backs. It might prudentially be the right thing to do and it is hard to see how it would be contractually the wrong thing to do; but that isn't the point. There is no contract. There is absolutely no guarantee that if we give up everything we have that we will get anything back. That is the nature of following Jesus and what it does is to show us starkly the extent to which we have grown accustomed to making compromises with the Gospel, striking deals where there is no deal to be had.

The nature of sacrifice, then, above all else, is that it is unconditional; it asks nothing; it expects nothing; and, perhaps most difficult of all, it consists in being open, being vulnerable, being more than active by being open. The reason that the cheque in the post and the admission of the stranger is necessary but not sufficient in terms of sacrifice is that these acts are positive acts; they are the lover offering goods and services to the beloved; we are back to the development assistance equivalent of chocolates and flowers. However these are appreciated and however good we feel in offering them, they are not enough; they are not what sacrifice is, they are not what love is.

It is massively significant that from the moment the arresting party arrives at the Garden of Gethsemane, Jesus is physically passive and verbally extremely economical, except in the trial scene in the Gospel of John which is somewhat theatrical. We are a culture of words and deeds, the most worthy of us being the most full of words and deeds; we find it very difficult to say nothing to God and to do nothing for God. That is why we find prayer so difficult; it is against our culture simply to leave ourselves open, vulnerable to the Holy Spirit.

In saying this I am not pretending that what I ask is easy. For all its deprivations, I look back with extreme fondness to the social homogeneity of my childhood when everybody in my mill town knew everybody, when hardly anybody owned a car and where we shopped in the open market not a supermarket. I loved the cohesion of two-channel television and football all being played at three o'clock on a Saturday afternoon, on the rhythm of the cricket season; and although I understand the contemporary benefits of pluralism and choice I think we have paid a high price. Sometimes I find the melting pot of London exciting and intellectually challenging but mostly I find it difficult: I just don't like riding in taxis where the drivers listen to foreign radio stations and foreign music instead of grumbling to me; I find it difficult to develop good, empathetic relationships with people with whom I only share a transaction, not a culture; I find it difficult to articulate disquiet without sounding prejudiced or actually being prejudiced. I don't think that all cultures are equally articulate, self-critical, altruistic or just; but to give up much of my comfort to save those who thrash out desperately between life and death in the Mediterranean seems to me to be of little ultimate consequence to me and of great consequence to them. I have read the history and read the individual stories and, yes, there are many people who want to live here because they will better themselves and their families, as distinct from refugees and asylum seekers but, ultimately, who am I to say?

We have three lives in the frame before us: the life of Jesus almost ended, the life of an orphan on a plank in the Mediterranean and our self. What do we say to the dying man who has refrained from rebuking his persecutors? What do we say to the child whose fate should not depend on the legal state of his parents? And what do we say to our comfortable self?

Every day in the great churches and cathedrals of this land Mary's prayer, the Magnificat, is said or sung during the Service of Evensong: "He has shown strength with his arm; he has scattered the proud in the imagination of their hearts; he has put down the mighty from their seats and has exalted the humble and meek; he has filled the hungry with good things and the rich he has sent empty away." I must confess that I have seen very little evidence of the Christian Church acting on the noble sentiments in the prayer in a way anything near adequate; but perhaps our problem is that we think that we are the humble and meek who deserve to be filled with good things. In British terms that may be true for some of us but in global terms we are the rich and the mighty; and, after the sacrifice of Jesus, it doesn't seem right that we should wait to be put down from our seats but should give them up with a degree of grace and good humour.

The end is very near. Jesus has said his last words and is about to die for us all, regardless of our race or place and perhaps we need help more than most because we are standing in front of the eye of the needle with too many packages, most of which we will have to abandon if we are to get through; and the best reason to abandon what we have is not because we will thereby be given some credit, earn some points on our heavenly score card, but because to do and, more important, to refrain from doing for its own sake is to imitate Christ.

### iii. When They Are Among Us: The Death of Jesus, Radical Islam and the Nature of Community

Jesus is dead. What does that mean for us?

Today Christians live in a state of uneasy truce about this question but in the middle of the sixteenth century Christians were being beheaded in public for saying what it meant to them; the executors were as sincere as the martyrs. The disagreement led, in the first instance, to civil war in what we now call Germany and France and, less than a century later, in England; and, in the intervening period it led to an international war, known as the "Thirty Years War" from 1618 to 1648. There is nothing in the current behaviour of the Islamic State that was not present in almost identical form in Europe between 1517 and 1648.

On the surface, to borrow the caricatures of their opponents, the strife was presented as a fundamental disagreement between the corrupted Roman Catholic Church and the reformed and Protestant churches about the nature of ecclesiastical authority, mirrored today in the Islamic disagreement between Sunnis and Shia about authority, but the underlying cause was much deeper.

Put crudely and combatively, the Roman Catholic Church claimed that Christians could not enjoy the fruits of our salvation through the death of Jesus without the mediation of the Church which had led it to the corrupt practice of selling indulgences, whereas reformers and Protestants emphasised the attainment of salvation through personal faith and the direct relationship between believers and Jesus. At the same time, and related to this, there was a disagreement about the relationship between our personal, earthly conduct and salvation: the Roman Catholic Church tended to emphasise the importance of Grace-driven good works whereas reformers and Protestants tended to base their hope on simple faith where conduct was irrelevant. That secondary issue has, to a great extent, disappeared but the basic issue has not gone away: we may agree that Jesus died for us and in some way that is associated with human wickedness but how we are saved and who is saved are by no means resolved.

In one respect the disagreement was somewhat technical as well as being violently partisan. Roman Catholics believed that they were saved because of how they conducted themselves, but how they conducted themselves depended upon their openness to the saving Grace of Jesus, Grace, in other words, that was the direct result of the death of Jesus. They were not Pelagians who simply believed that behaving well was enough because without the death of Jesus their conduct would have been irrelevant; without the death of Jesus they could not be saved and this was because they believed that the death of Jesus in some way redeemed humanity from its original imperfection, or "original sin" which all humanity shared since the "fall" of Adam and Eve. Reformers and Protestants, on the other hand, equally believed that their faith in the saving Grace of Jesus gave them the hope of salvation. The mechanics, the "how" this happened, became hopelessly technical but the outcome was the same.

Many Christians from both "camps" believed then and still believe now, based on the theology of St Anselm, that the mechanics of salvation involved God sending Jesus to earth so that he could suffer death by which God's anger with human beings was appeased, that the blood of Jesus literally atoned for human sin in a kind of quasi-judicial bargain—just look at the Holy Week hymns—which God made with himself or, to put it another way, human beings were made angelic in the Garden of Eden, fell from Grace and were rescued by the death of Jesus. This view depends upon the problematic nature of evil. Did God somehow allow—as he certainly could not invent—evil as a test which we failed, which God was bound to know we would fail, necessitating the Incarnation and death of Jesus which were intrinsic to the human story? God could not see the evil on earth and at a point in time decide that the Incarnation and death of Jesus were necessary because God does not live in time but lives not even for all time but outside time. So the Incarnation and death of Jesus always were.

I find these arguments difficult to comprehend. For me, the starting point is that God is love and that he created us in love; but that in order that we might freely love he created us imperfect, so that we could choose. That being so, we were bound to sin, to make wrong choices because that is our creaturely nature. To that extent the idea of "original sin" is not very far from the idea of intrinsic imperfection, the difference being that it shifts the argument away from the origin of evil to the nature of evil, from a concept of "fallenness" to a concept of necessary imperfection.

This God of love knew the difficulties we would face living with our imperfection and he therefore sent Jesus to be among us to show solidarity with our imperfection and to demonstrate a concrete hope that all was not lost, and could not be lost simply by virtue of how we were created. Throughout their history, the Chosen People had terrible problems in their relationship with God because he was almost always "somewhere up there" whereas Christians can look to the concrete being of God in Jesus and take inspiration from it. Further, this Jesus who lived in time left himself for us in the Eucharist and gave us the gift of the Church to provide us with constant support through the power of the Holy Spirit. This is why, incidentally, people who say they are Christians but don't participate in any form of church are deluding themselves. If we could be Christians without the Church then there does not seem to be any point in Jesus creating it. St Paul was lyrical about the nature of the Church as the body of Christ where all members played their different parts and where the absolute cardinal principle was unity. That is the great sadness of the sixteenth century. For all its imperfections, Paul would have wanted a brotherly accommodation between different Christians to preserve the unity of the Church, not some diplomatic stitch-up but, rather, a living together in unity in spite of our differences. The "30-Years War" did not end in unity, it ended because of mutual exhaustion; and because the civil powers were determined that it would not happen again, the idea of Christendom was abandoned in favour of the inviolability of sovereign states. This was the first great retreat of Christianity from the public sphere to the private; we lost the credibility to be the moderators of civic power and became subject to it.

Which leads back to the issue of who is to be saved. Sadly, some Christians believe that the only people who are saved by the death of Jesus are those who belong to a particular denomination: Roman Catholic doctrine, in spite of some equivocation, fundamentally believes that the only Christians who can be saved are those who are its members, with a grudging benefit of the doubt for Orthodox Churches; and among reformers and Protestants, although they are necessarily less uniform in their doctrinal approach, many believe that only the members of certain denominations will be saved; and some go further and say that only the "elect" of a denomination will be saved.

The central issue for us should not be how and why Jesus saved but the mystery of the "what" of being saved; we will never know the "mind of God" and any enquiry into the mechanics is always going to be futile. The disagreements about fundamental issues too often turn, as I said at the beginning, on the nature of religious authority, in Christianity and Islam, whereas the only authority we should acknowledge is the authority of God. This problem is usually viewed through the idea that God's authority is enshrined in a text which God has provided in a literal sense. This would be simple enough if sacred texts were so clear and obvious in their meaning that there was no room for genuine disagreement but we know to our cost that genuine disagreement is all too likely. But I would go further: I believe that genuine disagreement is not only inevitable but also necessary.

For me, the idea of unity is related to the idea of relationship, to the concept of love. We cannot inherit clear, unambiguous unity because that would take us back to the idea of unthinking angels; unity is to be worked for in the way that we work for relationship and love. Unity is what we strive to create for one another, not something we strive to impose.

Before we throw our hands up in horror at the conduct of Islamic State we not only need to remember our own cruelties perpetrated in the name of God, we also need to recognise that unity can only be built on the basis of a self-critical community which is what the Church should be. The more self-critical we are, the less likely we will be to try to impose our views on others. There is nothing in any view of the meaning of the death of Jesus that I have mentioned so far which should keep us apart as we all support each other to penetrate as deeply as we can into the mystery of our salvation. Theology is, quintessentially, a dangerous voyage of discovery, demanding risk, knowing that, like Jesus being tempted in the wilderness, God will not allow us to destroy ourselves in the effort. Theology is like being an athlete or a racing driver; if we haven't crossed the line totally exhausted or seen the chequered flag after testing our car to the ultimate, we haven't done theology properly. Unity, community and love are only achieved through risk, vulnerability and sacrifice. Most Christians recognise that the process of moving from theology to doctrine must be very slow and deliberative because, as we have seen, whereas we are saved from the ultimate danger of theology by God's promise, the danger of the doctrine is not only to ourselves by ossifying our enquiry into rigidity and pride but is also a danger to others whom we hurt when we use doctrine as an offensive weapon.

We might say that there needs to be some doctrine or else we will not know where the boundaries of the Church lie; we will not know who are members and who are not. So as Christians we recognise that Baptism is the defining mark of a Christian who is set aside in a special way for God. That idea has led on to the question of whether those who are not baptised can be saved. The great theologian Karl Rahner, tackling this issue head on, said that God self-communicates with everybody but that we are not all equally open to that self-communication but his inevitable conclusion is that we are all saved whether we are baptised or not. Jesus died so that all will be saved.

So what is the purpose of Baptism? Its purpose is to mark us out to prosecute the mission of Jesus, to carry the good news to the whole earth, to tell it of its salvation. To be a Christian, then, is not to be superior nor to be the sole beneficiary of salvation, it is to be given the privilege of proclaiming the good news so that all who suffer, or struggle, or see nothing in their lives, or see their lives as purely material, can be given the hope to which all are entitled. If we look round our problematic world we can see that we fall short of God's love for us in creation but I believe that almost all people know that they fall short; and what they need from Christianity is not a lecture on morals, they need hope.

Our task is to construct a church as the people of God living in a self-critical community of mutual support which then reaches out to provide hope and support for others. If we are not prepared for this difficult task then there is not much point in throwing our hands in the air when other communities are not self-critical. To be self-critical is to constantly explore our relationship with Jesus, to be a good host to the Holy Spirit dwelling within us, and to recognise the limitations of human understanding and human agency.

There has been much discussion recently about the nature of what is called Islamic radicalisation. Our response has largely been to try to institute forms of restraint whereas the response of many Islamic leaders has been to argue that the cause of radicalism is alienation from our society or indoctrination through sophisticated Islamic State propaganda; but both explanations miss the point. The only valid restraint which will change minds is self-restraint and the only shield against alienation is personal responsibility. The cultural emphasis on inspection, audit, risk assessment, targets, rules and social theory misses the ultimate truth that people make choices; and that those choices will be better if they are based on a self-critical examination of conscience. That will not guarantee a perfect world because, as I have said, we are imperfect, but it will provide a much sounder basis for choices which are always going to be provisional and open to doubt and change.

But none of this self-critical behaviour is possible without love. What makes a community is not rules nor contracts, it is love. No matter how many measures we take, no matter how many reports we write, no matter how we try to allocate blame or make appeals for joined-up policy, the answer is still love. Whether we are thinking about alienated young Muslims, abused children, people in poverty, the root cause of their ills is a lack of love. It is obvious that abuse is contrary to love but not so obvious, for example, that children in care need to be loved. It is obvious that people who are in poverty need practical help but they also need the love which will help them to develop their self-esteem and our esteem for them.

We talk about love all the time but we need to relate it to vulnerability which is the basic precondition for loving.

If we become a self-critical community then we will be in a much better position to recommend our conduct to others and to work with other communities so that they become more self-critical; but I would prefer us to be known, as the early Christians were known, simply as a community where members love one another. At one level this is the application of the golden rule that we must do to others what we would want done to us; but it is more than that because vulnerability and self-criticism are our best defence against pride.

Jesus is dead and our best responses to that death are wonder and hope. Beside this death all that we do and fail to do, all that we say and fail to say, is trivial. The wonder starts with the loving God who created us to love him and each other. As we think about the death of Jesus, let us try to forget the doctrine and the disputes, the why and the how, and simply wonder at the event.

And then let us move quietly from wonder to hope. We are not very good at the humility of hope which is why we have for so long put so much emphasis on trying to construct systems which, we believe, will guarantee our salvation. Indulgences were only the worst form of this; most of us spend our lives doing what good we think we can—and much less than we should—with the idea in the back of our minds that this is some kind of salvific insurance policy; but the pursuit of virtue is its own reward and the love of God is our purpose not our side of a salvation bargain.

Our salvation is rooted much deeper when it is grounded in hope. Again, thinking of how we talk about the death of Jesus, we often say that because Jesus overcame death that means that we will overcome death. That is true but it is not based on a doctrine or a contract; it is based on the promise of Jesus to us, the promise of hope which is a component of the mystery that is Incarnation, death and Resurrection.

So why should we be sad, knowing that we have such hope? The answer to that question, for me at least, is that I am sad because I believe that although Jesus died for our sins he also died as the result of our sins. Human beings committed the ultimate sin in killing God. Not that they knew it, which is why Jesus asked that his murderers should be forgiven; the sadness is that it came to this. Yet I would not wish for the alternative, I would not wish to be part of a world—even if I could—where such a thing could not happen because sadness is a necessary condition of imperfection; it is our privilege to be sad, to be here now rather than somewhere else, to recognise that to be here, now, is the best possible acknowledgment of the privilege of our Baptism.

To recognise that privilege, to stand here now, when the last drops of blood and water have been extracted by the sword of a Roman soldier, is the best possible preparation for mission. The birth of Jesus is beautifully touching and picturesque; the teaching of Jesus is both homely and profound; but the death of Jesus causes us to falter. We are so used to the story that we no longer feel the jolt that makes our footing uncertain. But as pilgrims we need to experience uncertain footing, we need to travel the road more cautiously, to take care that we do not march with too much sureness of foot.

One final thought as we confront the corpse of Jesus as it is taken down from the Cross. Those who lived through the Crucifixion never doubted that it was the pivotal event in salvation history. God could have sent Jesus to teach the good news and then called him back in a manner similar to the account of the Ascension but for us mortals that would not have been enough; what told was the shock of deprivation before the miraculous and mysterious restoration. That shock should dislocate ways of thinking and acting, it should change lives forever. So, as we take our leave of Jesus, we should try to identify with the shock which his followers felt so that we may change as they changed. Whether we were born into a Christian family and baptised as babies or whether God came to us as adults, we need to recognise the shock of death as well as the hope of salvation. Above all, in absorbing the shock, we should put aside familiar formulae which we have acquired in sacred works and in hymn books so that we can consider the death of Jesus afresh as the beginning of a renewed theological journey. The Cross is still everywhere in our society; to many non-believers it is an iconic cliché. To us, it must never become a cliché.

## iv. When They Are Part of Us: The Empty Tomb, Black Friday and the Nature of the Kingdom

Jesus is being laid in a new-hewn, empty tomb: no flowers, no hearse, no ceremonial, just basic embalming, a simple prayer and a farewell. He has left his kingdom on earth. What kind of kingdom is it and what kind of kingdom ought it to be?

We are caught between collusion and denial. We resort easily to condemning the materialist or the consumer society but deny that we are part of it, justifying our critique, although, as we have noted earlier, there is no room for such a critique where silence and our own behaviour would be best; but to denounce and collude simultaneously is much more serious, not because it is hypocritical, which it certainly appears to be, but because we are deluding ourselves which spares us the charge of hypocrisy. So often we are able to delude ourselves. Hardly a day goes by without a media outlet accusing somebody of being hypocritical for apparently saying one thing and doing another—a charge such outlets implicitly believe cannot be levelled at them—but in most cases the object of their condemnation is not hypocritical in the least; many people, and particularly politicians, have an immense capacity for persuading themselves that what they are doing is right; it is self-delusion which flourishes when we lack the capacity to be self-critical.

The mechanism of the eye of the needle works in a fascinating way in this context. Many politicians and commentators believe that the way to extinguish social and political controversy is to throw money at it. If you can load people up with enough packages they will give up the idea of getting through the eye of the needle; they will be secularised and sanitised. That is what many people of other religions than Christianity think about us. Set aside, for a moment, the argument about whether alcohol is fundamentally evil or what constitutes public modesty, the central point is that many people from other faiths and traditions view our society as licentious and decadent, sexualised, drunken, coarse and insensitive. Which presents us with the embarrassing question when we react to secularists: is this a Christian society or is it not? If we claim that it is a Christian society, then we have to take responsibility for what's happening; and if it is no longer a Christian society but is something else, a multi-cultural or a secular society, then how do we adjust to that? Unless we are a Church of the Cross then we will be nothing. It is only in the Cross that we can truly understand the mission of Jesus which it is our privilege to proclaim. There can no longer be what Bonhoeffer called "cheap discipleship" or what I might call comfortable religion. It just isn't enough that we like the beautiful words of the King James Bible or the Book of Common Prayer; this Church, founded by Jesus and infused with the Holy Spirit, isn't a culture fest, it's an enterprise to spread the good news under-written by the Cross.

The worst manifestation of how we are now came at the end of last November with Black Friday. I tried very hard to find the verb that links with the idea: did we witness it? Was it an imposition? Were we scandalised or disgusted? Well, in general all four terms might properly apply: we weren't involved, we didn't ask for it and the scenes on the television were horrid. But the problem with our attitude to anything in general is seriously compromised by our attitude to something in a particular way. Here are three replies that I heard in response to the question "What do you think about Black Friday? But, more interestingly, the answers to the follow-up question: "Did you have any involvement with it?"

- I was disgusted by it but my daughter isn't at all well off and it gave her the chance to buy a nice television; she has to spend a lot of time on her own.
- I think that the sight of people falling over each other and fighting was pretty shocking; but you can see why poorer people and older people might benefit from a bargain.
- I thought that it was barbaric but my sister got a lovely sofa and she said where she went it was all very calm.

In other words, on the whole Black Friday was a shocking event but there were all kinds of extenuating circumstances why people would be justified in becoming involved. And this provides us with the clue. We can all condemn the consumer society in general but most of us, at least, are complicit. We can all find good reasons why we do this and not that. I am, for example, particularly struck by the excuses church-going parents make for the absence of their children, such as attendance at sports or cultural events.

Perhaps it's a little harsh; but that is a rough summary of what the kingdom is like now. But what should it be like: how would we recognise the kingdom on earth as it is in heaven?

Looking at the Passion story for clues, I would identify seven marks of the presence, at least in nascent form, of the kingdom on earth as it is in heaven:

- Self-restraint, the refusal to judge others: exemplified by the way in which Jesus handled the quarrels of his followers; his refusal to enter into redundant dialogue with his accusers; and his silence after the rebuke of the disgruntled rebel who was crucified with him and after the jibes of those who passed by. These were responses to the opposite behaviours of his followers grandstanding; his accusers over-stating their case; and the self-justification of the criminal and by passers-by.

- Empathy, exercising the social imagination to create community: exemplified by the way in which Jesus understood the bewilderment of his followers; the way he cared for the servant who had lost his ear; and his understanding of the criminal who repented. Here the opposite behaviours are the need of his followers for clear-cut answers to meet their own needs; and Peter's aggressive action, not recognising the passive role of the servant. The repentant criminal's humility draws the salvation promise from Jesus.

- Humility, establishing a right relationship with God: exemplified by the relationship which Jesus articulated in the Garden of Gethsemane when he set out his anxieties but nonetheless put God's will first; the description by Jesus of his kingdom not being like the Roman Empire or the Jewish kingdom; and Jesus recalling the words of Psalm 22. The opposite behaviours are the way in which the authorities parade their judicial and military power; the use of God as a religious weapon; and the failure of the religious authorities to listen and think.

- Vulnerability, leaving oneself open to the other: we find that the whole of the life of Jesus is a pattern of vulnerability from the cradle to the Cross whereas those he meets are apt to be defensive.

- Generosity of spirit, giving people the benefit of the doubt: this is exemplified by the way in which Jesus paid attention to the women he met on his way to Calvary; the way in which he brought his mother and John together; and the way in which he forgave his persecutors. The opposite behaviour is demonstrated by the self-absorption and then flight of his followers in general and the denial of Peter in particular; the assumption by Judas that Jesus had in some way fallen short; and the legalism of Caiaphas and his colleagues.

- Perseverance, sticking to the task: the contrast here between Jesus and his followers is stark.

- Sacrifice, giving more than the law requires to correct flaws in society: again, we do not need a list here so much as the simple statement that Jesus gave his life for the world while his accusers and detracts simply wanted to keep what they had.

We might say that these features of human behaviour are the components of love. They do not vary greatly from St Paul's list in 1 Corinthians 13 where love is patient, kind, not envious nor boastful, not arrogant nor rude, does not insist on its own way, is not irritable or resentful, it does not rejoice in wrong-doing but in the truth. Love: "bears all things, believes all things, hopes all things, endures all things. Love never ends."

Jesus is being carried into the empty tomb by people who never had much but now believe they have nothing; their lives are destroyed forever; humiliation is added to their economically lowly state. Our paradoxical dilemma is that we have riches even beyond the imaginings of the greatest emperors and merchants of previous times which weigh us down but we also have the life of Jesus in front of us: there is so much that we could be, buoyed by the hope of eternal life and yet, even after the Resurrection, we cannot take seriously the lilies of the field.

But if we are to be builders of the kingdom of heaven on earth, to carry out the mission of Jesus, we cannot do so without a radical encounter with the Cross. The story is so familiar that it is often too easy to read: we don't feel the lashes and the thorns and the nails; we don't feel the taunts; we slide over the trials as we would over a newspaper account of something just a bit fishy. But no matter how well instructed we are by the Sermon on the Mount, no matter how awestruck we are by the feeding of the five thousand, no matter how we sit bolt upright at the raising of Lazarus, had the life of Jesus up to the night before Palm Sunday been all that we had, it would be nothing; Jesus would just be another holy man, an anti-establishment prophet, a miracle worker. It is no accident that the Gospels are so heavily geared towards the last five days of the life of Jesus, it is as if the previous chapters were just a prologue. It is only in the Passion and death of Jesus that we come into direct contact with the cosmic significance of the Incarnation which is why I am so saddened that so many people who turn up for crib services don't turn up for Holy Week and Easter services as if they were content to buy the biographies of great people and only read the first few chapters about school days and youth. Without the radical encounter with the Cross we are nothing; and certainly without it we would not have the means to be builders of God's kingdom on earth, for that kingdom, if it is to be a kingdom of love, needs to be modelled not so much on the life of Jesus when things were going relatively well but on his life when he faced terrible odds. When some of us go home we will eat buns with the Cross imprinted on them; I wish the Cross were printed on everything we buy, the equivalent of a health warning, because kingdom building is not episodic; through Baptism it has been built into our spiritual DNA so that it may encounter and counter the problems which arise from our physical DNA. Every line of the Scriptures on the last five days of the life of Jesus requires meticulous attention if we are to draw the strength from them to give us the resolve to invoke one of those aspects of love, and that is tenacity.

There are many who say that Christendom, as it was, is becoming secular, that attendance at church, not least on this day of all days, is falling, that the game is up, to which there are two responses. The first, to use management jargon, is that that we have become too obsessed with process rather than product; we write reports about things instead of doing things; we have become bureaucratic and rigid and sometimes, too, we have put more importance on religion than on Jesus.

The second response is much more critical. In the words of St Theresa of Avila: God has no body now but ours, no eyes, no feet on earth but ours; so we are the agents of the mission of Jesus, prosecuting that agency in the power of the Holy Spirit. On this day we are properly concentrating on the life of Jesus and, as part of the narrative, on the encounter of Jesus with the Father; and, to be flippant for just a moment, I don't suppose the Holy Spirit "minds" not being centre stage and, indeed, it is perhaps as well because the Holy Spirit gets rather a raw deal from the Church she inhabits: but we receive a whole new perspective on the death of Jesus and our obligation to build the kingdom if we stop thinking that it is a grim struggle which is bound to fail because society is against us. The Holy Spirit will bring the whole of this earth to Jesus if we give her room within us to work through our hands and our feet and our eyes; and, unlike the followers of Jesus, when we leave here today, bereft of the presence of Jesus, left in the new-hewn tomb, we will still be able to sit quietly and draw on the strength of the Spirit.

We therefore carry three truths into the world with which we have such an equivocal relationship: that God is love; that Jesus will keep his promise of salvation; and that the Spirit is with us.

We hear at funerals those ponderous words that we were made from dust and to dust we will return; and we read in Job that we came into the world with nothing and will leave it with nothing. That Jesus was put into an empty tomb is deeply symbolic for the writers who saw him as the Messiah. It was the custom of his times to bury rulers with their most treasured possessions to which the pyramids are testimony; but Jesus took nothing. Neither shall we. This truism is often cited as a very pragmatic reason for not being possessive. What's the point of accumulating wealth if we can't take it with us? A very laudable sentiment in its way but, like a lot of what I might call folk wisdom, it misses the point. We take nothing with us because nothing we have is ours to begin with. If we are to build the kingdom we have to get back to the idea that we are stewards of the earth and its riches, not owners of it and therein lies the deep contrast between Black Friday and Good Friday. Black Friday is not only vulgar and unsightly, it is a denial of who we are as creatures. Jesus gave himself for us and, in a very profound way, all we have to give to Jesus is ourselves for nothing else is ours, a very stark thought for us who live in a world of such plenty. In a very serious sense, we need to be able to live Lent and Easter together, fused at Pentecost. The sequential fasting and feasting takes the joy out of the fasting and takes the generosity out of the feasting. What we need is to be roared on by Pentecost so that our resolve can survive through the "green time".

I have almost ended and have not yet said a word about Mary, the Mother of Jesus as she suffers the worst fate of a mother, seeing her Son die before she dies. There has been much controversy in Christian history about Mary but nobody doubts that she possesses those same virtues which I described and which St Paul describes as the attributes of love. Some people find the encounter with Jesus problematic because of his dual nature as both divine and human and many, understandably, have looked to Mary, not least oppressed women, as the quiet, human, female figure. There need be no choice but as I find myself at a terrible loss between the time I leave Church on Good Friday and the time I return from the Easter Vigil, I focus on Mary's plight because she is the nearest human being to Jesus that there has ever been.

One final thought before these reflections end. I chose to frame them in the context of people far away, people approaching us, people living among us and people becoming part of us because this is a global reality which we find difficult but with which we need to come to grips. I chose the subject deliberately because what I have tried to show is that the timeless call of the Cross should not be entrapped by, but should become free of, culture. Very often in history Christianity has become an intrinsic, even valuable, and usually comforting aspect of culture which is what, for better or for worse, we have made. And that is the point. We have made culture and it is often so beautiful that we are charmed by our own creation. It would be harsh to label this as pride but it is another manifestation of the subtlety of the temptation to succumb to pride.

Mission is what Jesus has made for us. Every time I am asked to preach on the text that we should give up everything we have, including family and friends, for the sake of Jesus, I flinch; and when I preach such a sermon, as I have in an extended form today, I must be the first to acknowledge my failing; but to fail is not the same as failing to know what I must do and, knowing what I must do I merely ask you to think; someone who fails as I fail is in no position to tell anyone, to judge anyone. The language of preaching will always veer that way but there must always be a corrective; the step from encouragement to judgment is perilously short.

So, as we commit Jesus to his new-hewn, empty tomb, away from worldly goods, away from culture, law and, yes, religion, let us understand the profound counter-culturalism of the Cross. Never was there such a twist in the tail as this, a triumph born out of tragedy; never was there such a preposterous king as this, judicially murdered in the hope that that would be the end of it; never was there, in the words of St Paul, such a foolishness as this compared with traditional religious law and secular philosophy. The story of the Cross is the most astounding story that has ever been told but it becomes mere bathos if it is absorbed into and used to justify any culture. Since the Creator made us creatures to build his kingdom on earth as it is in heaven we know that we have not done well, that our solutions have been feeble and that we have always looked for excuses; but now, knowing what we know, there is no viable alternative to taking the story of the Cross at its literal word without equivocation: if we are to build the kingdom on earth then we will always do so in the shadow of the Cross as its stands, made ever darker by the rising light of the Resurrection.